Where We Stand

The Official Position Papers
of the Assemblies of God

Gospel Publishing House
Springfield, Missouri
Bound #02-0670
Looseleaf #02-0674

6th Printing 2003

Includes the latest position papers

Printed in the United States of America

Table of Contents

Introduction

The statements on the issues in this book were approved as the official statements of The General Council of the Assemblies of God by the General Presbytery, the ruling body of the Assemblies of God, over the past thirty years. (See the dates below which indicate the year approved.) As the need arose to make a statement on a controversial issue, a study was done and a report was given to the General Presbytery for approval. These statements were then printed as position papers. They are now available in bound and loose-leaf format for easier use.

The Inerrancy of Scripture, 1970
Can Born-Again Believers Be Demon Possessed? 1972
Divorce and Remarriage, 1973
Divine Healing: An Integral Part of the Gospel, 1974
The Discipleship and Submission Movement, 1976
Transcendental Meditation, 1976
Deacons and Trustees, 1976
Eternal Punishment, 1976
The Assemblies of God View of Ordination, 1976
The Doctrine of Creation, 1977
The Security of the Believer, 1978
The Rapture of the Church, 1979
The Believer and Positive Confession, 1980
A Biblical Perspective on Gambling, 1983

Abstinence from Alcohol, 1985

The Kingdom of God as Described in Holy Scripture, 1989

The Role of Women in Ministry as Described in Holy Scripture, 1990

Theology of Ministry, 1993

A Biblical Perspective on Assisted Suicide, 1998

The Baptism in the Holy Spirit: The Initial Experience and Continuing Evidences of the Spirit-Filled Life, 2000

Ministry to People With Disabilities: A Biblical Perspective, 2000

Homosexuality and the Bible, 2001

Apostles and Prophets, 2001

Assemblies of God Perspectives on the Sanctity of Human Life, Including Abortion and Euthanasia, 2002

1
The Inerrancy of Scripture

We believe the Bible is the Word of God written; it is the revelation of the truths of God conveyed by inspiration through His servants to us. As such, it is infallible and without error.

Implications of Statement

1. We refer to original autographs. While the science of textual criticism assures us of a trustworthy text, inerrancy can be claimed only for the original writings (Jeremiah 36:2).

2. We conceive the Bible to be in actuality the very Word of God. The divine Author prompted the original thought in the mind of the writers (Amos 3:8); He then guided their choice of words to express such thoughts (Exodus 4:12,15); and, lastly, He illumines the mind of the reader of such words in a way that the reader potentially may comprehend the same truth as was originally in the mind of the writer (1 Corinthians 2:12; Ephesians 1:17,18). Thus, both thought and language are revelatory and inspired.

3. We understand *inspiration* to mean that special act of the Holy Spirit by which He guided the writers of the Scriptures. Such superintendency made full allowance for the divergent backgrounds, abilities, and personalities of the writers, and

applies to all they wrote as it is found in the canon of Scripture.

4. We define *inerrancy* as meaning "exempt from error" and *infallibility* as a near synonym meaning "incapable of error, certain." If there is any difference in the shade of meaning between the two terms, inerrancy emphasizes the truthfulness of Scripture, while infallibility emphasizes the trustworthiness of Scripture. Such inerrancy and infallibility apply to all of Scripture and include both revelational inerrancy and factual inerrancy. It is truth (2 Samuel 7:28; Psalm 119:43,160; John 17:17,19; Colossians 1:5).

Historical Considerations

While discussion on the doctrine of inerrancy is primarily a phenomenon of recent years, a survey of church history suggests that the church has long held to a high view of inspiration, with the doctrine of inerrancy implicit in that view. During the Patristic Period, the Scriptures were considered to be the unique work of the Holy Spirit carrying forth a divine message. To the church fathers, inspiration extended even to the phraseology of the Bible. Thus, Clement of Alexandria underscores Christ's words in Matthew 5:18 by saying that not a jot or tittle shall pass away because the Lord has spoken it (Propterticus, IX, 82, 1). Gregory Nazianzus suggests that the smallest lines in the Scriptures are due to the care of the Holy Spirit, and that we must be careful to consider every slightest shade of meaning (Orat., 2, 105). Justin Martyr distinguished between human and divine inspiration, and spoke of the divine word that moved the writers of Scripture (Apology I, Ch. 36). Iranaeus thought of the Scriptures as "beyond all falsehood" (Apology, Ch. 18). There can be little doubt that the early fathers had a very high view of inspiration, and that this view extended to the minutia of Scripture.

During the medieval or scholastic period, the Bible became a mere source book for disputations instead of the living Word of God. As might be expected, the period was unproductive in respect to definitive statements on inspiration. Much more attention was given to the status of the Bible in its relationship to other authorities within the church. Although Abelard and Aquinas emphasized the human element in the transmission of God's revelation, there is no evidence to suggest that a less high doctrine of inspiration was necessitated by the mood of the Middle Ages.

The reformers, in a search for authority, readily accepted the doctrine of inspiration and, by implication, the doctrine of inerrancy. Zwingli appealed consistently to the Old Testament and New Testament in his defense of pure Christian doctrine. Calvin described the Scriptures as the "only record in which God has been pleased to consign His truth to perpetual remembrance, until we have a perfect conviction that God is its Author" (Institutes, 1, 7, 2, 4). Luther argued for a high view of inspiration, once the question of canonicity was settled, and thought of the Scriptures as being above error. While the reformers did not devote a decisive part of their theology to the subject of inspiration, it is conclusive that they accepted the full authority of the Scriptures.

The age of rationalism leveled its attack against the application of inspiration to the minutia of the Bible. In the spirit of the Renaissance, linguistic and textual studies flourished. The rationalistic approach suggested that if errors could be demonstrated to exist in the text of Scripture, the whole doctrine of inspiration would crumble. This kind of thinking ignited a rash of claims that the Bible was full of errors, its critics hoping thereby to destroy the whole doctrine of inspiration.

Unfortunately, orthodoxy countered with the same appeal to

rationalization. They argued that since the Bible is without error, it is thereby inspired. This does not mean that we should accept a lower view of inspiration, nor that we should reject the doctrine of inerrancy; it only suggests that our appeal must arise from the claims of Scripture alone. The Scriptures are inerrant because they are inspired of God—not inspired because they are inerrant. The first approach is biblical and leads to a correct view of inspiration and inerrancy; the second approach is rationalistic and opens the door to human speculations.

Exegetical Considerations

The starting point for a correct understanding of the doctrine of inerrancy is the self-witness of the Bible. The Bible clearly claims for itself divine authority and full inspiration, and implicit therein is the doctrine of inerrancy.

Jesus Christ, both a credible witness and messenger from God, vouches for the inspiration of the details of the Scriptures. In Matthew 5:18, Jesus said, "'I tell you the truth, until heaven and earth disappear, not the smallest letter, not the least stroke of a pen, will by any means disappear from the Law until everything is accomplished.'" Whether we take this reference literally, that the jot represents the smallest Hebrew letter and the tittle the minor stroke that distinguishes one letter from another, or figuratively, that the jot and tittle represent the particles of Scripture, the force is the same. Jesus thought of the Scriptures as being consequential even in their slightest detail. If Jesus did not believe in full inspiration and the quality of inerrancy, the force of His argument is lost.

Christ's insistence on the essential nature of every part of Scripture is further seen in John 10:34,35. Here Jesus points to a brief statement from the Psalms and argues that neither it nor the other parts of the Law can be broken. If Jesus had thought of the Scriptures as being only partially inspired and subject to errors of detail, He certainly would not have spoken as He did.

In Matthew 22:32 the validity of Christ's statement rests on the essential nature of scriptural detail, namely, the present tense of the verb *to be,* "I am." In questioning the Pharisees in Matthew 22:43–45, the force of the dialogue rests on the use of one word, *Lord.* In Galatians 3:16, the apostle Paul depends on a distinguishing of singulars and plurals for the force of his argument. Examples of minutia, involving tenses, particular words, and singulars and plurals, are meaningful only in light of a fully inspired Scripture that is infallible even in its detail.

One of the most forceful statements on the full inspiration of the Scriptures is found in 2 Timothy 3:16. This passage teaches that every or all Scripture is "God-breathed," or literally "breathed out" of God. Whether one translates the opening words of this verse "Every Scripture inspired of God" or "All Scripture is inspired of God," the meaning is the same. What is true of one Scripture is true of all or every Scripture; that is, they are uniquely the product of God.

One last passage deserves consideration. Second Peter 1:21 states that the Old Testament writers spoke "as they were carried along by the Holy Spirit." In its context this verse suggests the uniqueness of Scriptures when compared to humanly inspired statements. The men who wrote the Scriptures were carried along, or moved, by the Holy Spirit. The uniform witness of the Scriptures themselves is clear: God spoke the concept (revelation) to the mind of the writer; the Holy Spirit guided the transmission (inspiration) of that concept into the objective form of words; and, through the continual guidance of the Holy Spirit (illumination), we receive the original revelation as we read the Scriptures.

In addition to the above passages, mention should be made of the numerous claims of the Scriptures to be in reality "God's Word." The Old Testament is abundant with such phrases as "And God said," "This is what the Lord says," and "The Word of the Lord came." In other passages, Scripture is equated directly with divine authorship: "It says," "It is written," and "The Scripture says." This shows that God's voice, spoken to the prophets, is equated with the Scriptures, which were written by divine inspiration.

Objections to the Doctrine of Inerrancy

1. Since we do not have the original autographs, any doctrine of inerrancy is without value.

The answer is twofold.

First, the science of textual criticism has assured us, by the estimates of competent scholars, that our present texts (Greek and Hebrew) are without errors of significance. The text we work with is therefore trustworthy and deserving of the most careful and detailed study.

Second, to reject the doctrine of inerrancy transfers the question of truth from the objective into the realm of the subjective. Who is to decide what part of the Scripture is true and what part of it is false? What part is trustworthy and what part is untrustworthy? The Scriptures' claim to divine authority is lost when we subject them to rationalistic, subjective human appraisal.

2. The doctrine of inerrancy necessitates a doctrine of inspiration that eliminates human personality in the composition of the Scriptures.

We hold that God, by the superintendency of the Holy Spirit, so prepared the authors of His Word that they were able to write precisely what He intended to have written. The total personality of each author was utilized by the Holy Spirit in the conveyance of the divine message, thus allowing for variety and individuality, yet not destroying the message God desired to present (2 Peter 1:21).

3. The Bible contains errors in matters of science, history, morality, reasoning, quotations, etc., so as to render it untrustworthy.

First, while this is a popular claim, it is difficult to substantiate. Both science and time tend to vindicate the Scriptures.

Second, the Bible does not claim to be a textbook on nonreligious topics. Yet, when it does speak in these areas, its statements, though incomplete and expressed in popular terminology, are never in error.

Third, the Bible must be studied against the background of its day. Matters of culture, language, and literary procedure must be carefully considered. If the Scriptures are approached with an attitude of sincerity and intelligent inquiry, they will prove to possess the quality of infallibility.

4. A high view of inspiration does not necessitate the doctrine of inerrancy.

An appeal must be made in three directions. As has been seen, the testimony of history is convincing. The church generally has held to a high view of inspiration, holding to the inseparability of inspiration and inerrancy.

Second, a study of the Scriptures demonstrates the correlation between inspiration and inerrancy. It is difficult to imagine that the Bible writers thought of the Scriptures as being anything other than infallible and without error.

Finally, we appeal to logic. Since God is himself free from error, which is the clear testimony of the Scriptures (Psalms 31:5; 100:5; John 7:28; 8:26; Romans 3:4; 2 Corinthians 1:18; 1 John 4:6; 5:20; Revelation 6:10), and since He has chosen humans as the vehicle through which He would disclose His truth, it is wholly consistent that He should conduct the process of providing Scripture so as to avoid all error, and wholly inconsistent if any minute part of it should be in error.

2
Can Born-Again Believers Be Demon Possessed?

The spread of oriental religions and the occult in America has brought with it an increase in demon possession similar to that reported formerly by missionaries on foreign fields. All too often there has been too little teaching in this area. Many have felt all that is necessary is to preach Christ, and the demons will go away.

But the New Testament does more than command to preach Christ. It warns very definitely against the enemy of our souls and shows that demons are not to be treated lightly. It also emphasizes that deliverance is available through the "finger of God," the power of the Spirit, and the name of Jesus.

The Danger of Extremes

There is a danger, however, when emphasizing any neglected doctrine, to go to an extreme which is beyond the intent of the Scriptures. It is also possible to be sidetracked into making the neglected doctrine the whole ministry. This seems to be the case with some who become fascinated with the subject of demonology. They are trapped into giving most of their attention to it. The more demons they cast out, the more there seem to be to cast out, and the rest of their ministry is practically ignored.

This tendency to become more occupied with casting out demons than with exalting Christ seems inconsistent with the balance of Scripture. Also there seems to be no basis in Scripture for the accompanying preoccupation with external phenomena, such as vomiting up various substances in connection with the casting out of demons (forgetting that demons are spirit beings). In the one instance in which foaming is recorded, Scripture makes it clear that this was a consistent pattern prior to the time the demon was cast out and not a phenomenon occurring only at the time of exorcism.

One of the regrettable side effects of an unscriptural overemphasis on demonology is that scriptural teaching is sometimes brought into disrepute. This was one result of the so-called witchcraft of 16th and 17th century England and 17th century America. In England, cases were reported where children vomited up articles which supposedly proved evil spirits had entered into their bodies.

Then, in 1692, Cotton Mather, a brilliant Boston preacher who graduated from Harvard with honors, roused the people of Salem, Massachusetts, against "witches." Nineteen persons were hanged and 150 imprisoned because of the testimony of children who were supposed to be demon possessed (and who may have been moved by lying demons, though there may be other explanations). In the presence of the accused, these children would throw "fits" and would go into what seemed to be a trance. In this state they would name people who they said were responsible for their "suffering."

Though many of the accused showed a spirit and a faith worthy of Christian martyrs, judges who were men of personal integrity pronounced them guilty. As a result of the publicity given these trials, Americans of that day turned away from the supernatural and branded all that the Bible teaches about Satan and evil spirits as mere superstition.

It seems important, then, that we do not permit Satan to sidetrack God's people into an attention on demons or evil spirits that goes beyond the clear teaching of the Bible, thus producing a reaction that would turn people away from all that is supernatural and hinder the work of God.

Exercising caution, however, does not mean we should treat the matter of demonology lightly. The Bible clearly recognizes both the activity of demons and their great number. This is even more evident when we recognize that the word *devils* in our common English version really means "demons." Actually, the word *devil* (Greek, *diabolos,* "the slanderer") is appropriate only for Satan. This is not to say, however, that the devil does not work through demons. Satan is a created being, a finite spirit, and is not omnipresent. He does most of his work through demons scattered in various parts of the world. Jesus' work in casting out demons was at least a part of His work of healing those oppressed (exploited, dominated, under the tyrannical rule) of the devil (Acts 10:38). (It should be noted that the word *oppressed* as used here is stronger than in today's usage.)

A question that arises, then, is not whether demons are active today, but whether born-again believers can be demon possessed, have a demon, or need to have someone cast demons out of them. Can the Holy Spirit and a demon dwell in the same temple? Are not our bodies temples of the Holy Spirit?

What Writers Have Said

Most of the older writers say that genuine Christians cannot be possessed or indwelt by a demon.

An example is John L. Nevius, a Presbyterian missionary

who spent nearly 40 years in China, who saw many cases of demon possession, but never among Christians. He found that demons did not want to stay in the presence of true Christians.[1]

A pioneer Pentecostal missionary, Victor Plymire, gave similar insights from Tibet. He found also that demon worshipers did not find it easy to get demons to take possession of them.

More recently writers of various denominations have taken a different view. M. H. Nelson, a medical doctor, tells of numerous reports of Christians who apparently have suffered from demon possession. He suggests, however, that some of them may be in open rebellion against God. (Apparently, he believes in eternal security and still calls these rebels Christians.) He goes on to say, however, that though a demon may gain an influence over the mind and body of a Christian, it is very doubtful that the body of a Christian can be *possessed* by a demon.[2]

Others say that a demon can possess the Christian's body without possessing the Christian's inner being. This seems contrary to the biblical view of the body as the temple of the Holy Spirit. It also goes against the biblical view of the unity of body, soul, and spirit as far as responsibility is concerned. The fragmentation of the person into various aspects is a heathen idea. If a demon enters any area of the body or mind (or attitudes), it enters *you!*

What the Bible Says

Many Christians have had God-given deliverances from problems and believed they were delivered from demon possession. But we must search the Scriptures to see if their interpretation of what happened is really in line with what the Bible teaches.

Some, for example, teach that since the Bible speaks of a

spirit of cowardly fear, any deliverance from fear must be by the casting out of an evil spirit or demon of fear. But an examination of the same passage (2 Timothy 1:7) shows it speaks also of a spirit of power, of love, and of a sound mind or self-control. If people interpret fear to be an evil spirit needing to be cast out, to be consistent they would need to beseech three good spirits to come in.

The fallacy of this reasoning is obvious. Love and self-control are fruits of the Holy Spirit in our lives. By a spirit of love and of self-control is meant the attitudes that result from our cooperation with the Holy Spirit.

Actually, the word *spirit* in many cases means an attitude or a disposition. David spoke of a broken spirit (Psalm 51:17); Solomon of a humble spirit (Proverbs 16:19). Paul wanted to come to Corinth, not with a rod, but with love and a meek or gentle spirit (1 Corinthians 4:21). Peter spoke of the adorning of the heart with the imperishable gift of a meek and quiet spirit (1 Peter 3:4), actually meaning a quiet disposition. This is in line with the frequent use of the word *spirit* for one's own spirit and its expressions (Haggai 1:14; Acts 17:16; 1 Corinthians 2:11, etc.).

Thus, unless the context shows that an independent spirit-being is meant, it seems best to take most phrases such as a haughty spirit, a hasty spirit, a spirit of slumber, a spirit of jealousy, etc., to be sins of the disposition or lusts of the flesh (Galatians 6), and not demons.

A serious danger in considering all these sins of the disposition to be demons is that the individual may feel no responsibility for personal actions and feel that the necessity for repentance is removed. Actually, the Bible calls people to repent of these things and to put off these attitudes. The great conflict within us is not between the Holy Spirit and demons, but between the indwelling Holy Spirit and the flesh (that is, all the sensory apparatus that tends toward sin).

When the word *spirit* is used of demons, the Bible may speak of an evil or unclean spirit. Sometimes the words are used together; for example, "a spirit of an unclean devil" (Luke 4:33).

In many cases these demons caused sickness. But the New Testament does not ascribe all sickness to demons or evil spirits. In fact, many passages make a clear distinction between sicknesses and diseases not caused by demons and those caused by demons (Matthew 4:24; 8:16; 9:32,33; 10:1; Mark 1:32; 3:15; Luke 6:17,18; 9:1, etc.). In none of these examples is there any indication that any of these sicknesses caused by demons were of people in right relation to God. We must remember also that all of these examples took place before Pentecost.

The word *daimonizomai,* to be possessed of a demon, or, as some put it, to be demonized, is not as common. It is used as a verb only once and that of a Canaanite girl who was "badly demonized," or cruelly tormented by a demon. Everywhere else it is found as a participle which should be translated, "the demoniac(s)" (Matthew 8:28,33; 9:32; 12:22; Mark 5:15–18; Luke 8:35). Again, in no case is there any indication that any one of these "demoniacs" or demonized persons was right with God; and in most cases they suffered severe torment—and a dramatic change of personality.

Another great problem with the idea that demons may possess Christians is a concept that erodes faith and waters down our concept of God and the salvation He provides. God is our Father. He has "rescued us from the dominion of darkness and brought us into the kingdom of the Son he loves" (Colossians 1:13). "In which [we] used to live when [we] followed the ways of this world and of the ruler of the kingdom of the air, the spirit who is now at work in those who are disobedient" (Ephesians 2:2). But now God by His love has saved us and made us "fellow citizens with God's people and members of God's household" (Ephesians 2:19). It would seem contradictory for demons to indwell our bodies now that our bodies are temples of the Holy Spirit.

We were once servants of sin (Romans 6:17) but now we are free to live for Christ. It is still possible to sin, but if a believer sins, it is because of having become willing to do so, not because of having been invaded by a demon. The Book of Romans calls not for the casting out of demons but for a faith act by which one becomes what one is.

For a Christian to have a demon would bring a division that Jesus refused to admit. The Pharisees tried to say that Jesus cast out demons by Beelzebub, the prince of demons (Matthew 12:24). They supposed the kingdom of Satan might be divided against itself. Jesus rejected this. Luke 11:21,22 further implies that Jesus has bound Satan as far as Satan's power to enslave a believer is concerned. Only when a demon returns and finds the house *empty* is he able to reenter (Luke 11:24–26).

The idea of a true believer being inhabited by a demon also erodes the biblical concept of salvation and peace. It may produce terrible fear as Christians begin to wonder what demon will invade them next. This is certainly not in line with the freedom the Bible assures us we have. Early Christians had no such fear, nor did the Church of the second century.

Hermas, who wrote a very influential Christian book called *The Shepherd* about A.D. 139, rebuked corruption and encouraged Christian virtue. In the book he also spoke of evil spirits that were able to live and reign within a person, but denied that the Holy Spirit could live in the same person with these evil spirits.

The Scripture is full of assurance for the believer: "The one who is in you is greater than the one who is in the world"

(1 John 4:4). A believer is a person who is delivered from the devil. This is fundamental. Some point to Ananias and Sapphira as exceptions. But Ananias either apostatized before Satan filled his heart to lie to the Holy Spirit, or else he and his wife were among those who joined *themselves* to the church rather than being added to it by the Spirit (see Acts 5:13,14). At the time, at least, they were no more than *professing* Christians.

Resisting Evil Forces

It seems evident that the term *possessed* should not be applied to true believers. What the Bible does show is that Satan and his cohorts are external foes. We are in a warfare against Satan's forces and they are looking for opportunities to *attack* us. (See Ephesians 6:12.) The biblical emphasis is on what we must face in the very atmosphere around us. The call is never for us to get someone to cast the demons out of us. They are out there attacking us, testing us, not possessing us. The call is to be vigilant and to put our armor on and take our stand (2 Corinthians 10:3–6; Ephesians 6:10–18; 1 Peter 5:8,9).

Jesus defeated Satan by quoting the Word of God (Matthew 4). We too must take our stand on God's Word and resist Satan and his demons, in faith (James 4:7; 1 Peter 5:8,9). Then the shield of faith will quench every fiery dart of the enemy (Ephesians 6:16). (Here we recognize that just as God's deliverances sometimes come through angels, so Satan's attacks sometimes come through demons or through those who are demon possessed.)

That the attack is external is seen in the case of Job; and also in the case of Paul's thorn in the flesh, which he called a messenger (or angel—Greek *aggelos*) of Satan sent to buffet him (beat or strike him with the fist). (See 2 Corinthians 12:7.) Paul besought the Lord three times that it (the messenger of Satan) might be removed (more literally, "Keep away from him"), but God refused and said His grace was sufficient. The result was that Paul learned to depend on God in his weakness, reproach, or distress. Whether the messenger of Satan was a demon, a sickness, or a person, the Bible does not say. Just what it was, however, is beside the point here. The attack, the buffeting, was from the outside, and Paul sought for it to be kept away, not cast out. We note also that Paul sees in himself and in us the living presence of Christ as the only hope (Colossians 1:2,29).

We believe also that the gift of the discerning of spirits is for the purpose of discerning the spirit that may motivate people who are not indwelt by the Holy Spirit, not the discerning of supposed demons in believers. If the truth remains in us, we remain in the Son and in the Father (1 John 2:24). Only if we are cut off from the vine and cast forth as a dead branch can Satan or his demons claim us. Our redemption is a redemption of the whole person. The full price has been paid.

Christ's enemies accused Him of having a demon. It is a subtle trick of the devil that makes sincere people accuse Christians today of having a demon. Clearly, there are deliverances, but calling them deliverances from demon possession is unscriptural.

---

[1]J. L. Nevius, *Demon Possession*, Grand Rapids: Kregel, reprint from 1894, pp. 278, 290.

[2]M. H. Nelson, *Why Christians Crack Up,* Chicago: Moody Press, 1960, pp. 76, 77.

3
Divorce and Remarriage

Application of Biblical Principles

A. Marriage

1. Marriage is a basic human relationship.

a. Marriage is God-ordained. "God created man in his own image, in the image of God he created him; male and female he created them" (Genesis 1:27). The very nature of the way God created human beings to live on the earth indicates He intended man and woman for each other.

Their relationship was to be social as well as physical. "The LORD God said, 'It is not good for the man to be alone. I will make a helper suitable for him' " (Genesis 2:18).

The first woman was a "helper" (a counterpart) for the man, taken from his side, bone of his bones and flesh of his flesh, his perfect complement (Genesis 2:23). It is obvious that God meant them to share in both privilege and responsibility.

b. God intended marriage to be a lifelong, monogamous union. "For this reason a man will leave his father and mother and be united to his wife, and they will become one flesh" (Genesis 2:24). When this is quoted in Matthew 19:5, a Greek word for *united* is used that means "to be glued to, be closely bound to."

The Old Testament factually recognized that polygamy did exist. It notes that the first case of polygamy was in Cain's line (Genesis 4:19) and shows that monogamy was still the ideal (Psalm 128:3; Proverbs 5:18; 31:10–29; Ecclesiastes 9:9). Jesus also acknowledges that God's ideal in the beginning was monogamy (Matthew 19:8).

2. Marriage involves a covenant.

Marriage is a covenant, a solemn binding agreement made before God and people. "The LORD is acting as the witness between you and the wife of your youth, because you have broken faith with her, though she is your partner, the wife of your marriage *covenant*" (Malachi 2:14, emphasis added). Ezekiel applies the idea of marriage to the relationship between God and Israel. " 'I gave you my solemn oath and entered into a *covenant* with you,' declares the Sovereign LORD, 'and you became mine' " (Ezekiel 16:8, emphasis added). From what is said we see that the husband "gave [a] solemn oath" to (or pledged faith to) the wife and entered into a covenant not intended to be broken. The Hebrew word used, however, implies no sacrifice, thereby distinguishing it from the word used for the more sacred and binding "cut a covenant." The love involved is fundamentally the Hebrew *hesed*, "a loyal, covenant keeping love," which God shows us even when we are unworthy.

B. Divorce

1. God hates divorce.

a. "The LORD is acting as the witness between you and the

wife of your youth, because you have broken faith with her, though she is your partner, the wife of your marriage covenant. Has not the LORD made them one? In flesh and spirit they are his. And why one? Because he was seeking godly offspring. So guard yourself in your spirit, and do not break faith with the wife of your youth. 'I hate divorce,' says the LORD God of Israel, 'and I hate a man's covering himself with violence as well as with his garment,' says the LORD Almighty. So guard yourself in your spirit, and do not break faith" (Malachi 2:14–16).

This passage shows that divorce is treachery (deceitful unfaithfulness) against your companion. It is also a violent thing coming from a wrong spirit. Worst of all, it hinders the growth of a "godly seed." Broken homes do not tend to produce the healthiest offspring.

b. "Therefore what God has joined together, let man not separate" (Matthew 19:6). Divorce was not in God's original intention for humanity. God's purposes in marriage are not helped by breaking the yoke. They can only be carried out as the pair subjects themselves to Christ and each other. Such a relationship is beautifully described in Ephesians 5:21–31.

2. The Law restricted divorce.

The Law recognized the fact that divorce was taking place in Israel (as were many other practices common to the ancient world). In giving Israel the Law, God accepted people where they were, put restrictions on their wrong practices, and tried to direct them.

In their confrontation with Jesus about divorce, the Pharisees were obviously in error when they said Moses *commanded* that a man give a certificate of divorce when putting his wife away (divorcing her). Jesus said that Moses only "suffered," or permitted, them to do so—and then not for "every cause," as was commonly practiced at that time (Matthew 19:3,7,8).

This is borne out in Deuteronomy 24:1–4. The Hebrew that Moses used there is a simple sequence that does not command divorce. He simply recognizes that men were divorcing their wives. The passage literally says that when a man divorces his wife "because he has found in her an unclean matter [a Hebrew word connected with uncovered stools (Deuteronomy 23:12–14), with Noah's nakedness (Genesis 9:21–23), and with Edom under the figure of a drunken woman (Lamentations 4:21)—that is, some moral or sexual uncleanness apart from adultery, since adultery would call for her death under the Law] and has written for her a certificate of divorce and given it into her hand and sent her away from his house, and she goes out of his house and has another husband [it is assumed she would do this] and the other husband hates her and writes her a certificate of divorce and gives it into her hand and sends her out of his house, or if the other husband dies who took her to be his wife, her first husband who sent her away shall not be able to return and take her (again) to be his wife."

In other words, a man is to think twice before he divorces his wife even for what seems to be a good reason. He might want her back, but if she has married again, he could not have her.

3. Jesus forbade divorce as contrary to God's will and word.

He made this clear in Matthew 19:5,6 and Mark 10:6–9.

4. Paul forbade a Christian couple getting a divorce.

"To the married I give this command (not I, but the Lord): A wife must not separate from her husband. But if she does, she must remain unmarried or else be reconciled to her husband.

And a husband must not divorce his wife" (1 Corinthians 7:10,11).

Although Paul recognized that Christians were getting divorces, he commanded that they keep the way open for reconciliation.

5. Paul forbade Christians taking the initiative in getting a divorce because their partner is an unbeliever.

"To the rest I say this (I, not the Lord) [Paul did not have an actual saying of Jesus to back this up, though Paul was speaking under the inspiration of the Spirit]: If any brother has a wife who is not a believer and she is willing to live with him [as a faithful wife], he must not divorce her. And if a woman has a husband who is not a believer and he is willing to live with her, she must not divorce him. . . . But if the unbeliever leaves, let him do so. A believing man or woman is *not bound [not enslaved]* in such circumstances" (1 Corinthians 7:12–16, emphasis added).

Thus Paul indicates that the Christian cannot stop the unbelieving partner who insists on leaving (getting a divorce).

6. Jesus permitted a Christian to initiate a divorce when fornication was involved.

"I tell you that anyone who divorces his wife, except for marital unfaithfulness, causes her to become an adulteress, and anyone who marries the divorced woman commits adultery" (Matthew 5:32; see also Matthew 19:9). This is permission, however, not a command.

The Greek word for "fornication" *(porneia)* may include especially repeated acts of adultery, but usually means habitual sexual immorality of any kind, both before and after marriage. (A *porne* was a prostitute.) A few scholars would limit the meaning of fornication here to incest, but this is not the normal usage of the word.

Some would rule out this exception because it is not found in Mark and Luke, not wanting to build a teaching on just the two passages in Matthew. However, we accept the length of the Millennium as spanning 1000 years even though this time period is mentioned in only one Bible passage (Revelation 20:2–7). The same principle applies to other Bible teachings.

It is seldom, if ever, that any single passage gives all aspects of truth on any single theme. In order to come to an understanding of any truth, we must take the whole of what the Bible teaches.

C. Remarriage

1. The Law accepted the fact that divorce permitted remarriage.

This is clear from the passage in Deuteronomy 24:1–4 already quoted. The same passage shows that the Law put some limits on remarriage. Malachi 2:11 condemned remarriage to an unbeliever. A priest was forbidden to take a divorced woman as his wife (Leviticus 21:7).

2. Jesus in His basic teaching forbade the remarriage of divorced persons.

He condemned remarriage as an act of adultery, a sin against the covenant of the first marriage (Matthew 5:32; 19:9; Mark 10:11,12; Luke 16:18).

However, Jesus recognized that the basic problem is divorce itself, for He saw that the divorced could be expected to remarry. By doing so they would commit adultery and cause the new partner to commit adultery. Thus, the basic purpose in what Jesus said is to prevent divorce in the first place.

3. Matthew 5:32 added an exceptive clause.

"I tell you that anyone who divorces his wife, except for marital unfaithfulness [habitual sexual immorality], causes her to become an adulteress." This shows that a husband who divorces a sexually immoral woman does not cause her to commit adultery, since she is already guilty of adultery.

4. Matthew 19:9 also carried this exceptive clause.

In this verse the best manuscripts read: " 'I tell you that anyone who divorces his wife, except for marital unfaithfulness [habitual sexual immorality], and marries another woman commits adultery' "[1]

It should be emphasized that the exception has in view sexual immorality, not merely a single act. Wherever possible, sexually immoral practices should be dealt with through repentance, confession, forgiveness, and reconciliation, thus saving the marriage.

Some, including those who follow the traditions of the Roman Catholics, say that the exceptive clause does not apply to "and marries another, commits adultery." In this view, fornication, or habitual sexual immorality, gives the right to separation from bed and board but does not sever the bond of marriage or give any right to dissolve it. But this is difficult to fit in with other passages that deal with the responsibilities of husband and wife (1 Corinthians 7:25). Therefore, most Protestants have always taken the position that the exceptive clause does apply to "and marries another."

It should also be pointed out that in the extreme cases where divorce seems necessary, Jesus did not command remarriage. However, it is clear that in Matthew 19:9 Jesus assumes the man will remarry. The verse deals with divorce *and* remarriage, and the laws of grammar make the exceptive clause apply to both. The Greek word for "divorce" *(apoluo)* is used with regard to the Deuteronomy passage referred to in Matthew 5:31 and Mark 10:2–12. There, the "divorcing" clearly did dissolve the marriage bond. Jesus did not change the nature of divorce as dissolving marriage. He simply threw out all excuses, reasons, or causes except "fornication" *(porneia,* habitual sexual immorality). However, in no case does He command divorce or remarriage. They are merely permitted under this one condition.

Again, the objection is made that Romans 7:1–3 and 1 Corinthians 7:39 make no exception to the statement that marriage is dissolved by death. Thus some take this to mean that marriage is broken by death alone.

But these passages are stating basic principles and do not deal with the exceptions. Romans 7 recognizes that the husband under the Law could get a divorce, but the wife could not. Therefore, the wife was bound by "the law of the husband" (lit.) until his death. We must also keep in mind that under the Law the penalty for adultery was death. This penalty of death was given not to break the marriage relationship, but in recognition that it was already broken.

5. 1 Corinthians 7:15 also contains an exception.

"If the unbeliever leaves, let him do so. A believing man or woman is not bound in such circumstances; God has called us to live in peace."

"Not bound" is a strong expression. Yet some, insisting on the basis of Romans 7:2 that death alone can dissolve a marriage, interpret this passage to mean that the Christian is free to let the unbelieving partner go, but not free to remarry. However, we must remember that in Romans 7:2 Paul is not addressing the subject of divorce and remarriage. He is simply using the unique situation of the woman under the Law in which only death could loose her from her husband to illustrate believers' complete dependence upon Christ's vicarious death to loose them from the claims of the Law. Paul was aware that under the Law the husband had the option of divorcing his wife (Deuteronomy 24:1–4), which was not available to the wife. Only death could loose her from the law of her husband. Sound principles of exegesis will not permit one to assume that Paul's view on the subject of divorce and remarriage appear here.

If a believer is "not bound" when an unbelieving spouse, unwilling to remain in the marriage, follows through with a divorce, the believer must be considered set free. Since it is the unbelieving partner who determines to go and initiates the divorce, the believer's freedom seems to be more than a freedom to let the partner go, since the partner is going anyway. The plain meaning seems to be that the believer is set free to remarry when choosing to do so.

Paul, however, does discourage remarriage for the cause of ministering to the Lord. "Are you unmarried? Do not look for a wife. But if you do marry, you have not sinned" (1 Corinthians 7:27,28).

6. Remarriage is a new contract or covenant

Some say that a person who remarries is living in adultery. They say that though adultery is not an unforgivable sin, true repentance will demand quitting the sin, as the thief must quit stealing. They argue that for a person who has remarried, to live with the new partner involves them continually in acts of adultery. But to assume an analogy between marriage and thievery is erroneous. It is obvious that marriage always involves a contract, but thievery does not.

A remarriage entered into wrongly does indeed constitute an act of adultery against the previous contract. This breaks the old contract; the former partner is set free. The person who remarries is then obligated to be faithful to the new contract. Deuteronomy 24 showed it to be wrong to go back to the old marriage contract. (Hosea was later commanded to do so as an illustration of the love of God that would take back apostate Israel.)

The Bible shows that God expects contracts to be kept even when entered into wrongly. When Joshua wrongly entered into a contract with the Gibeonites, God not only expected him to fulfill it, He gave him miracles of a hailstorm and the long day to help him (Joshua 9 and 10). Isaiah warned Ahaz against making a covenant with the Assyrians, but he made it anyway (Isaiah 7). Then God warned Hezekiah against breaking it and going down to Egypt for help (Isaiah 30 and 31).

D. The place of the divorced and remarried in the church.

1. Membership is open to all born-again believers.

This would certainly include those who were divorced and remarried before they were saved. Paul indicates that those in various social and legal positions, such as the circumcised and those who were slaves, should be accepted in the condition in which they were when they were saved (1 Corinthians 7:17–24). "Brothers, each man, as responsible to God, should remain in the situation God called him to" (1 Corinthians 7:24).

God accepted the Gentiles at the house of Cornelius (Acts 10 and 11). Knowing the frequency of divorce and remarriage among the Romans of the time, it is very probable that some at the house of Cornelius were so involved.

Paul gives the Christian no option but to continue to live with the unbelieving partner who is willing to remain in the marriage. Again, it is very probable that many of these Corinthian believers were married to unbelievers who had previous spouses still living. If God accepts such believers, who are we to judge? However, in no case shall a person be accepted into membership while living in a common-law state of matrimony.

2. The offices of elder and deacon are not open to those who are remarried, except where the divorce occurred prior to conversion.

The offices of elder (corresponding to pastor) and deacon are restricted by the requirement that they shall be "the husband of but one wife" (1 Timothy 3:2,12). This is understood to mean that candidates for elder and deacon are to be persons in a faithful heterosexual marriage with neither partner having been previously divorced, except where the divorce occurred prior to conversion.

We must remember that the Bible does not indicate that everyone is to have a turn at these offices in the church. The Bible lays down specific requirements for elders and deacons. The requirement that they be the husband of one wife is in keeping with the requirement that they must have a good report from outside the church. Both for the sake of the witness of the church and for the sake of freedom from entanglements, those who administer the affairs of the local church must meet these and other qualifications. This in no way promotes a double standard of morality, but is simply a matter of qualifications for the specific ministries of elders and deacons.

Some would restrict the remarried from all the ministries of the Church. However, every member of the Body has a function, and the ministries are given by the Spirit (Roman 12:6–8; 1 Corinthians 12:11; Ephesians 4:16).

Application of Biblical Principles to our Bylaws as Revised and Adopted by the General Council in Session

Article IX, Section 5

a. Membership

1. Marriage entanglements before conversion. There are now among Christian people those who became entangled in their marriage relations in their former lives of sin and who do not see how these matters can be adjusted. We recommend that these people be received into the membership of local assemblies and that their marriage complications be left in the hands of the Lord (1 Corinthians 7:17,20,24).

2. Common-law marriages. We recommend that in no case shall persons be accepted into membership who are known to be living in a common-law state of matrimony.

b. Remarriage

Low standards on marriage and divorce are very hurtful to individuals, to the family, and to the cause of Christ. Therefore, we discourage divorce by all lawful means and teaching. We positively disapprove of Christians getting divorces for any cause except fornication and adultery (Matthew 19:9). Where these exceptional circumstances exist or when a Christian has been divorced by an unbeliever, we recommend that the question of remarriage be resolved by the believer in the light of God's Word (1 Corinthians 7:15,27,28).

c. Local Church Leadership

1. Standard for offices of bishop, or elder, and deacon. Since the New Testament restricts divorced and remarried believers from the church offices of bishop, or elder, and deacon, we recommend that this standard be upheld by all our assemblies (1 Timothy 3:12; Titus 1:5–9), except when the divorce occurred prior to conversion (2 Corinthians 5:17). However, we recommend that all other opportunities for Christian service for which these believers may be qualified be made available to them.

2. Prerogative of local assemblies. It is understood that recommendations are not binding, but local assemblies shall maintain the prerogative of setting their own standards (in accord with provisions of Article XI of the Constitution).

d. Performing Marriage Ceremonies

1. Ministerial Guidelines. We disapprove of any Assemblies of God minister performing a marriage ceremony for anyone who has been divorced and whose former spouse is still living, unless the case is included in the exceptional circumstances described in Article IX, B, Section 5, paragraph b. Any minister of our Fellowship who performs a ceremony for a disapproved marriage (indicated above), unless innocently deceived into doing so, may be dismissed from the Fellowship.

2. Violation of conscience not required. We realize that the remarrying of such persons included in the exceptive circumstances in Article IX, B, Section 5, paragraph b, could violate the conscience of a minister; and if this should be the case, the minister should not be expected to perform such ceremonies.

3. Same-sex ceremonies. No minister shall perform any type of marriage, cohabitation, or covenant ceremony for persons

who are of the same sex. Such a ceremony would endorse homosexuality, which is a sin and strictly forbidden in God's Word (Leviticus 18:22; 20:13; Romans 1:26,27; 1 Corinthians 6:9; 1 Timothy 1:9–11). Any minister of our Fellowship who performs a ceremony for these types of disapproved relations, unless innocently deceived into doing so, shall be dismissed from the Fellowship.

4. Counsel. An Assemblies of God minister is urged to counsel applicants for marriage ceremonies with scriptural guidelines for Christian marriage prior to performing the ceremony. A minister may not perform ceremonies for persons who, in the minister's opinion, approach marriage without proper forethought, wisdom, and sobriety.

e. Ministerial Credentials

We disapprove of any married minister of the Assemblies of God holding credentials if either minister or spouse has a former companion living unless the divorce occurred prior to conversion. (See below Article VII, Section 2, paragraphs i and j.)

Article VII, Section 2

i. Marriage Status.

We disapprove of any married persons holding ministerial credentials with the Assemblies of God or of district councils granting credentials to such, if either marriage partner has a former spouse living, unless the divorce occurred prior to conversion.

j. Annulments, marriage dissolutions, and divorces

The Executive Presbytery shall have the authority to determine whether an applicant's annulment of a former marriage is consistent with the scriptural position of the Fellowship relating to the granting or holding of ministerial credentials; or in the case of a divorce or a dissolution, whether the circumstances would more appropriately be classified as calling for an annulment; or if the divorce occurred prior to conversion. In those cases involving preconversion divorce, they shall be decided on an individual basis, just as those that deal with annulments are decided. The application must be accompanied by clear and satisfactory evidence of an illegal marriage through deception or fraud. Appeals from the decision of the Executive Presbytery may be made to the General Presbytery.

---

[1]Some manuscripts omit "and marries another," but others, including the Sinaitic manuscript, contain it, and the sense of the context calls for it. There is no manuscript evidence for leaving out the exceptive clause. (See John Murray, *Divorce*, p. 40.)

4
Divine Healing: An Integral Part of the Gospel

From its inception the General Council of the Assemblies of God has recognized divine healing for the whole person as an important part of the gospel. It is part of the good news that Jesus commissioned His disciples to proclaim.

The Assemblies of God constitution in its Statement of Fundamental Truths, section 12, states: "Divine healing is an integral part of the gospel. Deliverance from sickness is provided for in the atonement, and is the privilege of all believers (Isaiah 53:4,5; Matthew 8:16,17; James 5:14–16)."

Though it is impossible in a brief paper to cover all the facets and implications of this statement or answer all the questions which have been raised concerning it, we shall attempt to show that the statement is scripturally sound.

An Integral Part of the Gospel

As we observe the ministry of both Jesus and the apostles, it is evident that divine healing was not something peripheral. It was an important witness to Jesus as the revelation of the

Father, as the promised Messiah, and as the Savior from sin (see John 10:37,38).

The Bible shows a close connection between the healing ministry of Jesus and His saving, forgiving ministry. His power to heal was actually a witness to His authority to forgive sins (Mark 2:5–12). Again and again His healing miracles parallel His preaching of the gospel and show the same compassion (Matthew 4:23; 9:35,36).

People came from all directions both to hear Him and to be healed (Luke 5:15; 6:17,18). He never turned any away but healed all who came to Him (Matthew 12:15; 14:14), curing all varieties of sickness, disease, deformities, defects, and injury (Matthew 15:30,31; 21:14). He also delivered people from demons and the problems they caused (Matthew 4:24).

Jesus recognized that sickness is often the result of sin (John 5:14) or of the activity of Satan (Luke 13:16). He recognized also, however, that sickness is not always the direct result of sin (John 9:2,3). There were times when it was rather an opportunity for God to be glorified (Mark 2:12).

Miracles of healing were an important part of the works God sent Jesus to do (John 9:3,4). This is in line with the Old Testament revelation of God as the Great Physician, the Lord who heals (Exodus 15:26; Psalm 103:3, where the Hebrew participles used in both cases indicate it is God's nature to heal). Jesus showed that divine healing is still a vital part of God's nature and plan.

Healings also helped to identify Jesus as the promised Messiah and Savior. As the Great Physician, Jesus fulfilled the prophecy of Isaiah 53:4, which in the Hebrew is very emphatic: "Surely our sickness He himself has borne [lifted and taken away], and our pain He carried [as a heavy load]. ("Griefs" [KJV] is the same word used of *physical* sickness and disease in

2 Chronicles 16:12; 21:15,18,19; Isaiah 38:9. "Sorrows" [KJV] is the same word used of *physical* pain in Job 33:19.)

Matthew applies this specifically to the healing ministry of Jesus: "He himself took away our sickness and bore away our diseases" (Matthew 8:17, literal translation). Isaiah ties this in with the saving ministry of Jesus (Isaiah 53:5). His sufferings were for our sins and lead to our peace with God: "And by his wounds we are healed [healing has come to us]."

The context in Isaiah 53:6 and the application in 1 Peter 2:24,25 emphasize especially the healing or restoration from sin. However, in view of the emphasis on physical sickness in Isaiah 53:4, it is clear that these passages include healing from both the spiritual and physical effects of our sins and waywardness.

When John the Baptist was imprisoned, he began to wonder whether or not Jesus was actually the promised Messiah or just another forerunner like himself. Jesus responded by calling attention to messianic works which linked miracles and the preaching of the gospel to the poor. Again, healing was an important witness, an integral part of the gospel (Isaiah 61:1,2; Luke 4:18; 7:19–23).

Divine healing continued to be an integral part of the gospel through the ministry of the apostles and the Early church. Jesus sent out the Twelve and the Seventy to preach and to heal the sick (Luke 9:2; 10:9).

After Pentecost "many wonders and miraculous signs were done by the apostles" (Acts 2:43). Luke treats the Book of Acts as an extension of what Jesus did and taught, not only through the apostles but through a Church filled with the Holy Spirit (Acts 1:1,8; 2:4).

Miracles, however, were not limited to the apostles. The promise of Jesus was to all believers (John 14:12–14) who would ask in His name (that is, recognizing His authority and conforming themselves to His nature and purposes).

God used deacons such as Philip to preach and heal (Acts 8:5–7), and an otherwise unknown disciple, Ananias, to heal Saul (Paul) (Acts 9:12–18). Mark supports healing in the ministry of believers (Mark 6:13, 9:38,39; 16:15–18).

Gifts of healings are included among the manifestations of the Spirit intended to edify or build up the Church (1 Corinthians 12:7) and are tied in with the witness to Jesus Christ as Lord (1 Corinthians 12:3).

Provided for in the Atonement

Under the Law attention is given to the priests, whose ministry points to our great High Priest who is touched with the feeling of our infirmities (Hebrews 4:14,15). The priests, through the sprinkling of the blood of the sacrifices, made atonement for the sins of the people.

An examination of the atonement in the Hebrew Bible shows that in most cases it refers to a ransom price paid for redemption and restoration. This points to the redemption through Christ where He shed His blood in our behalf and in our stead. God has set Him forth to be a propitiation (literally, a mercy seat) through faith in His blood (Romans 3:25).

The reference to the mercy seat goes back to Leviticus 16, where the high priest went once a year to sprinkle the blood of a sin offering on the mercy seat, the solid gold lid placed on the top of the ark of the covenant. In the ark were the tables of stone of the Law, which the people had broken.

The broken Law called for judgment and death. But when the blood of a spotless lamb was sprinkled, representing the sinless life of Christ, God saw that sinless life instead of the broken Law and could give mercy and blessing.

The primary purpose of the atonement was cleansing from sin (Leviticus 16:30; see also Romans 5:11 where "atonement" [KJV] is the same word translated "reconciliation" in Romans 11:15 and 2 Corinthians 5:18,19). It is also clear, however, that atonement brought release from the penalty and consequences of sin in order to bring restoration to God's blessing and favor.

When the people complained after the judgment that followed the rebellion of Korah, Dathan, and Abiram, God sent a plague on the Israelites. Moses then sent Aaron out into the midst of the congregation, where he made atonement for them, and the plague was stopped (Numbers 16:47,48).

We read also that when the men of Israel were numbered, they were to give one-half shekel atonement money for their redemption and to prevent a plague upon themselves (Exodus 30:12,15). Atonement thus provided for the consequences of sin, including sickness.

The Bible makes it clear that people could not pay the price for their redemption, so God out of His love and for the glory of His own name provided the atonement (Romans 3:25; see also Psalms 65:3; 78:38; 79:9; Romans 3:21–28).

That this atonement provided not only for the sin but the consequences of sin is pictured by Hosea buying back his wife at a great cost to himself when she was to be sold in the slave market (Hosea 3:1–5; 13:4; 14:4).

It is further illustrated by the brazen serpent incident: All the people had to do was look at it in order to live (Numbers 21:9).

All this was accomplished through Christ at Calvary (John 3:14–16). There He made a full atonement for the whole person. The New Testament speaks of this as redemption, which has essentially the same meaning as atonement. Through Christ we have received redemption and the forgiveness of sins (Romans 3:24; Ephesians 1:7; Colossians 1:14; Hebrews 9:15).

Again, atonement provides for the consequences of sin. Even where sickness is not the direct result of sin, it is still in the world because of sin. Therefore it is among the works of the devil Jesus came to destroy (1 John 3:8) and is thus included in the atonement.

The Bible indicates, however, that until Jesus comes we groan because we have not yet received the redemption of our bodies (Romans 8:23). Only when the dead in Christ rise and we are changed do we receive the new bodies which are like His glorious body (1 Corinthians 15:42–44, 51–54).

From the parallel between redemption and atonement, we see therefore that the provision for our bodies is the redemption spoken of in Romans 8:23. We receive the forgiveness of sins now in connection with the redemption of our souls. We shall receive the redemption of our bodies when we are caught up to meet the Lord and are changed into His likeness (1 Corinthians 15:51–54; 2 Corinthians 5:1–4; 1 John 3:2). Divine healing is a foretaste of this, and, like all the blessings of the gospel, flows from the atonement.

Again, the language of Isaiah 53:4 specifically speaks of physical ills and indicates that Christ in His atonement was concerned about providing for sickness as well as sin. Matthew 8:16,17 not only confirms this, but shows that the atonement includes divine healing as a means of meeting the needs of those who come to Jesus.

The Privilege of All Believers

Just as salvation is by grace through faith (Ephesians 2:8), so all God's blessings and gifts are ours by His grace or unmerited favor. We do not earn them. We do not deserve them.

No one in the New Testament demanded healing. People came to Jesus beseeching Him. They did not look on healing as their right, but as a gracious privilege extended to them.

As the privilege of believers, the promise of healing does not rule out suffering for Christ's sake and the gospel's. We are expected to be prepared to follow His example (Hebrews 5:8; 1 Peter 2:19,21; 4:12–14,19).

Nor are we to look to divine healing as a substitute for obedience to the rules of physical and mental health. Jesus recognized the need of the disciples to get away from the crowds and rest awhile (Mark 6:31). Jethro saw that if Moses did not delegate some of his responsibilities to others, he would wear away (Exodus 18:18).

Neither is divine healing a means of avoiding the effects of old age. Moses did retain a clear eye and his natural strength until the day of his death (Deuteronomy 34:7). But this privilege was not granted to King David (1 Kings 1:1–4).

The gradual breakdown of old age, pictured so graphically in Ecclesiastes 12:1–7, is the common experience of believers as well as unbelievers. Healing is still available to the aged, but the part that is healed usually continues to age like the rest of the body. We do not yet have the redemption of the body.

Even we who have the firstfruits of the Spirit groan and travail in pain like the rest of creation, waiting patiently for the fulfillment of our hope (Romans 8:21–25). No matter what we do for this body, no matter how many times we are healed, if Jesus tarries we shall die.

However, the Bible does not tell us this to discourage us, but to make us realize that we must encourage and cultivate our life in the Spirit, for the Spirit quickens (resurrects), and that is our real hope (Romans 8:11). In fact, even though outwardly one is perishing, inwardly one is being renewed day by day (2 Corinthians 4:16).

Actually it is this inner renewal that makes us best able to have the faith to claim the privilege of divine healing. To the woman healed of the issue of blood, Jesus said, "Your faith has healed you" (Mark 5:34).

Paul at Lystra, when he saw that the hearing of the gospel had brought faith to be healed into the heart of a cripple, commanded him to stand up (Acts 14:9,10).

The inner renewal of the mind (Romans 12:2; Colossians 3:10) is seen also in the great faith of the Roman centurion who recognized the authority of Christ's word (Matthew 8:5–13) and the Syrophoenician woman who believed that even a crumb would meet the need (Matthew 15:28; Mark 7:24–30).

That divine healing comes through faith is further confirmed by the fact that unbelief hindered its reception at Nazareth (Mark 6:5,6) and at the foot of the Mount of Transfiguration (Matthew 17:14–20). There Jesus indicates the necessity also of expressing faith by praying and fasting (Mark 9:29).

Prayer is one of the chief means of healing in the Old Testament. Many of the Psalms include prayers for healing. Many of the prophets prayed for the healing of others. James 5:15 promises that the prayer of faith will save the sick and the Lord will raise them up.

Great faith then receives healing through the simple Word of the Lord.

But Jesus did not turn away from those who had little faith or weak faith. Those who are sick often find it is not easy to express faith, and Jesus did a variety of things to help them.

Some He touched (Mark 1:41; 8:22), took their hands (Mark 1:31; Luke 14:4), or laid His hands upon them (Mark 6:5; 8:25; Luke 4:40; 13:13).

Others He helped by a variety of acts, some of which called for faith and obedience on their part (Mark 7:33; 8:23).

Others found that to touch Him or His garments helped

them express faith (Mark 3:10; 5:28; 6:56; Luke 6:19).

Peter's shadow had the same effect for a time (Acts 5:15). So did the handkerchiefs and work aprons from Paul's tent-making shop (Acts 19:12).

The faith, however, had to be in the Lord, not in the means used to help them express their faith. This seems to be the reason for the great variety of means used, lest people get their eyes on the means rather than on God.

In the same class is James 5:14, which instructs the sick to call the elders of the church to anoint them with oil in the name of the Lord. It is not the oil (a symbol of the Holy Spirit) that brings the healing, but the prayer of faith.

The promise "anyone who has faith in me will do what I have been doing" is closely connected with prayer, asking in Christ's name (John 14:12–14; 16:23,24). His name, however, is the revelation of His character and nature. We have that in us only if we abide in Christ and His words abide in us (John 15:7). Then our will lines up with His, and we can ask what we will, and it shall be done.

Some have tried to limit healing (especially the promise of Exodus 15:26, the covenant of healing or health) to Israel. But the healing of the centurion's servant and the daughter of the Syrophoenician woman show that healing is the privilege of Gentiles also. In fact, there is healing for those who desire it and will respond to Jesus, even though He has not yet dealt with their sins (as in the case of the impotent man at the Pool of Bethesda, John 5:2–9,14).

Others have tried to set divine healing in opposition to or in competition with the medical profession. This need not be so. Physicians through their skills have brought help to many.

It is true that the Lord is the Great Physician. It is also true that the Bible condemns King Asa because "in his disease he sought not to the Lord, but to the physicians" (2 Chronicles 16:12, KJV). But Asa had already sought for help from Syria in an act of unbelief and disobedience when he refused to rely on the Lord (2 Chronicles 16:7). The emphasis is not that he sought physicians (which in this case may have been heathen physicians), but that he refused to seek the Lord.

It is evident that the physician had an honorable place in Israel (Jeremiah 8:22). Jesus also presented the medicinal use of oil and wine by the Good Samaritan in a favorable light (Luke 10:34).

When the woman with the issue of blood was healed, we are told she "had suffered a great deal under the care of many doctors and had spent all she had, yet instead of getting better she grew worse" (Mark 5:26). If it was wrong for her to go to physicians, this would have been the perfect place for Jesus to have said so. But He did not. Instead, He accepted the faith she now expressed and commended her for it. Even today God has performed many miracles for those given up by doctors.

Jesus also sent the 10 lepers back to show themselves to the priests (Luke 17:14). Under the Law the priests were in charge of diagnosis, quarantine, and health (Leviticus 13:2ff.; 14:2ff.; Matthew 8:4). Thus Jesus recognized that human diagnosticians have their place.

The priests, however, were agents of the Lord, and in this sense it is possible to take all healing as divine, whether instantaneous or gradual (see Mark 8:24). On the other hand, those healed in the Bible did not testify to divine healing until the healing was actually accomplished by divine power.

We recognize that there have been abuses today. But we must not let that cause us to retreat from a positive proclamation of the truth of the Scripture. The apostles were able to say, "What I have I give you" (Acts 3:6).

Gifts of healings are among the variety of gifts and manifestations of the Spirit set in the Church as the body of Christ (1 Corinthians 12:4–11,28–30). Like the other gifts, these seem to be administered through members of the Body for the edification of those who need them. (Just as the word of wisdom does not make a person wise, the gifts of healings do not make people healers. Rather as a fresh word of wisdom is given for each need, so a fresh gift of healing is given by the Spirit for each individual sickness.)

We find also, both in the ministry of Jesus and the apostles, that there were times when the gospel was being preached in new areas and new situations when miracles of healing were especially prominent. This seems to be the case when special miracles were done by the hands of Paul (Acts 19:11).

In humility we recognize that we do not understand all that pertains to divine healing. We still see through a glass darkly. We do not understand why some are healed and others are not, any more than we understand why God permitted James to be martyred and Peter delivered. Scripture makes it clear, however, that our part is to preach the Word and expect the signs to follow.

5
The Discipleship and Submission Movement

The current outpouring of the Holy Spirit has given multitudes all over the world a new appreciation of what Jesus means to believers. As a result many old barriers have been broken down. Fellowship with God and Christ in the Spirit has brought people together from various backgrounds. With this, a new hunger for the teaching of the Word of God has arisen.

Every day new groups are formed for the express purpose of prayer and Bible study. Some of these groups, however, have lacked leaders with a mature understanding of the Word. In many cases the pastors of the old-line churches to which some of these people belonged have been either too busy or too unsympathetic to the Pentecostal experience to give the counsel and help needed.

With the avowed intention of meeting this need for training and for developing leadership, well-known Bible teachers are promoting a new concept of shepherding, discipleship, and submission to authority. For a number of those cut off from old loyalties and for new converts who had no one to guide them, this teaching seems to have filled a vacuum with what appears to be good results. In other cases, however, there have been serious abuses. Much has been reported that is destructive and divisive. So much so that it has become necessary to examine the claims of this movement, especially with respect to its teachings concerning the Scriptures, the Church, and the believers.

The Scriptures

All these teachers seem to declare loyalty to the written Word of God as the inspired and infallible rule of faith and conduct. All seem to claim that any manifestation of the gifts of the Spirit must be judged by it. They recognize also that the Word must be applied to our present situation and to our daily needs and problems. Some, however, seem to attach unwarranted authority to the contemporary spoken word, the *rhema*, going so far as to hold that it is equal to the written Word, the *logos*.

It is true that the gifts of the Spirit such as the word of wisdom, the word of knowledge, prophecy, and interpretation may provide specific help, encouragement, and guidance for believers. But the danger comes when instead of searching the Scriptures and judging these words by the whole intent of the Word of God, selected passages are spiritualized or allegorized in a way that will support their teachings.

One example is the way John 10 has been interpreted. In John 10:1–6, Jesus contrasted the shepherd who comes into the sheepfold by the door with the thief who enters by climbing up another way. His hearers did not understand His meaning, so Jesus changed the picture and plainly said, "I am the door of the sheep. All that ever came before me are thieves and robbers" (John 10:7,8, KJV). As the Good Shepherd, also, He would lay down His life for the sheep.

A number today have misinterpreted the phrase "I am the

door." Jesus is *the* door, they say, and then they add that everyone needs an "undershepherd" who is *a* door. They teach that such an undershepherd will keep out the thieves and robbers, the false teachers who would lead believers astray and rob them of God's truth and blessings. At the same time, they hold the undershepherd is to be responsible for teaching, training, counseling, and guiding his "sheep" in a lifelong commitment.

It is true many new converts look to someone to keep them from error and to guide them into truth. However, where they rely altogether on another person to protect them from all error, they will cease searching the Scriptures and fail to develop their own ability to withstand false teaching. Both Paul and Peter warn against false teachers, but the New Testament does not indicate that the answer is to get a human shepherd who will protect the believer. Scripture teaches that all must fight the good fight of faith (1 Timothy 6:12). All must put on the whole armor of God and learn to use the shield of faith and the sword of the Spirit so they may stand (Ephesians 6:10–18).

Furthermore, a closer examination of John 10 rules out the idea of anyone being a door in the sense that Jesus is. He is *the* door for *all* the sheep. The true sheep listen to no one's voice but Christ's, for they know Him and they know that He alone laid down His life for them. He knows their need. He gives them eternal life (John 10:4,14,27,28).

The sheep of His flock hear His voice for themselves and know it. Thus to take John 10 and use it as a basis for interposing human shepherds between the convert and Christ or to use it as a basis for making human teachers a door is to establish a doctrine for which this passage gives no grounds.

Paul recognized that the elders (pastors) of the congregations in Ephesus had a responsibility to feed the flock, the church (local assembly) of God. He warned that wolves would enter among them, not sparing the flock. But he also warned that from among these elders or undershepherds themselves, men would arise and twist the Scripture to draw away disciples after them (Acts 20:28–30). That is, they will seem to be good teachers but will twist the truth at some points in order to build a following for themselves.

Thus believers need more than a human shepherd to protect them. They need to develop their own ability to search and understand the Scriptures under the guidance of the Spirit, who alone can lead into all truth (John 16:13).

The Church

Another aspect of this movement is its attitude toward the Church. Its leaders claim they are not starting a new denomination and suggest that respect be given to existing churches and pastors. But in practice they are saying that existing churches and pastors have failed. By the very fact that leaders in this movement are establishing a new set of shepherds, they are setting up new structures and forming a new denomination, regardless of how they may try to interpret their actions.

In line with this, some of these teachers claim their mission and the church's mission is no longer evangelism, but the setting up of a new order on earth in prospect of bringing in the Kingdom. But the New Testament does not indicate we can set up a purified external order in this age. The Church grows and develops, but the tares will be among the wheat until the harvest. Judgment that destroys the present world order is necessary before the kingdom rule can be established on earth, as Daniel 2, 2 Thessalonians 1, and Revelation 19 clearly indicate. It is necessary to avoid this postmillennial viewpoint which ignores the evangelistic purpose of the Church in the present age.

Some find the pattern for their new order of discipleship in the relationship of Jesus and His disciples, forgetting that this was done within Judaism before Jesus began to build His Church. Instead they should seek guidance for church patterns in the Acts and Epistles. There variety is evident to meet the need for every situation.

Along with this there is a current tendency to downgrade democracy in the church in favor of submission to authority. It is supposed that apostles and elders of the Jerusalem church exercised authority over the church in Jerusalem and other churches as well. A closer examination of the Scripture shows that when the seven were chosen to administer aid to the widows, the apostles merely stated the qualifications and asked the people to choose or elect seven men (Acts 6:3,5). In Acts 14:23 where Paul and Barnabas "ordained" (KJV) elders in every church, the Greek word for *ordain* means to choose or elect by the raising of hands. Though it is correctly translated "chosen" in 2 Corinthians 8:19, some say it cannot mean elect in Acts 14:23 because the apostles are the subject. There is no reason, however, why the verb may not indicate that Paul and Barnabas laid down the qualifications for elders (as in 1 Timothy 3:1–7) and then conducted an election. We see variety in the New Testament rather than one rigid type of organization. The purpose of organization was always to meet the need and accomplish the task, never just to organize for organization's sake.

There is no indication that the Jerusalem church exercised authority over other churches. When they sent Peter and John to Samaria, it was to express interest and give help. The same thing was true when Barnabas was sent to Antioch. It is helpful to notice that Barnabas did not turn to Jerusalem for advice when he needed help. He went directly to Tarsus and brought

Saul to work with him. But Saul did not stay under the authority of Barnabas, for both were under the authority of Christ and the Holy Spirit. Barnabas willingly allowed Paul to take the place of leadership later on.

Not only so, Paul withstood Barnabas on one occasion (Acts 15:36–41), and Peter and the delegates from James and the Jerusalem church on another (Galatians 2:11–14). His authority was the Word, his guidance by the Spirit and the Word. Paul's response to the request of James at Jerusalem to participate in an act of purification was concern for the truth, not mere arbitrary submission to authority (Acts 21:17–26).

The Bible does teach a submission to our leaders and to one another in love. But this is a matter of mutual concern and consideration for one another. The Bible also recognizes the need for leadership, but Jesus warned that whoever would be first should be the servant of all. There is no room in the church for anyone to lord it over another or over God's heritage (1 Peter 5:3).

Paul and his company did not claim dominion over the faith of their converts. Rather, they were helpers of their joy, but by their own faith these converts would stand (2 Corinthians 1:23,24). Peter (1 Peter 5:5) urged the younger to submit to the elder, but immediately added that all are to be subject one to another and clothed with humility.

No one is to take arbitrary authority over others even to protect them. For each is to be on guard, to be vigilant, in order to have victory over Satan (1 Peter 5:8).

The Believer

With regard to the position of the believer, the tendency of this shepherding movement seems to be to over allegorize the Scripture, pressing its analogies too far.

The believer is said to be a "dumb" sheep. This takes the external circumstances of the analogy to an extreme not warranted by the context or by the rest of the Bible.

In the Bible believers are compared to sheep in the sense that through Christ they go in and out and find pasture. Christ leads and feeds them. But Jesus also called His disciples friends. He explained His plans and purposes. He called for them to share in His work as fellow laborers. He promised another Comforter to be with each one to do the same work He had done of helping, teaching, and building. Christ is the one Mediator between God and humanity, yet through the Spirit a variety of gifts and ministries is available to build the believer. (See Romans 12:4–8; 1 Corinthians 12; Ephesians 4:11–13.)

The emphasis of this shepherding movement, that believers find themselves a shepherd to submit to in order to be rightly related to Christ, is usually based on Ephesians 4:16. Proponents of this view interpret this to mean we must be connected to the Body through joints or ligaments. This also is pressing the human side of the analogy too far.

The context shows that all are to come to the unity of the faith and of the knowledge of the Son of God. None are to be as children, tossed to and fro and carried about with every wind of doctrine. All are to speak the truth in love so they may grow up into Him in all things. Unlike the human body, when every part of the body of Christ is in its proper place, every part receives from Christ directly, so that the Body increases and edifies itself in love.

Similarly in John 15 Jesus is the whole vine. Every branch (every believer) is related to Him directly and receives the flow of His life directly, not through some other branch.

God has set pastor-teachers in the Church (Ephesians 4:11) as a part of the variety of ministry to the whole Body. To reject these ministries is to deliberately reject the wise provision of the Head of the Church who is the giver of these gifts. On the other hand, however, to suggest that a Christian does not have access to God or guidance from Him apart from a human shepherd is going to the opposite extreme and denies what the Bible teaches about the believer's direct access to God (Hebrews 4:14–16).

In this connection some have even suggested that the "shepherd" must be told all one's plans and decisions so one can thus be "covered." This terminology is misleading. The Bible used *cover* in the sense of blood atonement—something Jesus did once and for all—something that is available only through Him.

Others have tried to justify a shepherd-sheep relationship by comparing it to Paul's relationship to Timothy. But this was the relationship of an older to a younger minister and does not establish a pattern for the relationship between a pastor and people.

Still others use the analogy of a wife's obedience to her husband. But this is used of submission of the Church to Christ, not of one believer to another. To use it in that way is misinterpreting the analogy.

Conclusion

Perhaps we should recognize that the current shepherding-discipleship-submission movement did indeed grow out of real needs. In the midst of a permissive society, people do need authority. But we must point them to the basic authority of the Word. Then we also point them to Paul's admonition that they learn to know those who labor among us, who are over us in the Lord, and esteem them in love for their work's sake (1 Thessalonians 5:12).

In our impersonal society, people do need the closer fellowship of smaller groups. These can be provided through leadership training within the local church under the direction of the pastor. Ways of meeting this need can vary to suit the circumstances. But the kind of division seen in the Corinthian church, based on getting a following for a human leader, must be avoided.

In our complex society, people do need teaching and training. But more is needed than one person or even a local church can supply. The Bible calls for a plurality of ministry and gifts within the local church (1 Corinthians 12). It also suggests that others can be brought in as was Apollos (Acts 18:27,28). Others can be sent to Bible colleges for training.

Above all, we need to recognize that the sin of causing division in the church is a most serious breach (Romans 16:17,18; Titus 3:9–11). In the urgency of this age the unity of the larger body is also very important if we are to accomplish the mission of the Church. The united effort of Assemblies of God missions is witness to the effectiveness of cooperation among many local assemblies. Much is being done that small groups working independently of each other are not doing and have never been able to do.

Finally, Jesus Christ must be kept central. He is the great Shepherd of the sheep. The only covenant we need is the one sealed in His blood. We can do God's will in a way that is well pleasing in the sight of God only through Him (Hebrews 13:20,21).

6
Transcendental Meditation

Among present attempts to bridge the gap between Eastern and Western philosophies are those of Hare Krishna and Transcendental Meditation. Transcendental Meditation, or TM as it is commonly called, in particular has received widespread publicity recently in America. It has gained sufficient attention to arouse the curiosity of many. People who previously knew nothing of the mystical practices of the East now search for materials on TM.

The Nature of Transcendental Meditation

A surface definition of Transcendental Meditation pictures it as a natural practice of relaxation for two 20-minute periods each day. During the process one repeats a word, known as a *mantra*, in such a way that its rhythmic repetition aids the relaxation effort. The promoters of TM present it as a "scientific" practice based on biological and psychological laws. They repeatedly declare that it is a non-religious activity in which people of all faiths may participate with great benefit.

After initiation and careful instruction in TM, for which one pays a fee, faithful use of the technique reportedly produces near-miraculous results in all areas of life—physical, psychological, social, and spiritual. Advocates of TM present what purports to be research data, and numerous testimonials from politicians, educators, sports and theatrical celebrities, as well as religious leaders, to support their claims.

However, an in-depth study of Transcendental Meditation reveals that not all of its story appears on the surface. Serious examination of TM materials shows it is more than a relaxation tool. It is a religious activity.

Transcendental Meditation has its root in Hinduism. All of its teachings about reality, God, humanity, and salvation are from the Vedas, the scriptures of the Hindus. The inclusion of the ritualistic initiation ceremony and the use of the secret *mantra* in TM are in keeping with the mystical practices of the cults of the East. Maharishi, world leader of TM, explains the benefits of the technique in religious rather than scientific language.

Transcendental Meditation, therefore, raises questions in the areas of psychology, theology, and sociology. These questions present the Church with a challenge which it cannot ignore.

The Roots of Transcendental Meditation

It is clear that Transcendental Meditation is a religious activity in point of origin. Aspects of it can be traced to Hinduism.

There are seemingly millions of gods in Hindu worship, but three stand out among them as most prominent. The first is Brahma, the creator of all things material. The second is Shiva, the god of destruction, disease, and death, as well as the god of vegetable, animal, and human reproduction. In Indian thought, death is but a prelude to rebirth. Thus the god of death is also the god of sexuality. The third is Vishnu, the god of love and benevolence. However, above these is the all-pervading, impersonal god-force, the being called Brahman. The literature of TM refers to Brahman as Creative Intelligence.

Hinduism provides various means for worship of the gods. These include ascetic practices, ritualistic devotions, and meditation. Meditation has enjoyed considerable attention as a means of worship through the centuries. The main feature of all yoga is meditation. In Hindu tradition meditation is necessary even for the gods if they are to be united with the Being and thus escape the cycle of birth, death, and rebirth.

By definition, then, meditation is emphasized in TM as the best means of "transcending" or experiencing unity with Being. Until recently, the last revival of Transcendental Meditation was during the Middle Ages. Sankara, the most outstanding scholar of medieval Hinduism, was its chief proponent. Modern efforts to restore the Eastern art of meditation received greatest impetus with Swami Brahmananda Saraswati, generally referred to as Guru Dev, one of four major religious leaders in India. The popular leader of TM, however, is Maharishi Mahesh Yogi, a disciple of Guru Dev.

Reportedly, Maharishi was commissioned by Guru Dev to develop a simple form of meditation. Following a time of seclusion in the Himalayas, he introduced TM in 1955. Failing to attract much attention in India, he exported his teachings to England. Among his most noted converts there were the Beatles. Maharishi began his work in America in 1959. He founded the Maharishi International University in Fairfield, Iowa, as the educational arm of TM in 1973.

The Teachings of Transcendental Meditation

It is manifestly evident that Transcendental Meditation is religious in nature because of the ideas upon which the technique is built. Its theological presuppositions are those of Hinduism.

Teachings About God

The Maharishi holds that the Being, or Creative Intelligence, is eternal, infinite, unknowable, sexless, and impersonal, following the tradition of Hindu theology. The Being is without attribute, quality, feature, or form. In Hindu thought a clear distinction is not made between God and His creation.

Teachings About Reality

Maharishi holds that all creation is one with Being. He illustrates this pantheistic view by declaring that Being permeates all that exists, as butter permeates milk, or as sap permeates a tree. Basic reality consists of the relative and the absolute, but they are simply two aspects of one essence. The absolute is that aspect of Being which, in its essential nature, remains unmanifested, while the relative is that aspect in which the Being manifests itself in creation.

In the view of Maharishi, Being indwells everything in creation in a way that It constitutes the only reality there is. The trunk, branches, leaves, flowers, and fruit of the tree constantly change, but the sap, which is like Being, remains the same. That which is always changing has no real quality of its own. Thus the world is only an illusion. It just seems to be real.

Teachings About Humanity

Thus, in the view of Maharishi, since Being manifests itself in the many forms of life in creation, It dwells in the heart of all people. Each person's soul, then, is one of a great ocean of souls that make up Brahman. One needs to know oneself as a part of all life in the universe. One's relationship to this universal life is like that of a cell to a body. Each one must come to experience every being in creation as dear as one is to oneself.

Teachings About Salvation

According to Maharishi, humanity's ignorance of the above facts is the sole source of all their problems. They are bound up in a world of illusion and ignorance. Thinking falsely that creation is real, they are unaware of identity with Being. As long as they remain in such ignorance, they are bound to a life of *karma,* action that keeps them endlessly in the cycle of birth, death, and rebirth. Salvation comes with the knowledge of the illusion of life and of oneness with Being.

Further, whatever one is presently is a result of *karma,* the actions in one's previous life. As long as a soul has not merged itself in knowledge with Creative Intelligence, it will continue as an individual and will keep on receiving the fruit of the *karma* of the past life. All suffering is due to not knowing the way to unfold the divine glory present within one's heart.

Lack of knowledge of how to "dive" within oneself is the root of all ills in human life. Without such experiences, one lacks energy and intelligence. One is tired, worried, and tense. For contacting divine consciousness within, Maharishi's technique, of course, is Transcendental Meditation.

The Methods of Transcendental Meditation

It is further evident that Transcendental Meditation is more than just a relaxation technique because not only are its presuppositions religious but so are its methods. Maharishi describes his meditative art itself as that which unfolds the divine in a person.

The Art of Meditation

Maharishi carefully gives his own definition of the term *meditation.* It is not to be confused with concentration. That is the reverse of what his technique requires. The mind must be totally passive in meditation. No conscious effort can be exerted. The mind is simply allowed to naturally "dive" into the great ocean of Creative Intelligence. All activity of human thought, the very content of human knowledge, is in the relative sphere of reality, not the absolute. Therefore, in meditation the mind is unconsciously infused with the power of Being. Successful living demands a continuous intake of such power.

That suspension of thought is necessary to achieve the sense of unity with Being is illustrated by Maharishi in his discussion of ethics. He recognizes that each of the religions of the world has its code of ethics. However, these are related to the changing cultures of the times. Thus there is no absolute, written standard of right and wrong. Nothing but a mind which is influenced by Creative Intelligence through TM can possibly determine actions in accordance with unchanging ethics.

The Initiation Ceremony

The initiation ceremony in Transcendental Meditation is distinctly religious in nature. It consists of a traditional Hindu *puja,* or worship ritual. At the rite the TM beginner brings an offering of six flowers, three pieces of fresh fruit, and a white handkerchief. His teacher places these on an altar before a picture of Guru Dev. Aided by candlelight and incense, the teacher chants a song of thanksgiving in Sanskrit to a long line of departed Hindu masters. He worships the Hindu *Trimurti* of Brahma, Vishnu, and Shiva as the manifestations of the formless Brahman. The primary focus of attention, however, is on Guru Dev, late master of Maharishi. The presence of his picture suggests the idea of an idol which is indeed worshiped.

The Mantra

As the final act of the initiation ceremony, the TM teacher kneels at the side of the convert and begins to repeat a secret *mantra* selected especially for him or her. While TM advocates declare that the *mantra* is a harmless, meaningless word chosen only for its hypnotic benefits, it is a word taken from the Vedas, which has been used traditionally to invoke the assistance of the various Hindu deities. It may seem meaningless to the uninformed, but the *mantra* has a definite religious meaning in the Hindu context.

The Problems of Transcendental Meditation

A serious consideration of these facts, then, suggests that Transcendental Meditation poses questions in the areas of psychology, theology, and sociology.

Psychological Issues

Possible psychological problems stem from the emphasis on mental passivity in TM. The technique requires that one's mind be left totally undirected during meditation. Ordinary thinking must be transcended altogether. What transpires in TM is supposedly beyond the level of intellectual comprehension.

For the Christian, the methods of TM are not a revival of the quietistic practices which have appeared periodically through history. The technique promotes mystical experiences divorced from either knowledge or reason. Thus TM encourages a passive state of mind which could open the door for demonic activity in the life of an individual. Transcendental Meditation is no less harmful than is idolatry. Demons were involved in idol worship in Bible times (Deuteronomy 32:17; 1 Corinthians 10:19,20).

Another psychological difficulty of TM is that it offers quick and easy solutions to anxiety without going to the root of the problem. It ignores the possible causes of psychological stress, offering only temporary relief. Some research by scholars outside the camp of TM indicates that the benefits which appear to come from meditation are short-lived.

Theological Issues

The theological problems which TM presents are manifold. Maharishi has termed his theological teachings as the Science of Creative Intelligence, or SCI. All that SCI teaches about God, reality, humanity, and salvation stands opposed to the teachings of the Bible. It denies the existence of a personal God. The Bible shows that God is personal. He knows (Matthew 6:8,32), loves (John 3:16), wills (Matthew 6:10), and acts (Genesis 1:1).

Further, SCI denies the Creator-creature distinction fundamental to Biblical revelation. Contrary to the pantheistic premise of SCI that God is all and all is God, God is distinct from His creation. Creation is but the handiwork of God (Psalm 19:1). In confusing God with creation, SCI repeats the sin of early human beings (Romans 1:23,25).

SCI says that God is an unmanifested Being. The Bible makes clear that He has revealed himself in nature, conscience, history, miracles, prophecy, Scripture, and finally through His Son Jesus.

Maharishi views people not as sinners helpless to save themselves from God's judgments but as beings capable of experiencing their own divinity. The doctrine of SCI presents no concept of humanity's need of a mediator. People become their own savior through merely practicing TM.

There is no talk in SCI of repentance. Punishment follows sin inevitably, according to the law of *karma*. There is no room for mercy and grace. One's present is dictated by one's *karma,* or action of the past. Thus the present is accepted fatalistically.

In spite of teachings so different from those of Christianity, Maharishi claims that Christians, or followers of any religion, may practice TM without conflict. But this is because he operates from a Hindu base, which has a myriad of gods, both good and evil, in its theology. To accept one more god creates no problem. He says it matters little what name people give their religion or what ritual they follow in their church, temple, mosque, or pagoda.

It is the Maharishi's view that Hinduism covers the world's religions by its giant umbrella. Accordingly, the Hindu is the most religiously tolerant of any person on earth. To Hindus the Vedas are the oldest of the scriptures. Whatever truth the sacred books of the world contain appeared first in the Vedas. Thus the basic truth of one religion is the basic truth of all other religions.

Sociological Issues

Due to Maharishi's bold plans for the propagation of the Science of Creative Intelligence, there are sociological problems associated with Transcendental Meditation. He presents his doctrine as a cure for all the world's ills, physical, psychological, spiritual, economic, political, social, and even environmental.

In 1972 Maharishi inaugurated a World Plan to make SCI and the TM program available to everyone on earth. He estimates that one teacher for SCI for every 1,000 people will be sufficient to accomplish the task. A program is now under way to establish 3,600 World Plan Centers for the project. Maharishi International University, video-tape programs, and television stations owned by TM will also serve to further the plan.

Besides the university, four other organizations have been

formed as arms of the World Plan. The Students' International Society works with youth. The International Meditation Society appeals to the general population of adults. The Spiritual Regeneration Movement is for those interested in a spiritual approach to life, but especially retired persons. The Foundation for the Science of Creative Intelligence is designed for the business and professional community.

The advocates of TM declare an interest in more than merely the health and happiness of individuals. Their ambitions reach to no less heights than that of changing social institutions. To achieve such purposes, Maharishi proposes to use whatever is in vogue in a society at a given time. This may be religion, education, or politics.

What is most suited as a tool for promoting TM in this generation? According to Maharishi, it is politics. Thus his energies are devoted to making TM available through the agencies of government. Already the teaching of TM on an experimental basis is available in some schools of the United States at federal expense. Classes in SCI and TM have been legalized for use in the public schools of Illinois, New York, Massachusetts, Florida, and California. In some areas concerned citizens have raised legal questions regarding the propriety of government support for such projects.

The Challenge of Transcendental Meditation

Thus Transcendental Meditation presents a challenge to the Church on three fronts. The first is to a new emphasis on correctness of doctrine. Those who know that doctrine and practice cannot be separated will avoid the temptation to use the TM technique in regard to its theological moorings.

The Church must also emphasize anew the work of the Holy Spirit in the life of the believer. TM is but a treacherous substitute for genuine, biblically-based experiences in the Holy Spirit.

Likewise, the Church must proclaim again the great principle of sabbath rest taught from the beginning in the Bible. The madness of modern people at work and play increasingly violates the sabbath principle. God offers people the correct tool for physical, mental, and spiritual renewal by providing one day in seven for rest and worship. The research of some outside the TM camp has shown that the technique offers no physical benefits which cannot be achieved equally well by the simple act of rest. By following God's original plan for rejuvenation, the Christian has no need for the method of Transcendental Meditation.

Psalm 1:2 enjoins the believer to meditate upon the Word of God. Herein is the true content of genuine meditation. And the benefits of such meditation are not transitory but eternal!

7
Deacons and Trustees

God's method by which the church of Jesus Christ has moved forward down through the centuries is that God selected a person to be the leader (the pastor) and then gave the leader others (deacons) to serve as support to the leader and as fellow servants to the congregation.

It is understood that God has always chosen to give the leadership the vision for the work of the Lord. For a pastor and board to work together for the enlargement of the kingdom of God is a beautiful experience.

Terminology Used With Church Boards

Deacons

The deacons are chosen from among the congregation to "serve the church" in the practical, spiritual, and temporal matters of that body of believers.

Trustees

The trustees are chosen from among the congregation to be custodians of the church property and serve as signatories.

Board of Advisors

The Board of Advisors shall be chosen to assist the pastor in those churches which have an insufficient number of adults to qualify as deacons.

Official Board

The pastor and deacons shall be the official board of the local church. In the event a church does not have a Board of Deacons, the official board shall be that board elected to serve with the pastor.

Qualifications

Deacons

A person's life and character must pass certain criteria before qualifying one to serve. The Scriptures dictate the qualifications.

1. The deacon must be chosen from "among you" (Acts 6:3), a lay member of the local congregation for at least 1 year.

2. The deacon must be of good reputation, "of honest report" (Acts 6:3, KJV). The confidence and trust of the congregation and community are essential.

3. The deacon is in a spiritual ministry, "full of the Spirit" (Acts 6:3), according to Acts 2:4, and continuing to be "filled" (Ephesians 5:18).

4. The deacon is required to make decisions in practical and temporal matters as well as giving support to the pastor in spiritual matters, so sound direction and wise counsel need "wisdom" (Acts 6:3).

5. The deacon must be willing to be involved in the work of

God through the church; the deacon is to "serve" (Acts 6:2, KJV).

6. The deacon is to be "sincere" (1 Timothy 3:8), i.e., steadfast and serious.

7. The deacon is "not double-tongued" (1 Timothy 3:8, KJV), i.e., must be as good as one's word, dependable.

8. The deacon is "not indulging in much wine" (1 Timothy 3:8), but is temperate, not depending on physical stimulants.

9. The deacon is "not pursuing dishonest gain" (1 Timothy 3:8), but faithful with the tithe, generous, and not motivated by money.

10. The deacon is proper in doctrine, keeping "hold of the deep truths of the faith with a clear conscience" (1 Timothy 3:9), fully subscribing to the tenets of faith of the Assemblies of God.

11. The deacon is a mature believer, "and let these also first be proved" (1 Timothy 3:10, KJV).

12. The deacon has not experienced matrimonial mix-ups, but is in a faithful, monogamous marriage (1 Timothy 3:12).

13. Deacons lead their homes in Christ, "ruling their children and their own houses well" (1 Timothy 3:12, KJV).

14. Spouses of deacons (or deaconesses) must be an example of the Christian life, "not malicious talkers but temperate and trustworthy in everything" (1 Timothy 3:11).

15. At the discretion of the local congregation, a female meeting other stated qualifications may be selected to serve as a deaconess.

Trustees

Trustee boards in churches are frequently granted capacities similar to that of a Board of Deacons. If the Board of Trustees is granted such capacities, it is recommended that the qualifications shall be the same as a Board of Deacons.

Board of Advisors

Members of the Board of Advisors shall subscribe to the tenets of faith of the Assemblies of God, support the local church in attendance and finances, and shall have been approved by the district officiary.

Official Board

If the official board is other than a Board of Deacons or Board of Trustees, the qualifications shall be determined by the constitution and bylaws of the local congregation as long as the scriptural standards of leadership are maintained.

Relationships of All Boards

To the Pastor

The board member is the pastor's advisor, helper, and prayer partner, a loyal supporter of the pastor, assisting in fulfilling the vision and goals God has given the pastor for the church.

The pastor is the chairperson and a voting member of the church boards.

To Each Other

Board members are a team, working together within the scope of their assignment with the view to achieving the successful advancement of the church.

Board members should seek to develop a close relationship through mutual prayer, worship, and cooperative co-laboring with the pastor and staff.

To the Congregation

Board members should promote goodwill in the congregation and should strengthen the people's confidence in the pastor's leadership. The spiritual interest and welfare of the congregation are their concern and responsibility.

To the Community

Board members should be the church's public relations people in the community. Their lives should be a testimony of true Christianity, conducting themselves in a manner that will honor Christ.

Responsibilities of Boards

It is generally understood that the pastor, by virtue of office, is president of the corporation and chair of the board.

Deacons

The deacons shall act in an advisory capacity with the pastor in all matters pertaining to the assembly in its spiritual life and in the administration of the ordinances. They shall act in the examination of applicants for membership and also in the administration of church discipline.

At the discretion of the pastor, individual board members may be assigned portfolios of responsibility in the functioning of the local church.

It is expected that the official board shall serve as the nominating committee for selection of a pastor.

Trustees

The trustees serve as the official, legal servants in matters of business. Normally the president (pastor) and the secretary of the Board of Trustees sign legal documents in behalf of the church, particularly as property and financial contracts are involved.

The trustees, serving as custodians of the church property, shall include its proper maintenance and insurance, etc., and shall act on behalf of the church in selling and acquiring property.

Board of Advisors

Inasmuch as the district officiary serves as the official board of the local assembly when a Board of Advisors serves, this board shall act in an advisory capacity to the pastor in the routine functioning of the local church.

Official Board

The official board shall serve as it has been defined in the above guidelines.

Appendage

Elder or Eldership

After research, we conclude, because of the use of the word in the original Greek (Acts 20:17,28; 1 Timothy 5:17; James 5:14, etc.), that the words "elder" or "eldership" refer to the office of pastor, bishop, or overseer. It is beyond the scope of our assignment to speak to this office.

Process by Which Eligibility Is Determined

A. When a nominating committee is provided for in the local constitution and bylaws, the following procedure is recommended:

1. Spiritual qualifications shall be considered as stated under

"Qualifications."

2. The nominee shall be one who faithfully supports the local church in attendance and finances.
3. The nominee should understand the Assemblies of God church government.
4. Before a nominee is presented, the pastor should discuss philosophy and vision and determine the nominee's willingness to serve.

B. The selection of board members shall be by a vote of the local congregational membership after nominees have been approved.

Conclusion

The pastor is God's gift to the church; board members are the church's gift to the pastor.

8
Eternal Punishment

The position of the Assemblies of God concerning eternal punishment is set forth in its "Statement of Fundamental Truths" as follows:

Section 15. The Final Judgment. There will be a final judgment in which the wicked dead will be raised and judged according to their works. Whosoever is not found written in the Book of Life, together with the devil and his angels, the beast and the false prophet, will be consigned to everlasting punishment in "the fiery lake of burning sulfur: This is the second death" (Revelation 21:8; compare Matthew 25:46; Mark 9:43–48; Revelation 19:20; 20:11–15).

Here we note that the punishment is with the devil and his angels, that it is everlasting, and that it is in the lake of fire which is called the second death. This paper will attempt to give further definition and explanation to each of these points.

The Wicked Share Satan's Doom

The Bible makes it clear that the lake of fire was not intended for people but for the devil and his angels (Matthew 25:41). God's purpose and desire for humanity has always been good. The first heaven and earth were created good (Genesis 1:31). The Law was given for the good of humankind (Deuteronomy

6:24). God does not will that any should perish (2 Peter 3:9). In fact, God works in all things for the ultimate good of those who love Him and respond to His call (Romans 8:28). Nevertheless, God will not allow Satan to spoil the new heaven and the new earth which are to come. God will shut him off in the lake of fire. Those who follow Satan must share Satan's doom (John 16:8,11), for they have Satan, not God, as their father (John 8:44).

Those who share Satan's punishment are further referred to as the "wicked" (Matthew 13:49, 50). This is a general term for all who are actively evil and worthless. They include the cowardly (cowardly because of lack of faith), the unbelieving, the vile (the disgusting, detestable), murderers, sexually immoral, those who practice magic arts (those who use enchantments, harmful drugs), idolaters, and all liars (Revelation 21:8). (See also Matthew 8:12; 13:41,42; 22:13; 23:15; 25:30,33; Luke 13:27; Revelation 21:27; 22:15.) Paul sums it up by including all who do not know God with a personal knowledge of salvation plus all who do not keep on obeying the gospel (2 Thessalonians 1:8).

The Punishment of the Wicked Has No End

The first Bible reference given in the "Statement of Fundamental Truths"—Matthew 25:46—uses the phrase "everlasting [Greek, *aionion*] punishment." Some have denied that this means eternal in the sense of absolutely unending. In the same verse, however, Jesus used the same word of life "eternal" *(aionion)* in a manner that is directly and exactly parallel. In other words, the punishment will be as eternal as the eternal life. This leaves no room for any later restoration of the wicked. In Matthew 25:41 the punishment is defined as "everlasting [Greek, *aionion*] fire."

Jesus characterized the intermediate state of the wicked after death (hell, Hades) as one of fire (Luke 16:23,24), but this is to be distinguished from the eternal fire. Jesus' words in Luke 16 show us that the wicked remain conscious and are aware of their state and of what they have missed. But the eternal fire is to be identified with what Jesus called *Gehenna* or literally "the gehenna of fire" (Matthew 5:22,29,30; 10:28; 18:8,9; 23:15; Mark 9:43,45,47; Luke 12:5). This fire is not only to be eternal, but is also said to be of such a nature that it can never be quenched (Mark 9:43). This clearly indicates that there can be no possible end to the fire or the punishment. The punishment is as eternal as the fire. If the fire brought an annihilation of the wicked, there would be no reason for the fire being eternal.

Jesus also referred to the same fire as a "fiery furnace" (Matthew 13:42,50) where there will be terrible remorse shown by weeping and gnashing of teeth. But remorse is not repentance. The remorse of Judas did not save him from eternal loss as the "one doomed to destruction" (John 17:12; Acts 1:16–20). Jesus identified this weeping and gnashing of teeth as taking place in "outer darkness" (Matthew 8:12; 22:13; 25:30, KJV et al.). This darkness indicates a final separation from God and from the Lamb who is the light of the New Jerusalem (Revelation 21:23).

Another New Testament passage refers to eternal punishment as "eternal judgment," that is, a judgment that is valid eternally (Hebrews 6:2). Still another passage speaks of "ruin" (literally, "death," "separation") and "destruction" (eternal loss) (1 Timothy 6:9). This "everlasting destruction" (or separation) is "from the presence of the Lord and from the majesty of his power" (2 Thessalonians 1:9). In these passages the word "death" is thus used in the sense of spiritual death or separation from God. The sinner is even now dead in trespasses and sins and therefore without Christ, or separated from Christ (Ephesians 2:1,12). Eternal judgment brings a final and eternal separation from God and from Christ.

The Second Death

The Bible calls this final separation from God "the second death." In the Book of Revelation the lake of fire is so described (Revelation 20:14). Jesus also identified Gehenna as a second death when He warned: "Do not be afraid of those who kill the body but cannot kill the soul. Rather, be afraid of the One who can destroy both soul and body in hell [Gehenna]" (Matthew 10:28; see also Luke 12:4,5). This clearly refers to another death after the physical death of the body. It is also clear that this death is different in order and in kind. As physical death is separation from the body and from the environment of this life, so the second death is a final and eternal separation from God and from the life to be enjoyed in the new creation. Among those consigned to this second death will be all who take the mark of the beast (Revelation 14:9–11). These will be tormented with fire and brimstone in the presence of the angels and Christ. That is, though shut off from the new creation in the lake of fire, they will be able to see the Lamb of God they rejected, just as Lazarus was able to see across the great gulf between Hades and Abraham's bosom (Luke 16:23). Again, they will not be annihilated, for "the smoke of their torment rises for ever and ever. There is no rest day or night" (Revelation 14:11). They will be forever denied the rest promised to the saints.

None of these passages indicates any promise of rehabilitation or restoration once the final judgment is pronounced. No sanctifying agent is revealed in connection with the lake of fire or Gehenna. The fire is parallel to the "worm" of Mark 9:44,46,48 (KJV). It is looked at as punitive, not purifying. There will be no second chance. This should stir the Church to proclaim the message, "Now is the day of salvation" (2 Corinthians 6:2).

9
The Assemblies of God View of Ordination

The view of ordination in the Assemblies of God is predicated upon biblical principles and is consonant with the evangelical view. The following characteristics comprise the Assemblies of God view.

Ordination can be defined as the public ceremony by which the Movement acknowledges the divine call, commission, and qualification of a person to ministry in the Assemblies of God; extends its blessings, fellowship, and opportunities; receives the person's pledge of dedication, faithfulness, and loyalty; and invokes divine enablement for success in life and ministry.

Ordination is held to be spiritual and functional rather than sacerdotal. It is important as a public acknowledgment of God's prior call and commission, but it is not essential. All Christians are equal, but ministers are set apart for special, full-time Christian service and leadership. When necessary, the laity can perform all of the functions of ministry except those for which the State requires an ordained minister.

Ordination is performed only after a careful examination of candidates as to qualification on six essential points:

1. The genuineness of their Christian experience

2. The sufficiency of their spiritual, moral, emotional, social maturity

3. The reality of their divine call

4. The correctness of their doctrine

5. The adequacy of their preparation and practical abilities

6. The acceptability of their allegiance to the Movement's policies and programs

Authority and power for ministry are conferred directly by Christ through the Holy Spirit, not through those who perform the ordination ceremony. No particular individual or group is essential to the ordination process. Those who participate are dispensable instruments. The stress is upon an immediate spiritual connection with Christ rather than a historical episcopal (apostolic) succession. The living Lord of the Church is making direct, dynamic appointments in His body today.

Ordination is held to be of concern to the whole Church, not just the local assembly. This is indicated by the fact that the apostles, whose ministry was international in scope, presided in each of the five New Testament ceremonies of ordination. Therefore, in the Assemblies of God the ordination is conducted at district level by the superintendent with the imposition of hands and prayers of the district presbytery. It is recognized by the Executive Presbytery of the General Council and is signatured by the general superintendent and general secretary. Also, since ministers participated in each of the New Testament ceremonies, presbyters and other senior ministers are involved in Assemblies of God ordination in the laying on of hands and prayer.

The Assemblies of God stresses the importance of the spiritual quality of the ordination ceremony as opposed to a formal ritual. Typical Assemblies of God ordinations include fasting, prayer, and the laying on of hands, preaching, a charge, and other elements which were seen in the New Testament ceremonies of ordination.

Ordination is available to men or women who meet the biblical qualifications proposed for bishops in 1 Timothy 3:1–7 and Titus 1:5–9, and who are fulfilling one of the types of proclamation-oriented ministry given to the Church by Christ in Ephesians 4:11. These are apostles, prophets, evangelists, pastor-teachers (bishops/elders). Those fulfilling a ministry as directors of youth, music, or Christian education may qualify for a Certificate of Ministry or specialized license but are not afforded ordination if they do not fulfill the basic preaching-pastoral ministry. Those fulfilling a ministry of temporalities (deacons) are appointed to a tenure of service but without credentials.

Benefits of Ordination

Benefits to the Minister

A first benefit is that ordination serves as a goal which represents a high level of spiritual, moral, emotional, social, intellectual, and ministerial maturity. This is not an end in itself, for the ordained minister will need to continue to grow in all of these areas personally and professionally.

A second benefit is that ordination provides candidates the opportunity of corporate judgment as to the genuineness of their Christian experience; the sufficiency of their spiritual, moral, emotional, and social maturity; the reality of their divine call; the correctness of their doctrine; the adequacy of their preparation and practical abilities; and the acceptability of their allegiance to the Movement's policies and programs.

A third benefit is that ordination is recognized as a mature level of personal and professional accomplishment in all of the areas mentioned in benefit number two above. Thus, ordination becomes the goal, test, and testimony of personal and professional maturity and effectiveness.

Ordination provides a fourth benefit in that it opens opportunities of ministry in the Assemblies of God movement. It is an essential key for acceptance in pastoral, evangelistic, administrative, teaching, chaplaincy, and other ministries.

A corollary to this is that ministry in the Movement provides reasonable assurance that the fruit of one's ministry will be preserved.

A fifth benefit of ordination is that it qualifies the minister to meet civil requirements for certain functions of ministry such as funerals, weddings, and serving on certain community, state, and federal boards or agencies, etc.

A sixth benefit of ordination is that it allows a minister to participate fully in the life of the Movement—supporting, contributing to the formulation of policies and programs, refining doctrine, holding office, and many other general or specific benefits.

Benefits to the Movement

In the first place, ordination benefits the Movement by insuring that its ministry is comprised of individuals who are qualified by virtue of the genuineness of their Christian experience, the reality of their divine call, and the sufficiency of their spiritual, moral, emotional, and social maturity to have an effective ministry.

A second benefit to the Movement is that ordination provides a checkpoint to insure a ministry which has sufficient and correct understanding of Bible content and doctrine in order to edify the body of Christ and not bring disharmony.

Ordination benefits the Movement by guaranteeing an effective level of practical ability for the ministerial functions of preaching/teaching: worship leading, administering the ordinances and performing the ceremonies, pastoral care, and the administration (oversight and planning) for the departments, deacons, committees, staff, finances, public relations, building programs, etc.

And finally, ordination benefits the Movement by ascertaining that its ministers have an acceptable knowledge of and loyalty to the policies and programs of the Assemblies of God.

Qualifications for Ordination

The qualifications for bishops, as set forth in 1 Timothy 3:1–7 and Titus 1:5–9, are the norm for all ministers today, along with stated qualifications taken from the General Council Constitution and Bylaws. In addition, the following groups of attributes are recommended for the ordained minister.

Spiritual Attributes

The following spiritual attributes are essential to a most productive ministry: A devotional spirit; love (for God, the ministry, people, 1 Thessalonians 1:3; 1 Timothy 6:11,12; 1 John 3:16); faith (Romans 12:3–8; 2 Corinthians 3:5,6; 5:18–20; Ephesians 3:7; 4:11; Colossian 1:23–29; 1 Thessalonians 1:3); humility (Proverbs 15:33; Romans 12:3); convictions (Jude 3); dedication (total commitment to Gods will); a ministerial spirit (an aptitude to give service; to be solicitous over the well-being and growth of people spiritually, morally, socially, etc.); and faithfulness (1 Corinthians 4:1,2, in stewardship of time, spiritual preparation, business matters, etc.).

Moral Attributes

The following moral attributes are essential to a most productive ministry: integrity (basic honesty and wholeness of character, spiritual honesty [Psalm 51:6], intellectual honesty, honesty in preaching, and in everyday dealings) and moral purity (Isaiah 52:11; Galatians 1:10; 2:11–14; 1 Timothy 6:11–14; 2 Timothy 1:7,9).

Emotional Attributes

It is quite likely that more inefficiency and failure in the ministry are caused by emotional and personality deficiencies than by ill health, moral defection, and lack of training, education, or talent. Because of this it is most important that candidates for ordination be very mature in self-understanding and emotionally healthy. If they have unresolved emotional problems, violent mood swings, personality conflicts, or fail under duress, it will greatly affect their attitudes in the pulpit as well as determine their attitudes in all of their interpersonal relationships. At least the following seven emotional attributes of character are important to the minister: A sanctified temperament (Galatians 5:22,23); a sense of proportion (balance of humor and seriousness); enthusiasm; realism; a sense of the beautiful (Philippians 4:8; Titus 1:15); sympathy (Romans 12:15; Hebrews 5:1); and patience (Romans 5:1–5; 2 Peter 1:5–8).

Intellectual Attributes

The following intellectual attributes are important for the minister: Studiousness; regimentation (reasonably well-organized); moderation (in views rather than radical extremes, 1 Corinthians 9:25; Galatians 5:23; Philippians 4:5; Titus 1:8;

2 Peter 1:6); logic; imagination; power of concentration; memory (John 14:26); and wisdom (James 1:5).

Social Attributes

Among the social attributes which are essential to the minister are the following: Sociability, knowledge of human nature, lack of prejudice, a cooperative attitude, a conciliatory disposition, respect for authority, teachability, and loyalty (to family, church, the Movement, associates, and friends).

Practical Attributes

It is essential to a productive ministry that the minister develop practical ability to perform the functions of the ministry with skill. It is important that ministers study Bible and theology in order to educate their heads, but it is important that they study practical theology in order to educate their mouths and hands as well. The minister should cultivate the spiritual and practical abilities requisite to the functions of preaching/teaching, worship, administering the ordinances, pastoral care, and administration.

The Process of Ordination

Ordination in the Assemblies of God is an orderly process which involves prescribed key personnel, advancement in ministerial levels, examination, and the ordination service itself.

Organizational Structure and Ordination

The key personnel in the organizational structure with respect to ordination of a minister are the pastor, presbyter and sectional committee, and district superintendent and district presbytery. The pastor is essential to the process as the one who grooms the candidates spiritually, trains them for ministry, and recommends them to the presbyter and/or examining committee. The district council ordination committee examines the candidates ultimately, and the district superintendent and the district presbytery ordain them.

The General Council Executive Presbytery recognizes the ordination by the district, and the General Council executive officers witness to the ordination by their signatures and seal on the ordination certificate.

Steps to Ordination

Those seeking ordination in the Assemblies of God ask of their pastor both counsel and a letter of recommendation to the sectional presbyter. The presbyter arranges for candidates to fill out an application for additional credentials with the district and be examined by the sectional committee. Upon the committee's approval, candidates are granted initial credentials by the district. A candidate must maintain an acceptable ministry at the licensed level for a minimum of 2 years and be at least 23 years of age before being invited to write for ordination. This is to insure personal and professional maturity ("not be a recent convert," 1 Timothy 3:6). Upon application for ordination to the sectional presbyter, candidates are examined again by the sectional committee. Upon the committee's approval, candidates are allowed to meet the district committee by whom they are examined once more. Upon the district's approval, candidates are ordained in a special service at the district council and receive an ordination certificate from the General Council. This credential is renewed annually by the minister filling out a questionnaire, which is filed with the district and the General Council.

Examination for Ordination

The sectional committee and/or the district council ordination committee by written examination and oral interview shall examine candidates upon the following points:

1. The genuineness of their Christian experience
2. The reality of their divine call to the ministry
3. The sufficiency of their spiritual, moral, emotional, and social maturity
4. The sufficiency and correctness of their understanding of Bible content and doctrine
5. The adequacy of their preparation and practical abilities
6. The acceptability of their knowledge of and allegiance to the Movement's policies and programs

The Ceremony of Ordination

The Assemblies of God stresses the importance of the spiritual quality of the ordination service as opposed to a formal ritual. While we do not believe as the sacramentalists do that a supernatural grace and power are communicated by our words and hands, we do believe fully that Christ can and will (if He hasn't already) impart the grace and power necessary to the fulfillment of the ministry as we pray and lay hands on the ordinand. Thus the ordination service provides—in addition to its public acknowledgment that the ordinand has been called, commissioned, and qualified for mature ministry—an opportunity for the minister to make a fuller consecration and receive the maximum grace and power for service. It provides opportunity for one of the most significant spiritual experiences of the ordinand's life.

Typical Assemblies of God ordination services include fasting, prayer for the candidates with the imposition of hands by the elders, preaching, a scriptural charge, and other New Testament elements of worship.

Responsibilities of Ordination

Ordination to full gospel ministry is a most responsible step for all concerned. Grave responsibilities fall to the movement which ordains, to the minister who is ordained, and to those who are ministered to by the ordained.

Responsibilities of the Movement

It is the responsibility of the Movement to ordain only ministers who are highly qualified on the biblical qualifications as represented in the six points of examination.

It is the Movement's responsibility to solicit the highest levels of personal life and ministerial proficiency among its ordained ministers.

It is the Movement's responsibility to provide means of spiritual, moral, emotional, social, intellectual, and professional growth among its ordained ministers.

It is the Movement's responsibility to provide opportunities for fruitful ministry.

Responsibilities of the Minister

As a minister, it is one's responsibility to achieve, with the Lord's help, the highest level of qualifications on the biblical qualifications as represented in the six points of examination.

As a minister, it is one's responsibility to maintain the highest level of personal life and ministerial proficiency that the Lord enables. It is advisable to review the definition of ordination, the biblical qualifications, and the six points of examination each year when filling out the ordination questionnaire, as a self-check and as an incentive to continue growing.

As a minister, it is one's responsibility to enter into opportunities of ministry with dedication, love, faith, anointing, and faithfulness in order to render service acceptable to one's constituency, to the Movement, and to the Lord.

Responsibilities of Those Receiving Ministry

It is the responsibility of those receiving ministry:

1. To accept the minister as God's messenger (Luke 10:16; 1 Corinthians 4:1; Galatians 4:14).

2. To pray for the minister (Romans 15:30; 2 Corinthians 1:11; Ephesians 6:18,19; Hebrews 13:18).

3. To love and respect the minister (2 Corinthians 8:7; 1 Thessalonians 3:6; 5:12,13).

4. To follow and obey the minister (1 Corinthians 11:1; 16:16; Philippians 3:17; Hebrews 13:7,17).

5. To provide the minister with generous financial support (1 Corinthians 9:7–14; Galatians 6:6; 1 Timothy 5:17,18).

Enhancing the Ordained Ministry

No vocation is more worthy of a goal of excellence than the gospel ministry. Since ordination is the goal, test, and testimony of maturity and proficiency in life and ministry, it is the primary point at which concentrated effort should occur. The following suggestions are made in the interest of enhancing the ministry through the process leading to ordination and afterward as well.

1. All who receive initial credentials should also receive a copy of the General Council position paper on ordination for careful study as they progress to ordination.

2. Credentials committees should take their work very seri-

ously. They should be sensitive to the voice of the Holy Spirit as to who should be ordained (Acts 13:2; 14:26; 20:28). They should maintain high standards of qualification and not be reluctant to extend the probationary license period for another year or longer on any doubtful candidates. They should examine candidates for Certificate of Ministry and all step-ups very carefully on the six points that have repeatedly been dealt with in this paper.

3. An extensive questionnaire should be developed on character, emotional problems, views on human relations, spiritual and practical matters, etc., which could be administered by presbyters to those seeking credentials and step-ups. This tool could be the basis of one or more counseling sessions by the presbyter, a committeeman, or a designated sectional counselor. Such a questionnaire would become a worksheet in the minister's file with space for notes of strengths, weaknesses, and recommendations by the committee. This would contribute to better analysis, continuity, and follow-up until the candidate is ordained. It would be kept in a confidential file until the candidate reached ordination and would then be destroyed.

4. Require ministers anticipating ordination to write, during their period of license, their credo on doctrine and the functions of the ministry. This would be read by the presbyter and sectional committee and kept on file until the candidates' ordination and then returned to them. The credo, and questionnaire mentioned above, would be utilized to help candidates achieve self-understanding and the ability to express their beliefs clearly. Also these documents would provide the credentials committee insight into the personality, beliefs, strengths, and needs of individual candidates. Further, they would be used for counseling and growth of the candidates, and not as tests for them to pass.

5. Supplement the work of the home pastor and the presbyter and sectional committee and keep on file until ministerial counseling service at sectional or metropolitan level. This would not necessarily require a professionally trained counselor doing in-depth or long-term counseling. Mature ministers could staff the counseling service on a rotating basis or a superannuated minister or ministers could be appointed to provide the service. These elders could provide excellent counsel out of years of experience, have a continuing ministry, and some remuneration if a fee were advisable. This would provide a much-needed service for ministers in general, and for young ministers and their companions in particular, as they recognized the need for help in their lives and ministries. This service would help relieve the workload of presbyters; help young preachers to achieve personal, domestic, and ministerial growth; and increase the harmony and progress in the assemblies.

6. Make the ordination ceremony a truly important spiritual experience. We know that much fasting and prayer was standard procedure in the Early Church. We would be careful to retain not just the outward symbolism, laying on of hands, but also the spiritual exercises of fasting and prayer in our ordination service (Acts 13:3).

7. Stress the importance of both basic and continuing education. While we do not require certain formal studies or degrees for ordination (resolution adopted by 1951 General Council, p. 9; see Constitution Art. X., par. d., 1975 GCM, p. 83), the Movement is committed to the importance of education for ministry, and the majority of those being ordained today are graduates of Assemblies of God Bible colleges. Those who cannot attend a resident Bible college are urged to study through extension classes, correspondence programs, institutes, semi-

nars, and reading programs (2 Timothy 2:15).

8. Stress at all opportunities (Assemblies of God Theological Seminary, Bible colleges and institutes, etc.) substantive spiritual, moral, ethical, emotional, social, intellectual, and practical matters.

9. Keep Assemblies of God Bible colleges and the Assemblies of God Theological Seminary staffed with administrators and faculty members who are proven to be mature in character and emotional, social, and spiritual life; dedicated to Bible holiness, Pentecostal distinctives, doctrines, and Assemblies of God policies and programs; proven in ministerial success; and currently anointed, active in ministry, and in touch with the vital issues of the ministry.

"The Spirit of the Lord is on me, because he has anointed me to preach good news to the poor. He has sent me to proclaim freedom for the prisoners and recovery of sight for the blind, to release the oppressed (Luke 4:18).

10
The Doctrine of Creation

"In the beginning God created the heavens and the earth" (Genesis 1:1). The Bible begins with creation, and the fact that God is Creator is always in view from Genesis to Revelation.

Even though the Bible is not primarily a book of science, it is as trustworthy in the area of science as when it speaks to any other subject. We can have confidence in what it says concerning the origin of all things because "all Scripture is God-breathed and is useful for teaching, rebuking, correcting and training in righteousness" (2 Timothy 3:16). The Bible is not the changing word of human beings, but the unchanging Word of God (1 Thessalonians 2:13).

The Bible Shows God as the Creator

Scripture focuses our attention not so much on the act of creation as on God himself as the Creator. In Genesis 1:1 to 2:3 God is the subject of most of the sentences. We read that God created, God said, God saw, God divided, God called or named, God made, God set or appointed, God blessed, God rested, and God sanctified.

Creation is the revelation of an intelligent, loving, personal

God. In contrast to pantheism He is distinct from His creation (Psalm 90:2). In contrast to deism He continues to be personally interested in His handiwork; for He upholds, sustains, and preserves it (Nehemiah 9:6).

The rest of the Bible continues this emphasis on God as the Creator, bringing it into many facets of our relationship to Him. We are to worship and serve Him as the Creator (Isaiah 40:26,28,31). We are warned not to strive against our Maker (Isaiah 45:9). We are to commit the keeping of our souls to Him in well doing, as unto a faithful Creator (1 Peter 4:19). We also recognize that our help comes from the One who made the heavens and the earth (Psalms 121:2; 124:8; 146:5,6), and there is nothing too hard for Him (Jeremiah 32:17).

The Bible further emphasizes the fact that God is the Creator of all things. Repeatedly in both the Old and New Testaments this is brought to our attention (Exodus 20:11; Nehemiah 9:6; Psalm 146:6; Acts 14:17; Revelation 4:11; 10:6).

This is one of the distinctive elements of the biblical revelation. In contrast to ancient heathenism and modern materialism, the Bible teaches a genuine beginning. Most heathenism was dualistic, teaching that the universe in some form existed eternally alongside the gods. In the heathen myths the gods are seen as having created something, but always from preexisting materials. The very declaration that God is the Creator sets Him apart from the idols (Psalm 96:5).

Materialists teach that matter and its laws are eternal and are the sum total of all existence, thus ruling out the idea of God altogether. But the Bible declares that God is the Creator of all things and that He existed before all things (Psalm 90:2). Thus we have a genuine beginning when God brought the universe into existence out of nothing.

Another important fact of biblical revelation is that creation was the cooperative work of the Trinity.

The Old Testament shows that the Spirit of God had a part (Genesis 1:2).

The New Testament further reveals that Jesus, who is the one Mediator between God and humankind (1 Timothy 2:5) in our redemption, was also the Mediator in Creation. Christ, who is called "the firstborn" because He has first place, the place of the heir (Colossians 1:15), was the active Agent in creation. "Through him all things were made; without him nothing was made that has been made" (John 1:3). The Greek word translated "through" *(dia)* is a word of secondary agency, used, for example, where God spoke by the prophets. So God created by or through Jesus. Jesus was the living Word through whom God spoke the worlds into existence. He was the One who made humankind from the dust of the earth. He is before all things and is the Creator of the invisible angelic world as well (Colossians 1:16).

The Biblical Account of Creation Reveals Progress and Climax

Progress and a climax were a part of the biblical account of creation. Progress can be seen in the increase of personal attention God gave in His creative work. Of the vegetation we read that God said, "'Let the land produce vegetation. . . .' And it was so" (Genesis 1:11,12). Of the animals we read that God said, "'Let the land produce . . . .' And it was so" (vv. 24,25). But of the human race God said, "'Let us make man. . . .' So God created man . . . ; male and female he created them" (vv. 26,27). The human race is thus a special and distinctive creation, the climax, and to human beings is given dominion.

All this evidence of sequence, balance, correspondence, progress, and climax shows careful, intelligent planning. That

God created by plan absolutely rules out any idea that part of creation came into being by mere chance. God exercised His wisdom and control at all times (Psalms 136:5; 148:5; Isaiah 45:12; 48:12,13) and brought it all to a complete and well-designed end (Genesis 1:31).

The Biblical Account Shows Distinct Steps of Creation

It is evident that God carried out His plan in distinct steps. This is indicated by the mention of succeeding days in Creation and by the mention of the evening and morning. That is, here is an evening, this part is over; here is a morning, a new beginning.

Genesis 2, instead of being another creation record as some claim, is an amplification of activity not mentioned in Genesis 1. That is, the first chapter simply states that God created man, male and female created He them. The second chapter gives further details about part of the sixth creation day. There we see that God took the dust of the earth and formed Adam. Then He breathed into him the breath of life. This act indicates that humans are distinct from animals and that God did not form Adam from some previously existing animal (1 Corinthians 15:39). The creation of animal life from the dust of the ground (Genesis 2:19) only indicates that God used the same source of material for both.

After creating Adam, God put him in the Garden and gave him work to do. Then "the LORD God caused the man to fall into a deep sleep; . . . he took one of the man's ribs" and made a woman (Genesis 2:21,22).

This Bible record of creation thus rules out the evolutionary philosophy which states that all forms of life have come into being by gradual, progressive evolution carried on by resident forces. It also rules out any evolutionary origin for the human race, since no theory of evolution, including theistic evolution, can explain the origin of the male before the female, nor can it explain how a man could evolve into a woman.

Only God Can Create

It is also evident that no part of God's creation, whether human, angel, or devil, is creative in the sense God is. The Hebrew word for *create (bara')* always has God as the subject of the verb. This word is used for God's work of creation and is also used to indicate that God would do something unusual and unprecedented. When the earth opened up to swallow the rebellious Korah, the phrase "brings about something totally new" is literally "create a creation" (Numbers 16:30). It is used when God said to Israel at Sinai: "I will do wonders never before done [*bara'*, created] in any nation in all the world" (Exodus 34:10).

Of miracles and the fulfillment of prophecy in Isaiah's day, when events showed the foolishness and weakness of the people's trust in idols, God said, "'From now on I will tell you of new things. . . . They are created now, and not long ago'" (Isaiah 48:6,7). Thus even in the first chapter of Genesis, the word *create* is used only of completely new and unprecedented acts of God; that is, of the creation of the heavens and the earth in the beginning, of the creation of the first animal life in the sea (1:21), and of man and woman in God's own image (1:27). Other times the word *made* (Hebrew, *'asah*) is used. The word *create (bara')* thus emphasizes that God alone is the Creator, and His acts of creation are unique and unprecedented.

God Had Purpose in Creation

God had purpose in creation. He created "for his own ends" or for His own pleasure (Proverbs 16:4; Revelation 4:11) and for

His glory (Isaiah 43:7). He wanted the earth to be inhabited (Isaiah 45:18). All creation is thus an expression of His will and His power.

People are beings who are in the image of God (Genesis 1:26,27): free, rational, capable of self-appreciation and self-expression, capable of moral and spiritual understanding, created for fellowship with God. They will find their proper place in creation only as they are in right relation to God through the redemption accomplished in Jesus.

The Creation Account Is Factual and Historical

The account of creation is intended to be taken as factual and historical. Our understanding of God as Creator is rooted in a revelation that is historical in nature, just as our understanding of God as Redeemer is rooted in the revelation of God's dealings with Israel in history and in the historical events of the life, death, and resurrection of His Son. All the New Testament accepts it this way. The first man Adam, for example, is recognized as a historical person (Romans 5:14; 1 Corinthians 15:45; 1 Timothy 2:13,14).

Some have contended that the first two chapters of Genesis are poetical and are to be taken as parables. But a comparison of poetical references to Creation (Deuteronomy 32 and 33; Job 38:4–11; Psalms 90; 104:5–9) shows that the Genesis account is not poetry but prose. It should be noted, however, that poetry in the Bible often describes actual, historical events, so the use of poetry does not make an event a parable or myth.

It is significant that although creation events are not stated in modern scientific terminology, they are given in unusually acceptable statements, thus providing a solid record for all peoples in all times (Ephesians 1:18).

In summary then, we see that the Bible points us to God as

the Creator in every step of creation. "By faith we understand that the universe was formed at God's command, so that what is seen was not made out of what was visible" (Hebrews 11:3). "For he spoke, and it came to be; he commanded, and it stood firm" (Psalm 33:9).

11
The Security of the Believer

The Assemblies of God has declared itself regarding the security of the believer in its bylaws (Article VIII Section 1):

In view of the biblical teaching that the security of the believer depends on a living relationship with Christ (John 15:6); in view of the Bible's call to a life of holiness (Hebrews 12:14; 1 Peter 1:16); in view of the clear teaching that one's part may be taken out of the Book of Life (Revelation 22:19); and in view of the fact that one who believes for a while can fall away (Luke 8:13); The General Council of the Assemblies of God disapproves of the unconditional security position which holds that it is impossible for a person once saved to be lost.

This paper seeks to explain further why this position has been taken.

In the matter of the security of the believer, The General Council of the Assemblies of God stands between the extreme positions of Calvinism and Arminianism. It accepts the scriptural elements found in both teachings.

The Calvinist stresses, rightly, God's sovereignty and divine prerogative, while the Arminian stresses, also rightly, one's free will and responsibility. The two positions, however, must be considered together if they are to be properly understood. The

General Council of the Assemblies of God believes in the sovereignty and divine prerogative of God untainted by arbitrariness or caprice. It also believes in the free will and responsibility of human beings.

In order to explain the position taken by the Assemblies of God on the security of the believer, four points need to be emphasized:

1. Salvation is available for everyone (John 3:16; Romans 10:11–13; 2 Peter 3:9).

2. Salvation is received and kept by faith (Romans 3:28; Galatians 2:20,21; Ephesians 2:8; Philippians 3:9; Hebrews 10:38; 1 Peter 1:5).

3. Continued sin will adversely affect the believer's faith (Romans 3:5–8; 1 Corinthians 3:1–3; Hebrews 3:12–14; 12:1; 1 John 1:8; 3:8).

4. The believer's salvation is forfeited by rejecting Christ (John 17:12; 1 Timothy 4:1; 5:12,15; Hebrews 6:4–6; 10:26,27,38; 2 Peter 2:20; 1 John 5:16).

Salvation Is Available for Everyone

Two questions may be asked: "Are some predestined to be saved and others to be lost?" and "Who are the elect?" The answer is clear when it is recognized that the message of the gospel is one of "whoever will come." No one reading the New Testament can miss the impact of this great truth.

However, in Romans 9–11 there are some statements that seem to imply that free will is excluded in the matter of the believer's salvation and that God in His choice of the elect exercises His divine sovereignty entirely apart from human volition. For example:

"Yet, before the twins were born or had done anything good or bad—in order that God's purpose in election might stand:

not by works but by him who calls. . . 'Jacob I loved, but Esau I hated. . . . I will have mercy on whom I have mercy, and I will have compassion on whom I have compassion.' It does not, therefore, depend on man's desire or effort, but on God's mercy. . . . Therefore God has mercy on whom he wants to have mercy, and he hardens whom he wants to harden" (Romans 9:11,13,15,16,18).

When this passage is considered in the light of all that God's Word teaches concerning election, however, it is evident that the will is involved in one's election. Jacob was chosen before having done good or evil, but God's choice was on the basis of what He foreknew Jacob would do.

This truth is brought out in Peter's letter to "the strangers scattered throughout Pontus, Galatia, Cappadocia, Asia, and Bithynia." These believers were recognized to be "elect according to the foreknowledge of God" (1 Peter 1:1,2, KJV).

This same truth is stated in Romans 8:29. Paul wrote, "For those God foreknew he also predestined to be conformed to the likeness of his Son."

God determined beforehand the conditions on which He would show mercy. And on the basis of His foreknowledge believers are chosen in Christ (Ephesians 1:4). Thus God in His sovereignty has provided the plan of salvation whereby all can be saved. In this plan a person's will is taken into consideration. Salvation is available to "whoever will come."

Salvation Is Received and Kept by Faith

The Bible clearly states that we are saved by grace through faith (Ephesians 2:8) and that the just shall live by faith (Habakkuk 2:4; Romans 1:17; Galatians 3:11; Hebrews 10:38). As the believer's salvation is received, not by an act of righteousness but by an act of faith, so the believer's salvation is maintained, not by acts of righteousness but by a life of faith!

Being a Christian then is not a matter of works; it is a matter of faith. This must be emphasized. In no case are sinners accepted by God on the basis of any good that they have done. They are saved totally and solely by grace through faith. By faith sinners accept the fact that Christ died in their stead. By faith they throw themselves upon the mercy of God and accept Christ as their Savior. By faith they see themselves clothed with the righteousness of Christ—a standing imputed to them through no merit of their own (Philippians 3:9). They know that they are accepted through faith, and this knowledge gives them peace and joy.

The state of believers must not be confused with their standing, however. They stand secure because of faith. Their standing is the result of God's grace which they have accepted by faith. They stand justified, clothed with the righteousness of Christ!

The believer's state, or the working out of the righteousness of Christ in the believer, is another matter. It involves spiritual growth, a progressive sanctification by obedient cooperation with the Holy Spirit (Romans 6:12,13; 8:13; Colossians 3:1–5; 2 Peter 1:5–7). During this maturing process the believer must learn by mistake as well as by victory. Nevertheless, security is never in doubt as long as faith in Christ is steadfast, for one is kept by faith.

Spiritual growth varies in excellence and degree according to the yieldedness and attention one affords to the Spirit who is at work within. Yet all the while the perfecting processes go on, the believer is credited with the perfection through the imputed righteousness of Christ by faith. Through the process of "becoming conformed" the believer is secure; salvation is sure. "Therefore, there is now no condemnation for those who are in

Christ Jesus" (Romans 8:1).

The believer's security, then, is solely through faith, both in the receiving of salvation and in the keeping of salvation. This security is made possible through the mercy of God in imputing the righteousness of His own Son to the fallible and faulty believer who maintains a living faith in Christ. "God made him who had no sin to be sin for us, so that in him we might become the righteousness of God" (2 Corinthians 5:21).

Continued Sin Will Adversely Affect the Believer's Faith

The Bible makes it clear that in this life Christians do sin and that the Christian's recourse upon having sinned is forgiveness through Christ (1 John 1:8,9; 2:1).

On the other hand, it is unnatural for Christians to continue in sin. That is, as long as they have the life of Christ within them, they cannot habitually sin. (See 1 John 3:8,9, where the Greek tense is the continuous present.) The one who practices sin is of the devil. Whoever is born of God does not practice sin, does not keep on habitually sinning. The child of God cannot keep on sinning the way the child of the devil does. Instead, believers should grow spiritually and lay aside sin, recognizing that continued sin will adversely affect their faith.

Does this imply that a Christian can sin and still be saved? The first impulse of many may be to say no. Yet it is necessary in this connection to consider the fact that worry, pride, envy, and bitterness are accepted as common failings. Few would suggest that believers committing these sins are lost.

Moreover, if it be insisted that God demands present sinless perfection from believers, then the question must be raised: "Is one's standing in Christ based upon personal righteousness or upon the righteousness of Christ imputed by faith?" If believers are saved only as long as they maintain a flawless life, then salvation is not of grace, but of works!

Then too if people are accepted by God only if they are without fault, Christian living is not free from condemnation as Paul insisted in Romans 8:1. It is rather a continual exercise in soul-searching and penance, full of fear and condemnation and void of the joy and confidence that a knowledge of salvation can bring. (See Romans 5:9–11 where it is clear that the God who loved us enough to provide for our salvation loves us enough to provide for us all the way to glory. This assurance gives us joy in Him.)

A related question is: "What would happen to a believer who commits a sin at that moment Jesus returns?" Those who maintain that a Christian who commits a sin cannot still be saved would teach that such a believer is lost and doomed for eternity. What despair!

Believers are not in a revolving door, moving in and out of the grace of God! Secure in the hand of God, neither death nor life, angels nor demons, nor any powers, neither the present nor the future, not height nor depth, nothing in all creation will be able to separate them from the love of the Father!

This must be said, however, with further emphasis that it is not the natural thing for Christians to sin. They cannot keep on sinning the same old sins. Having been born of the Spirit, every believer is a new creature for whom old things have passed away and new things have come (2 Corinthians 5:17, NASB).

It is thus now unnatural to sin. The old life is a thing of the past, a latent force within, subdued and reckoned dead by the new Presence (Romans 6:11). What was the custom and practice before now becomes unnatural and contrary to the new impulses of the heart.

"No one who is born of God," John said, "will continue to sin." That is, sin is foreign to the new nature. The new nature that is ours by faith does not sin. Thus when the old nature temporarily and unexpectedly regains ascendancy, the whole new being revolts against this unnatural intrusion. The immediate recourse is to Christ.

The believer who has sinned turns to Christ, not with the despair of a lost soul, but with the secure knowledge that as the child of God who has an Advocate with the Father—who is faithful and just to forgive and cleanse from all unrighteousness. Thus the believer exercises the prerogative as a child of God, never needing to doubt this standing that is based upon the infallible righteousness of Christ by faith.

Having stressed the sovereignty and grace of God, it is also imperative to bring the free will and responsibility of the believer into focus. God does not withdraw the power of choice from the person who believes. By the exercise of free will the believer becomes a child of God and by the continued exercise of free will remains a child of God. To keep on believing is the believer's responsibility.

Believers must also be careful that they do not take a light attitude toward sin. They dare not use the grace of God as a license to sin.

"Shall we go on sinning so that grace may increase?" asked Paul (Romans 6:1). The answer is an emphatic negative. Paul knew and taught that continued sin will adversely affect a believer's faith, and faith is the very thing that makes a relationship with God possible.

Continued sin becomes presumptuous, high-handed, and is evidence of rebellion. (See Numbers 15:30,31.) Rebellion is the opposite of the trust and obedience of faith.

Believers must be on guard, constantly "looking diligently lest any man fail of the grace of God" (Hebrews 12:15, KJV). The Bible's exhortation is: "Examine yourselves to see whether you are in the faith; test yourselves" (2 Corinthians 13:5).

Why such precautions and concern? These repeated warnings are meaningful only when it is recognized that the loss of faith means the eternal loss of the soul. For while it is true that the believer's salvation is neither earned nor maintained by righteous deeds, it is equally true that this salvation obtained by faith can be lost by unbelief!

Sin and unbelief are closely related. Sin jeopardizes faith, and loss of faith means loss of standing. Hebrews 3:12–14 bears this out. The writer warned his readers against unbelief, which will lead to a departure from the living God. He mentioned the deceitfulness of sin as the cause of unbelief and reminded them that they are partakers of Christ only if they hold the beginning of their confidence unto the end.

Standing in Christ is by faith. Remove faith, and there is no longer any standing. This is why Scripture admonishes believers to "see to it . . . that none of you has a sinful, unbelieving heart" (Hebrews 3:12).

Salvation Is Forfeited by Rejecting Christ

God does not let anyone go easily. (See Romans 10:21 where Paul was speaking of Israel, but the principle applies.) But believers can be lost if they disregard the continuing checks of the Holy Spirit and reach the point where they reject Jesus as their Savior.

It is possible to believe for a while and in a time of temptation to fall away (Luke 8:13). It is possible for the weak brother to perish for whom Christ died (1 Corinthians 8:11). It is possible for a name to be written in the Book of Life and then removed from it (Revelation 22:19).

It is not always possible to determine whether a person has turned away from Jesus as Savior. Therefore it is well to leave judgment of these matters in the hands of the omniscient God. Of this we can be certain, however: if God does not give up in His efforts to bring the prodigal back, neither should the church of Jesus Christ. Too often people write off an individual when God has not.

The Bible does recognize the possibility of forfeiting salvation, but it never ceases to offer hope for anyone who wants to respond to the entreaty of the Holy Spirit. Jesus' invitation is without qualification. He speaks to all when He says, "Come to me, all you who are weary and burdened, and I will give you rest" (Matthew 11:28).

Again the Bible speaks to all when it says, "Everyone who calls on the name of the Lord will be saved" (Romans 10:13).

12
The Rapture of the Church

Under the section "The Blessed Hope" in the Statement of Fundamental Truths of the Assemblies of God is the following statement:

"The resurrection of those who have fallen asleep in Christ and their translation together with those who are alive and remain unto the coming of the Lord is the imminent and blessed hope of the Church (1 Thessalonians 4:16,17; Romans 8:23; Titus 2:13; 1 Corinthians 15:51,52)."

Jesus Taught That He Will Return

Jesus taught that He will return to earth. He was careful to warn His disciples to be constantly prepared for this (Matthew 24:42–51; 25:1–13; Mark 13:37; Luke 12:37).

They understood that the present age will end with His coming (Matthew 24:3). The assurance of His return was one of the truths with which He comforted His followers before His death (John 14:2,3).

At the time of Christ's ascension two angels came to the group of watching disciples to repeat the promise that He will return. They declared it would be in the same manner that He went away (Acts 1:11). This clearly means His second coming will be literal, physical, and visible.

The Epistles Teach That Jesus Will Return

The New Testament Epistles refer often to the Second Coming, and the theme of imminence runs through all the passages of Scripture dealing with this subject. Though there would be a period of time between the first and second comings (Luke 19:11), the whole body of teaching concerning the return of the Lord emphasizes that it will happen suddenly, without warning; that believers should be in a state of continual readiness (Philippians 4:5; Hebrews 10:37; James 5:8,9; Revelation 22:10).

Believers in the early days of the Church lived in this state of expectancy (1 Corinthians 1:7; 1 Thessalonians 1:9,10). Paul's "we" in 1 Corinthians 15:51 and 1 Thessalonians 4:17 shows that he maintained the hope he would be alive when Jesus comes back.

Removal of Believers From Earth

A comparison of passages of Scripture relating to the Second Coming shows that some speak of a visible event seen by all mankind and involving the judgment of sinners. Others describe a coming known only to believers and resulting in their deliverance from earth.

The latter is referred to among evangelicals as the Rapture. This word is not in the English Bible, but has been used so widely that one of the definitions of "rapture" in *Webster's Third New International Dictionary Unabridged* is "Christ's raising up of His true church and its members to a realm above the earth where the whole company will enjoy celestial bliss with its

Lord." The word *raptured* could well be used to translate the expression "caught up" of 1 Thessalonians 4:17. Jesus said His coming will result in one individual being taken from a location while another is left. This indicates a sudden removal of believers from the earth, with unbelievers left to face tribulation (Matthew 24:36–42).

Jesus spoke of His return as a time when the nations of the earth shall mourn as they see Him (Matthew 24:30). The apostle Paul spoke of the Lord's return as a time of judgment and wrath upon the wicked (2 Thessalonians 1:7–10).

In 1 Thessalonians 4:13–18, he considered a different aspect of the Second Coming. This brief passage is the most direct and clear teaching on the Rapture in the New Testament. It speaks only of believers, living and dead. Nothing is said about the wicked seeing Christ at this time. Paul described Jesus as coming in the air, but nothing is said about His feet touching the earth, as we are told elsewhere they will at His return (Zechariah 14:4). It is the moment when 1 John 3:2 will be fulfilled, and we shall be like Him.

The same Greek word used in 1 Thessalonians 4:17 for "caught up" is used in Acts 8:39 to describe Philip's being "taken away" after baptizing the Ethiopian. The latter verse states that the Spirit of the Lord took Philip away—identifying the source of the power that will remove believers from earth at the Rapture.

In 2 Thessalonians 2:1 Paul called the Rapture "our being gathered to him." The Greek word for "gathered" is the same as the one used for "meeting" in Hebrews 10:25, referring to the assembling of Christians for worship. It is a picture of the saints congregating around Christ at His coming for them.

The supernatural removal of godly individuals from earth is not unknown in Scripture. The outstanding event in the life of

Enoch was his miraculous disappearance from earth after years of walking with God (Genesis 5:21–24). The author of Hebrews called this experience a translation, bypassing death (Hebrews 11:5).

Although some aspects of Elijah's translation differed from Enoch's, it also involved the sudden removal of a believer from the world without experiencing death (2 Kings 2:1–13).

First Corinthians 15:51–54 deals with the same event as 1 Thessalonians 4:13–18. Here also Paul spoke of the changes that will take place in both living and dead believers at the Rapture. He called this a mystery (1 Corinthian 15:51), a truth previously unrevealed but made known to him by the Holy Spirit.

In Philippians 3:21 Paul connected the Lord's coming to the time when "our lowly bodies" will be changed—another reference to the Rapture.

Passages which pertain to the Rapture describe the coming of the Lord *for* His people. Passages which refer to the revelation of Christ describe the coming of the Lord *with* His saints. Colossians 3:4 speaks of believers appearing *with* Christ at His coming. Jude 14 also foresees the Lord's return *with* His people to execute the judgment referred to in many other passages relating to His public appearing.

Since Scripture does not contradict itself, it seems reasonable to conclude that the passages describing Christ's coming *for* the saints and *with* the saints indicate two phases of His coming. We believe it is scripturally correct to assume that the intervening period between the two is the time when the world will experience the Great Tribulation, involving the reign of Antichrist and the outpouring of God's wrath on the wicked (Daniel 12:1,2,10–13; Matthew 24:15–31; 2 Thessalonians 2:1–12).

Christians and the Great Tribulation

Although God's people may endure severe trials before the Lord comes, the Church will be raptured before the period called the Great Tribulation.

In 2 Thessalonians 2 Paul indicated certain things must take place before the Day of the Lord (of which the Great Tribulation is a part) can begin. An individual called the man of sin (Antichrist) will appear. The mystery of iniquity has been at work since Paul's time but is being restrained by the power of the Spirit working through the true Church. Only when the Church is removed from earth by the Rapture can this man come forward publicly.

In 1 Thessalonians 5, following the passage on the Rapture in chapter 4, Paul taught about the Day of the Lord. He warned of the destruction it will bring to the wicked (vv. 2,3). He was quick to assure Christians that those who abide in Christ will not be overtaken by it (v. 4).

Still speaking of the Day of the Lord, Paul wrote: "For God did not appoint us to suffer wrath but to receive salvation through our Lord Jesus Christ" (v. 9). It seems clear that he meant the deliverance of believers from the judgments of the Day of the Lord, including the Great Tribulation.

Christians are told repeatedly in the New Testament to be watchful for the Lord's appearing. Never are they taught to watch for the Great Tribulation or the appearance of Antichrist. To expect that such things must happen before the Rapture destroys the teaching of imminence with which the New Testament is replete.

Believers are told to wait "for his Son from heaven," not the Great Tribulation (1 Thessalonians 1:10). When the signs of the end of the age are evident, they are to look up and lift up their heads in expectation of their redemption, not the Great Tribulation (Luke 21:28).

The signs of the Lord's coming will be fulfilled before His public appearing, but they do not have to be fulfilled before the Rapture. Any teaching that certain events must transpire before the Rapture is out of harmony with the doctrine of imminence.

It is consistent with God's dealings with His people in the Old Testament to believe that the Church will be removed from the world before the Great Tribulation. God did not send the Flood until Noah and his family were safe in the ark. He did not destroy Sodom until Lot was taken out.

The weight of Scripture supports a pre-Tribulation Rapture. Wherever teaching about the Second Coming occurs in the New Testament, imminence is underscored. To interpose other events before the Rapture does violence to such teaching.

While Christians are looking forward to the coming of the Lord, it is well to remind themselves of Paul's words to Titus: "The grace of God that brings salvation has appeared to all men. It teaches us to say 'No' to ungodliness and worldly passions, and to live self-controlled, upright and godly lives in this present age, while we wait for the blessed hope—the glorious appearing of our great God and Savior, Jesus Christ, who gave himself for us to redeem us from all wickedness and to purify for himself a people that are his very own, eager to do what is good" (Titus 2:11–14).

13
The Believer and Positive Confession

The Assemblies of God from its early days has recognized the importance of the life of faith. It has been given prominent emphasis because Scripture gives it prominence.

The writer to the Hebrews points out that without faith it is impossible to please God. Then he describes faith as believing two things—that God is, and that He rewards those who diligently seek Him (Hebrews 11:6).

All the blessings which God has for His people are received through faith. Salvation (Acts 16:31), baptism in the Holy Spirit (Acts 11:15–17), divine preservation (1 Peter 1:5), inheritance of the promises which include healing and provision of material needs (Hebrews 6:12), and motivation for witnessing (2 Corinthians 4:13) are among the many provisions of God's grace.

Today, as in every generation, it is important for believers to be mindful of the example in Scripture of being strong in faith (Romans 4:20–24). They must be on guard against anything which would weaken or destroy faith. They need to pray for its increase (Luke 17:5) and constantly seek to cultivate it through reading the Word of God (Romans 10:17). The life of faith is the life of victory (1 John 5:4).

Occasionally throughout church history people have taken extreme positions concerning great biblical truths. Sometimes teachers have advocated these extremes. On other occasions followers have gone beyond the teachings and reflected adversely on the cause of Christ.

Positive and *negative confession* are expressions which in recent years have received acceptance in an extreme form in some circles. Both the definition in writing and the pattern of usage give some insight into the implications of these terms.

The fact that extremes are brought into focus does not imply rejection of the doctrine of confession. It is an important truth. The Bible teaches people are to confess their sin (1 John 1:9). They are to confess Christ (Matthew 10:32; Romans 10:9,10). They are to maintain a good "confession" (Hebrews 4:14; 10:23, American Standard Version).

But when people, in emphasizing a doctrine, go beyond or contrary to the teaching of Scripture, they do not honor that doctrine. Conversely, they bring reproach upon it and the work of the Lord. For this reason it is important to call attention to these excesses and show how they are in conflict with the Word of God.

Some Positions of the Positive Confession Teaching

The positive confession teaching relies on an English dictionary definition of the word *confess:* "to acknowledge, or to own; to acknowledge faith in." Confession is also described as affirming something which is believed, testifying to something known, and witnessing for a truth which has been embraced.

This view goes a step further and divides confession into negative and positive aspects. The negative is acknowledging sin, sickness, poverty, or other undesirable situations. Positive confession is acknowledging or owning desirable situations.

While there are variations of interpretation and emphasis concerning this teaching, a conclusion seems to be that the unpleasant can be avoided by refraining from negative confessions. The pleasant can be enjoyed by making positive confessions.

According to this view, as expressed in various publications, believers who refrain from acknowledging the negative and continue to affirm the positive will assure for themselves pleasant circumstances. They will be able to rule over poverty, disease, and sickness. They will be sick only if they confess they are sick. Some make a distinction between acknowledging the symptoms of an illness and the illness itself.

This view advocates that God wants believers to wear the best clothing, drive the best cars, and have the best of everything. Believers need not suffer financial setbacks. All they need to do is to tell Satan to take his hands off their money. They can have whatever they say whether the need is spiritual, physical, or financial. It is taught that faith compels God's action.

According to this position, what one says determines what one will receive and what one will become. Thus people are instructed to start confessing even though what they want may not have been realized. If you want money, you are to confess you have it even if it is not true. If you want healing, you are to confess it even though it is obviously not the case. People are told they can have whatever they say, and for this reason great significance is attached to the spoken word. It is claimed that the spoken word, if repeated often enough, will eventually result in faith which procures the desired blessing.

It is understandable that some people would like to accept the positive confession teaching. It promises a life free from problems, and its advocates seem to support it with passages of Scripture. Problems develop, however, when Bible statements are isolated from their context and from what the rest of Scripture has to say concerning the subject. Extremes result which distort truth and eventually hurt believers as individuals and the cause of Christ in general.

When believers study the life of faith and victory God has for His people, it is important, as in all doctrine, to seek for the balanced emphasis of Scripture. This will help to avoid the extremes which eventually frustrate rather than help believers in their walk with God.

Believers Should Consider the Total Teaching of Scripture

The apostle Paul gave an important principle of interpreting Scripture which calls for "comparing spiritual things with spiritual" (1 Corinthians 2:13, KJV). The basic thrust of this principle is to consider everything God's Word has to say on a given subject in establishing doctrine. Only doctrine based on a holistic view of Scripture conforms to this biblical rule of interpretation.

When the positive confession teaching indicates that to admit weakness is to accept defeat, to admit financial need is to accept poverty, and to admit sickness is to preclude healing, it is going beyond and is contrary to the harmony of Scripture.

For instance, King Jehoshaphat admitted he had no might against an enemy alliance, but God gave him a marvelous victory (2 Chronicles 20). Paul admitted weakness and then stated that when he was weak, he was strong because God's strength is made perfect in weakness (2 Corinthians 12:9,10).

It was after the disciples recognized they did not have enough to feed the multitudes and admitted it that Christ marvelously provided a more than adequate supply (Luke 9:12,13).

It was after the disciples admitted they had caught no fish that Jesus directed them to a most successful endeavor (John 21:3–6).

These people were not told to replace negative confessions with positive confessions which were contrary to fact. They stated conditions exactly as they were rather than pretending they were something else. Yet God marvelously intervened even though they made what some would call negative confessions.

Comparing Scripture with Scripture makes it clear that positive verbal expressions do not always produce happy effects nor do negative statements always result in unhappy effects. To teach that leaders in the early days of the Church such as Paul, Stephen, and Trophimus did not live in a constant state of affluence and health because they did not have the light on this teaching is going beyond and contrary to the Word of God. Doctrine will be sound only as it is developed within the framework of the total teaching of Scripture.

The Greek word translated "confess" means "to speak the same thing." When people confess Christ, it is to say the same thing as Scripture does concerning Christ. When people confess sin, it is to say the same as Scripture does concerning sin. And when people confess some promise of Scripture, they must be sure they are saying the same thing about that promise as the total teaching of Scripture on that subject.

The words of Augustine are appropriate in this regard: "If you believe what you like in the gospel and reject what you don't like, it is not the gospel you believe, but yourself."

Believers Should Consider Adequately the Will of God

When the positive confession doctrine indicates one can have whatever one says, it fails to emphasize adequately that

God's will must be considered. David had the best intentions when he indicated his desire to build a temple for the Lord, but it was not God's will (1 Chronicles 17:4). David was permitted to gather materials, but Solomon was to build the temple.

Paul prayed that the thorn in his flesh might be removed, but it was not God's will. Instead of removing the thorn, God gave Paul sufficient grace (2 Corinthians 12:9).

God's will can be known and claimed by faith, but the desire of the heart is not always the criterion by which the will of God is determined. There are times when the enjoyable or pleasurable may not be the will of God. James alluded to this when he wrote, "Ye ask, and receive not, because ye ask amiss, that ye may consume it upon your lusts" (James 4:3, KJV). The word translated "lusts" does not refer to perverted desire but to pleasure or enjoyment, that which the heart desires. Several translations use the word "pleasure" rather than "lust."

In Gethsemane Jesus asked that if it were possible the cup might be removed. That was His desire, but in His prayer He recognized the will of God. He said, "Yet not my will, but yours be done" (Luke 22:42).

The Bible recognizes there will be times when believers will not know what to pray for. They will not know what the will of God is. They may even be perplexed as Paul sometimes was (2 Corinthians 4:8). Then, rather than simply making a positive confession based on the desires of the heart, they need to recognize the Holy Spirit makes intercession for them according to the will of God (Romans 8:26,27).

God's will must always have priority over the believer's plans or desires. The words of James should be kept constantly in view: "You ought to say, 'If it is the Lord's will, we will live and do this or that' " (James 4:15).

Getting what the believer wants is not as simple as repeating a positive confession. Pleasant things might be out of the will of God; and, conversely, unpleasant things might be in the will of God. It is important for the believer to say as Paul's friends did, "The Lord's will be done" (Acts 21:14)—more important than to demand a life free from suffering.

Believers Should Recognize the Importance of Importunate Prayer

When the positive confession view teaches that believers are to confess rather than to pray for things which God has promised, it overlooks the teaching of God's Word concerning importunate prayer. According to some who hold this view of positive confession, God's promises are in the area of material, physical, and spiritual blessings; believers are to claim or confess these blessings and not to pray for them.

The instruction not to pray for promised blessings is contrary to the teaching of God's Word. Food is one of God's promised blessings, yet Jesus taught His disciples to pray: "Give us today our daily bread" (Matthew 6:11). Wisdom is a promised blessing of God, yet Scripture states, if anyone "lacks wisdom, he should ask God, who gives generously to all without finding fault" (James 1:5). Jesus called the Holy Spirit the promise of the Father (Luke 24:49), and yet He also taught that God would give the Holy Spirit to those who ask (Luke 11:13).

While there were times God told people not to pray, as in the case of Moses at the Red Sea (Exodus 14:15), there are many Scriptures reminding believers to pray, and that, without ceasing (Romans 12:12; Philippians 4:6; 1 Thessalonians 5:17).

Jesus emphasized the importance of importunity in prayer. The illustration of the persistent friend who came at midnight asking for bread to set before his guests became the basis for Christ's statement, "Ask and it will be given to you" (Luke

11:5–10). The parable of the widow and the unjust judge became the occasion for our Lord to emphasize importunity in prayer (Luke 18:1–8). These people were commended for importunity and not for prayerless positive confession.

While God's ways are above our ways, and we cannot understand the reason for every command in Scripture, we do know that in His wisdom God has ordained prayer as part of the process included in meeting a need. Rather than an indication of doubt, importunate prayer can be an indication of obedience and faith.

Believers Should Recognize They Can Expect Suffering in This Life

The positive confession teaching advocates reigning as kings in this life. It teaches that believers are to dominate and not be dominated by circumstances. Poverty and sickness are usually mentioned among the circumstances over which believers are to have dominion.

If believers choose the kings of this world as models, it is true they will seek the trouble-free life (although even kings of this world are not free from problems). They will be more concerned with physical and material prosperity than with spiritual growth.

When believers choose the King of kings as their model, however, their desires will be completely different. They will be transformed by His teaching and example. They will recognize the truth of Romans 8:17 which is written concerning joint-heirs with Christ: "We share in his sufferings in order that we may also share in his glory." Paul even went so far as to glory in his infirmities instead of denying them (2 Corinthians 12:5–10).

Though Christ was rich, for our sakes He became poor (2 Corinthians 8:9). He could say, "Foxes have holes and birds of the air have nests, but the Son of Man has no place to lay his head" (Matthew 8:20).

While God in His providence has endowed some with the ability to accumulate greater wealth than others, something is tragically lacking if there is not a willingness to do the will of God and surrender all, if need be, including creature comforts.

Jesus never ceased to be God, and through the power of the Holy Spirit performed many miracles; yet He was not free from suffering. He knew He must suffer many things of the elders (Matthew 16:21; 17:12). He desired to eat the Passover with the disciples before He suffered (Luke 22:15). After His death, the disciples recognized that Christ's suffering was a fulfillment of prophecy (Luke 24:25,26,32).

When believers realize that reigning as kings in this life is to take Christ as the model of a king, they will recognize suffering can be involved, that sometimes it is more kingly to stay with unpleasant circumstances than to try to make all circumstances pleasant.

Paul had been shown he would suffer (Acts 9:16). Later he rejoiced in his sufferings for the Colossians. He saw his suffering as filling up "what is still lacking in regard to Christ's afflictions, for the sake of his body, which is the church" (Colossians 1:24).

God promises to supply the needs of believers, and He knows how to deliver the godly out of temptation; but reigning in life as Christ did may also include suffering. Committed believers will accept this. They will not be disillusioned if life is not a continual series of pleasant experiences. They will not become cynical if they do not have all the desires of their heart.

They will recognize the servant is not greater than the Master. To follow Christ requires denying ourselves (Luke 9:23). This includes denying our selfish desires and may include admitting our problems.

Problems are not always an indication of lack of faith. To the contrary, they can be a tribute to faith. This is the great emphasis of Hebrews 11:32–40:

> And what more shall I say? I do not have time to tell about Gideon, Barak, Samson, Jephthah, David, Samuel and the prophets, who through faith conquered kingdoms, administered justice, and gained what was promised; who shut the mouths of lions, quenched the fury of the flames, and escaped the edge of the sword; whose weakness was turned to strength; and who became powerful in battle and routed foreign armies.
>
> Women received back their dead, raised to life again. Others were tortured and refused to be released, so that they might gain a better resurrection. Some faced jeers and flogging, while still others were chained and put in prison.
>
> They were stoned; they were sawed in two; they were put to death by the sword. They went about in sheepskins and goatskins, destitute, persecuted and mistreated—the world was not worthy of them. They wandered in deserts and mountains, and in caves and holes in the ground.
>
> These were all commended for their faith, yet none of them received what had been promised. God had planned something better for us so that only together with us would they be made perfect.

To hold that all suffering results from negative confessions and indicates a lack of faith contradicts the Scripture. Some heroes of faith suffered greatly, some even died through faith, and they were commended for it.

Believers Should Recognize the Sovereignty of God

The positive confession emphasis has a tendency to include statements which make it appear that believers are sovereign and God is the servant. Statements are made about compelling God to act, implying He has surrendered His sovereignty, that He is no longer in a position to act according to His wisdom and purpose. Reference is made to true prosperity being the ability to use God's ability and power to meet needs regardless of what the needs are. This puts human beings in the position of using God rather than their surrendering themselves to be used of Him.

In this view there is very little consideration given to communion with God in order to discover His will. There is very little appeal to search the Scriptures for the framework of the will of God. There is little emphasis on the kind of discussion with fellow believers which results in two or three agreeing what the will of God might be. Instead, the desire of the heart is viewed as a binding mandate on God. It is seen as constituting the authority of the believer.

It is true that Jesus said, " 'And I will do whatever you ask in my name, so that the Son may bring glory to the Father' " (John 14:13). But Scripture also teaches that the asking must be in harmony with the will of God. "This is the confidence we have in approaching God: that if we ask anything according to his will, he hears us. And if we know that he hears us—whatever we ask—we know that we have what we asked of him" (1 John 5:14,15).

"Be still, and know that I am God" (Psalm 46:10) is still an important injunction today. God is God. He will not surrender His glory or sovereignty to anyone. No one will compel God to action.

The authority of the believer exists only in the will of God, and it is the believer's responsibility to discover and conform to the will of the sovereign God even down to individual desires. Paul's words are still applicable: "Therefore do not be foolish, but understand what the Lord's will is" (Ephesians 5:17).

When believers recognize the sovereignty of God and properly become concerned with the will of God, they will not talk in terms of compelling God or using God's power. They will speak of becoming obedient servants. They will desire to become yielded instruments in the hands of God.

Believers Should Apply the Practical Test

In reviewing the efforts of those who advocate this positive confession teaching it is evident that the basic appeal is to those who are already Christians living in an affluent society. They encourage a spiritual elitism in which adherents say, "We believe the same things you do. The difference is that we practice what we believe."

A practical test of a belief is whether it has a universal application. Does the teaching have meaning only for those living in an affluent society? Or does it also work among the refugees of the world? What application does the teaching have for believers imprisoned for their faith by atheistic governments? Are those believers substandard who suffer martyrdom or grave physical injury at the hands of cruel, ruthless dictators?

The truth of God's Word has a universal application. It is as effective in the slums as in suburbia. It is as effective in the jungle as in the city. It is as effective in foreign countries as in our own nation. It is as effective among deprived nations as among the affluent. The test of fruit is still one way of determining whether a teacher or teaching is of God or of human origin. "By their fruit you will recognize them" (Matthew 7:20).

Believers Should Accurately Deal With the Word *Rhema*

Because there is very little literature among those who espouse the positive confession teaching concerning the Greek word *rhema,* it is necessary to consider it as used primarily in oral communication.

A distinction is generally made by proponents of this view between the words *logos* and *rhema.* The first, it is claimed, refers to the written word. The second, to that which is presently spoken by faith. According to this view whatever is spoken by faith becomes inspired and takes on the creative power of God.

There are two major problems with this distinction. First, the distinction is not justified by usage either in the Greek New Testament or in the Septuagint (Greek version of the Old Testament). The words are used synonymously in both.

In the case of the Septuagint both *rhema* and *logos* are used to translate the one Hebrew word *dabar* which is used in various ways relative to communication. For instance, the word *dabar* (translated, "word of God") is used in both Jeremiah 1:1 and 2. Yet in the Septuagint it is translated *rhema* in verse 1 and *logos* in verse 2.

In the New Testament the words *rhema* and *logos* are also used interchangeably. This can be seen in passages such as 1 Peter 1:23 and 25. In verse 23, it is "the *[logos]* of God which . . . abides forever" (NKJV). In verse 25, "the *[rhema]* of the Lord endures forever" (NKJV). Again, in Ephesians 5:26 believers are cleansed "by the washing with water through the *[rhema]*." In John 15:3 believers are "clean because of the *[logos]*."

The distinctions between *logos* and *rhema* cannot be sustained by biblical evidence. The Word of God, whether referred to as *logos* or *rhema,* is inspired, eternal, dynamic, and miraculous. Whether the Word is written or spoken does not alter its essential character. "All Scripture is God-breathed and is useful for teaching, rebuking, correcting and training in righteousness, so that the man of God may be thoroughly equipped for every good work" (2 Timothy 3:16,17).

A second problem also exists among those who make a distinction between the words *logos* and *rhema*. Passages of Scripture are sometimes selected without regard to context or analogy of faith. In this kind of application of the so-called *rhema* principle, adherents are more concerned with making the Word mean what they want it to mean than in becoming what the Word wants them to become. In some instances it becomes obvious they love God more for what He does than for who He is.

It is important for believers to avoid any form of Christian existentialism that isolates passages of Scripture from the context or makes some passages eternal and others contemporary.

Conclusion

In considering any doctrine it is always necessary to ask whether it is in harmony with the total teaching of Scripture. Doctrine based on less than a holistic view of biblical truth can only do harm to the cause of Christ. It can often be more detrimental than views which reject Scripture altogether. Some people will more likely accept something as truth if it is referred to in the Word of God, even if the teaching is an extreme emphasis or contradicts other principles of Scripture.

God's Word does teach great truths such as healing, provision for need, faith, and the authority of believers. The Bible does teach that a disciplined mind is an important factor in victorious living. But these truths must always be considered in the framework of the total teaching of Scripture.

When abuses occur, there is sometimes a temptation to draw back from these great truths of God's Word. In some cases people even lose out with God altogether when they discover that exaggerated emphases do not always meet their expectations or result in freedom from problems.

The fact that doctrinal aberrations develop, however, is not a reason for rejecting or remaining silent concerning them. The existence of differences of opinion is all the more reason why believers should continue diligently to search the Scriptures. It is why servants of God must faithfully declare the whole counsel of God.

14
A Biblical Perspective on Gambling

Gambling, both legal and illegal, is a phenomenon gaining unprecedented acceptance. Because it is so widespread, Christians must look at this activity to determine the ethical and moral implications.

Gambling Defined

Advocates of gambling often try to place this activity in the same category as other ventures which involve risk. They describe farming, business, insurance, and even investments as gambling because the outcome is unpredictable and losses can occur. In this way they hope to transfer the respectability of legitimate ventures to gambling.

L. M. Starkey, Jr., has made the following helpful observation:

> Life does have its normal risks which one must accept with faith and courage. These normal risks are in no sense equivalent to the risks in a game of chance. Gambling devises artificial risks in the hope of excessive gain far beyond what the investment of

time, money, or skill would justify. In gambling the chance is unrelated to any creative effort called for by the farmer or the stockbroker in the responsible investment of his mental, monetary, and physical funds.[1]

To distinguish gambling from risks involved in legitimate venture it will be helpful to recognize three factors integral to gambling: (1) An incentive consisting of money or merchandise is offered. (2) The prize is acquired primarily on the basis of chance. (3) A payment of money or other consideration is required to become involved in the chance taken.[2]

Gambling then is recognized as any activity in which wealth changes hands, mainly on the basis of chance and with risk to the gambler. Creative effort, useful skills, and responsible investment are not integral factors.

Because gambling exists in many forms and people in increasing numbers are exposed to its temptations, the responsible Christian must form an opinion concerning its propriety. The legalization of gambling by government or its acceptance by some religious organizations cannot be a criterion for evaluation. The Christian attitude must be determined by the principles of Scripture.

God's Attitude Toward Gambling

God's people in Bible times apparently were not greatly tempted with gambling. It seems the vice manifested itself only when Israel was dominated by heathen nations. When gambling did occur God clearly indicated His attitude concerning it.

During their Babylonian captivity the Israelites came under the influence of people who gambled. As a result some of the captives also became involved. To these people God through

Isaiah said, "Ye are they that forsake the Lord, that forget my holy mountain, that prepare a table for that troop, and that furnish the drink offering unto that number" (Isaiah 65:11, KJV). As indicated in some modern translations of the Bible, the Hebrew words translated "troop" and "number" were names of the heathen gods "Gad" and "Meni." To the heathen, Gad was the giver of good luck. Meni was the god of bad luck.

The translation of Isaiah 65:11 by James Moffat is as follows: "But ye who have forsaken the Eternal, ye who ignore his sacred hill, spreading tables to Good Luck, pouring libations to Fate, I make the sword your fate."

E. H. Plumptre, late Dean of Wells, has pointed out that Gad was worshiped as the greater fortune, the giver of good luck. Meni was worshiped as the lesser fortune. George Rawlinson, who at one time served as professor of Ancient History at Oxford, has indicated the name Meni "designated a deity who apportions men's fortunes to them."

The sin for which some of the Israelites were condemned was trusting in luck rather than God. Isaiah made it clear that trust in God and trust in luck cannot coexist. If people rely on chance it is evident they do not rely on God. Isaiah described those who trusted in gambling as "they that forsake the Lord" (Isaiah 65:11).

Biblical Principles

A careful reading of Scripture makes it clear there are numerous biblical principles which indicate gambling is an evil to be avoided. When people recognize God's authority they will honor the principles which indicate gambling is evil.

1. Gambling is wrong because it is a disregard of responsible stewardship.

The Bible clearly teaches that all things belong to God. "The earth is the LORD's, and everything in it, the world, and all who live in it" (Psalm 24:1). Since all things belong to God, people are placed in the position of stewards who must give a proper accounting for everything given to them in trust.

The first step in a faithful administration of this stewardship is the giving of self to God. Believers must recognize they are not their own (1 Corinthians 6:19). They have been redeemed with a price, not of silver or gold, but with the precious blood of Jesus (1 Peter 1:18,19). The churches of Macedonia set a worthy example of personal dedication when "they gave themselves first to the Lord" (2 Corinthians 8:5). Life, with all it involves, is a stewardship to be administered for the glory of God.

People who honestly dedicate themselves to God will also recognize that all they possess must be handled as a stewardship. The Parable of the Talents (Matthew 25:14–30) indicates that the good and faithful servants administered the talents entrusted to them in such a way that the master was pleased. The wicked and slothful servant failed in his administration and suffered the appropriate consequences.

When people recognize their stewardship responsibilities they will not consider gambling in any form a proper administration of divinely bestowed resources, time, and ability. Even the ethics of the world will not tolerate those who gamble with resources put in their trust. Christian responsibility transcends all other responsibility, and for the Christian, gambling is wrong. It is a total disregard of the principle of stewardship. It is a prostitution of God-given assets which should be used to glorify God and advance His kingdom.

2. Gambling is wrong because it involves a chance of gain at the expense and suffering of others.

The nature of gambling is such that a person has a chance of gain only because others have suffered loss. The economic benefits come only to a very few. The financial loss is borne by many who usually can least afford it. The fact that people involved in gambling are commonly referred to in derogatory terms by its promoters is an indication of the status to which they are reduced. Whether or not the financial loss is excessive, gamblers are basically the losers while the operators of gambling establishments are the winners.

The suffering caused by gambling is totally inconsistent with the teaching of Scripture concerning love. Not only is the Christian to love those who are lovable, but even enemies. God's people are to love their neighbors as themselves. The principle of love will prevent Christians from gambling because of the damage it does to others. The principle of love will cause Christians to oppose any effort by the state or any other organization to legalize any activity based on a weakness of people which degrades society.

William Temple, late Archbishop of Canterbury, stated the Christian position well when he wrote:

> Gambling challenges that view of life which the Christian church exists to uphold and extend. Its glorification of mere chance is a denial of the divine order of nature. To risk money haphazardly is to disregard the insistence of the Church in every age of living faith that possessions are a trust, and that men must account to God for their use. The persistent appeal to covetousness is fundamentally opposed to the unselfishness which was taught by Jesus Christ and by the New Testament as a whole. The attempt (inseparable from gambling) to make profit out of the inevitable loss and possible suffering of others is the antithesis of that love of one's neighbor on which our Lord insisted.[3]

3. Gambling is wrong because it is inconsistent with the work ethic of Scripture.

Throughout Scripture the importance of work is empha-sized. In several places the correlation between working and eating is stated. The Old Testament reminds us, "He who works his land will have abundant food" (Proverbs 12:11).

In the New Testament the same principle is stated with great forcefulness. To the Thessalonians Paul wrote: "When we were with you, we gave you this rule: 'If a man will not work, he shall not eat' " (2 Thessalonians 3:10).

Not only does the Bible require that one should work for the necessities of life, but it also warns against the something for nothing, get-rich-quick approach. "One eager to get rich will not go unpunished" (Proverbs 28:20). "He that hasteth to be rich hath an evil [envious] eye, and considereth not that pover-ty shall come upon him" (Proverbs 28:22, KJV). "Dishonest money dwindles away, but he who gathers money little by lit-tle makes it grow" (Proverbs 13:11).

In the wisdom of God work was assigned in the Garden of Eden even before the Fall (Genesis 2:15ff; cf. 1:28). Though sin resulted in a change of the nature of work (Genesis 3:17,19), the responsibility of working was never rescinded. Any effort to circumvent the work ethic of Scripture can result only in failure. Gambling, whether to secure wealth in a hurry or to place bread on the table, is inconsistent with what the Bible teaches about work.

4. Gambling is wrong because it tends to be habit forming.

Gambling, like other evils, has a tendency to become an addiction. As in the case of alcoholics and drug addicts, com-pulsive gamblers are dominated to the extent that they risk not only money, but everything meaningful in life. They have lost control of themselves.

This condition is contrary to the teaching of Scripture. The Word of God points out that a Christian will refuse to be brought under the power even of lawful things (1 Corinthians 6:12). The person indwelled by the Holy Spirit will be characterized by temperance, or self-control (Galatians 5:23).

Those who have studied gambling addiction seem to agree there are six symptoms characteristic of compulsive gambling: (1) The activity becomes chronically repetitive. (2) It becomes a mania which precludes all other interests, including the home. (3) A pathologic optimism replaces the ability to learn from previous losing experiences. (4) The ability to stop in a winning situation no longer exists. (5) In spite of initial decisions to gamble only so much the addict invariably risks too much. (6) The activity seems to produce an enjoyable tension consisting of both pain and pleasure.

It is obvious that habitual gamblers are under the control of the compulsion to gamble. Rather than being servants of God, they are servants of a desire they cannot handle. Paul described the condition clearly when he wrote, "Don't you know that when you offer yourselves to someone to obey him as slaves, you are slaves to the one whom you obey?" (Romans 6:16). Because of the degrading possibility of addiction, gambling should be considered an evil.

Christian Responsibility in Relation to Gambling

When the various truths of God's Word are considered, Christians cannot adopt a neutral stance toward gambling. There are responsibilities which they cannot ignore.

When the Bible instructs believers, "whatever you do, do it all for the glory of God" (1 Corinthians 10:31), it certainly precludes gambling. God is not glorified when people put their trust in chance rather than in the Lord.

When God's Word teaches that we should "avoid every kind of evil" (1 Thessalonians 5:22) it precludes gambling. There is no way in which a practice can be considered anything other than evil when it violates principles of God's Word concerning stewardship, consideration of others, and the dignity of honest labor.

Those who want to live according to Scripture will refrain from participation in any form of gambling. As the salt of the earth (Matthew 5:13) they will also do all within their power to discourage the legalization of gambling, whether to raise money for charity, church , or state.

---

[1]L. M. Starkey, Jr., *Money, Mania, and Morals* (Abingdon Press, 1964).

[2]Virgil W. Peterson, "Obstacles to Enforcement of Gambling Laws," *The Annals of the American Academy of Political and Social Science* (May 1950).

[3]William Temple, "Gambling and Ethics," issued by The Churches' Committee on Gambling, 215 Abbey House, London.

15
Abstinence from Alcohol

The General Council of the Assemblies of God has histori-cally opposed the consumption of alcohol in any form. Early documents of the Church declare, without reservation or com-promise, a position of total abstinence.

In more recent years, however, this mark of separation from the world and this token of dedicated service to God has been questioned by some. Yet the continued effective work of reach-ing the lost and of challenging all believers to be always filled with the Holy Spirit is seriously jeopardized by a careless atti-tude concerning the consumption of alcoholic beverages.

For two reasons we urge all believers to avoid the Satanic tool of alcohol, which destroys lives, damns souls, and blights society: (1) A studied review of the Scriptures affirms a stern warning against intoxicating drink and a call to separation from this evil for the purpose of better service to God and humanity. (2) Current social abuses and the public outrage over the high cost of alcohol in terms of human misery, death, and destruction of property cry out with urgency for the church of Jesus Christ to oppose firmly any use whatsoever of a beverage that so insidiously afflicts and binds the bodies and minds of men and women.

The Scriptures Record Tragedies Caused by Alcohol

Although there is disagreement among Bible scholars about the true nature of the drink referred to by the various Hebrew and Greek words for "wine," it is only too evident that some persons in the Old Testament drank fermented wine. Noah, after saving his family from the destruction of the Flood, planted a vineyard, made wine, became intoxicated, and brought disastrous results on himself and his family (Genesis 9:20–27). Noah was no doubt surprised, upon his return to sobriety and clear thinking, to realize his simple act of taking a drink had ended in such shame. The two daughters of Lot made their father drink liquor until he became drunk; then they committed incest with him (Genesis 19:30–38).

Ahasuerus was powerful. He ruled over a great kingdom and had a beautiful wife. But his foolish action before his drinking guests resulted in the deposition of his queen and the dissolution of their marriage (Esther 1:9–22). Belshazzar, in a state of drunkenness, committed sacrilege with the sacred vessels from the Jewish temple. That very night he was killed as a fulfillment of prophecy (Daniel 5).

Drunkenness, according to Scripture, is a sin. But what about such references in the Old Testament as "wine, which cheers" (Judges 9:13) and "wine that gladdens" (Psalm 104:15)? We believe such references are accommodations to human weakness and hardness of heart (cf. Matthew 19:8). The spirit and intent of Scripture emphasize the evil consequences of alcohol.

Scriptural Principles and Examples Recommend Abstinence

Alcohol destroys the body. Even in small amounts it begins its subtle work of destruction, taking its toll on mental and physical reactions. God knew this fact very well when He gave instructions that priests and kings (spiritual and secular leaders) should refrain from any use of alcoholic beverages.

In the Old Testament instruction to the Levites, the spiritual leaders of Israel, priests were commanded to abstain from wine or intoxicating drink when they went into the presence of the Lord to minister (Leviticus 10:8–11). This requirement of abstinence was given so the ministering priest would be able to distinguish between the holy and the unholy, between the clean and the unclean, and so he could be a teacher of all the statutes of God.

Today, all born-again Christians have been made priests to God (1 Peter 2:9; Revelation 1:6). As such we should always give our best and be at our best in His service. We believe the standard of abstinence demanded of the Old Testament priest should be the standard of every Christian today. We too must distinguish between right and wrong. We must be Spirit-led teachers in a society that greatly needs divine instruction and godly example.

Secular leaders are also to abstain from alcohol. "It is . . . not for kings to drink wine, not for rulers to crave beer, lest they drink and forget what the law decrees, and deprive all the oppressed of their rights" (Proverbs 31:4,5). If the prohibition is absolutely essential for spiritual and secular leaders, it is certainly essential for every believer. We who are kings and priests unto God (Revelation 1:6) must live according to His standards.

A Little Alcohol Is Too Much

The Christian who advocates or condones "drinking in moderation" is providing Satan an opening he would not have with an individual committed to total abstinence. By medical definition, alcohol is a drug. The moderate drinker is naive not to recognize the peril of eventually becoming addicted.

The condition of the drunkard is tragic; and God's Word gives clear warning of the final tragedy. The individual who refuses to have anything to do with such a dangerous taskmaster is wise indeed. No alcoholic ever intended to become an alcoholic upon taking the first drink. And no individual who persistently refused to take the first drink ever became an alcoholic. The church of Jesus Christ must take a bold stand against this evil that in the end "bites like a snake and poisons like a viper" (Proverbs 23:32).

The effects of alcohol are vividly described in Proverbs 23. There is a physical and emotional impact. "Who has woe? Who has sorrow? Who has strife? Who has complaints? Who has needless bruises? Who has bloodshot eyes?" (Proverbs 23:29). The answer is obvious: "Those who linger over wine" (v. 30). But the woe, the sorrow, the contention, the complaints, the injuries, are not reserved for the drunkard in the gutter. They begin all too frequently with a social drink.

Just like every other temptation of Satan, the drinking of alcoholic beverages has its attraction. Hence the warning of Holy Scripture: "Do not gaze at wine when it is red, when it sparkles in the cup, when it goes down smoothly!" (Proverbs 23:31). The warning is so strong because the attraction of the temptation soon turns the pleasure seeker into a pathetic embarrassment to the human race: "Your eyes will see strange sights and your mind imagine confusing things" (23:33). Even the normal physical protection systems of pain and caution are defeated by alcohol (23:34,35).

"Wine is a mocker and beer a brawler; whoever is led astray by them is not wise" (Proverbs 20:1). God's will is for His people to abstain from this deceitful betrayer that mocks and destroys basic human dignity.

God Calls His People to Holiness

The standard for God's people is no less in the New Testament than in the Old. The Old Testament warnings about the abuses and excesses of alcohol become in the New Testament a call to holy living through the power of the Holy Spirit. Our bodies are the temples of the Holy Spirit (1 Corinthians 6:19). We need to cleanse them from all profane habits, including alcohol. Opening up the human temple to the possible influence and control of alcohol is absolutely contrary to the biblical admonition to keep those temples filled with the Holy Spirit (Ephesians 5:18). The only safe way is to leave alcoholic beverages alone.

First Timothy 3:3 states that a bishop must be one "not given to wine" (KJV). A spiritual leader should set the highest example for all Christians to follow. The apostle Paul willingly invited his fellow believers to follow his example, even as he followed the example of Christ (1 Corinthians 11:1). A minister who drinks alcohol risks disobedience to the Word of God.

Some well-meaning people have misused the instruction given by Paul to Timothy in 1 Timothy 5. When Paul suggested that Timothy "stop drinking only water, and use a little wine because of your stomach and your frequent illnesses" (5:23), he was not recommending wine as a social drink. The fact that Paul had to mention the medicinal use of wine indicates rather strongly that Timothy was committed to abstinence as a lifestyle.

The call to holy living and to total abstinence is most appropriate for a Movement that looks with expectation for the soon return of Jesus Christ and the eventual inauguration of His kingdom on earth. Jesus warned His disciples, as well as all who would live between their time and the end time, "Be careful, or your hearts will be weighed down with dissipation, drunkenness and the anxieties of life. . . . Be always on the watch, and pray that you may be able to escape all that is about to happen, and that you may be able to stand before the Son of Man" (Luke 21:34,36). As we watch and pray for the return of Jesus, our senses should be as sharp and clear as they can possibly be.

The Use of Alcohol Weakens the Christian's Testimony

The use of alcohol violates some basic principles laid down for all believers, whether ministers or laypeople. One of these important principles is the biblical caution not to offend a weaker believer or cause a younger Christian to fall.

The apostle Paul deals with the responsibility of the stronger believer toward the weaker believer in Romans 14. "It is better not to eat meat or drink wine or to do anything else that will cause your brother to fall" (v. 21). It takes a stronger act of the will to abstain from the consumption of alcohol than to participate in this social practice of the world. Yet believers who take their Christian responsibility seriously cannot avoid the obvious importance of total abstinence to their Christian testimony.

This truth is especially significant when it is applied to the young people of the world who are turning to alcohol in unprecedented numbers as an acceptable mind-altering drug. They are going beyond moderation, no matter what their parents and elders say. If Christian parents and adults use alcohol even in moderation or just to be socially accepted, the next generation will use it with less care and self-control. The best example our generation can set for the next generation is to practice and teach total abstinence.

Jesus spoke very clearly to the disciples about the responsibility of the older generation to its children and youth: "Things that cause people to sin are bound to come, but woe to that person through whom they come. It would be better for him to be thrown into the sea with a millstone tied around his neck than for him to cause one of these little ones to sin" (Luke 17:1,2). We must not set an example that will send others to hell and destruction.

As believers we must draw a line on the use of alcohol. If we draw the line at the point of moderation, our ministers will soon find it necessary to exhort congregations to forsake drunkenness. If we draw the line at total abstinence, we will save a multitude of young and old from the sin of alcoholism.

Social Drinking Is Satan's Cruel Deception

The term *social drinking* suggests that the consumption of alcohol in respectable surroundings is in some way different from drinking in other environments. There was a time when it would have been unthinkable that we would have to speak out against social drinking among Christians. The fact that such a problem has grown to the currently distressing proportions shows what a powerful and insidious influence the present age exerts on the church of Jesus Christ. The Holy Spirit can deliver from the shackles of social drinking, and we plead with all Christians who have fallen into this bondage to cry out for God's help immediately.

Many people who experience psychological problems (and some of them unfortunately are Christians) are tempted to seek an easy solution in "a little bit" of alcohol. But what was used as a supposed cure has caused even greater problems. We are set free through Jesus Christ, not through a drug that dissipates and destroys us when we submit to its influence.

Every one of the 13 million problem drinkers in the United States today started on the road to alcoholism with a social drink or an innocent first taste. Half of the fatal automobile accidents in this country are caused by drinking drivers. According to government estimates, the economic cost of alcoholism—including lost production, automobile accidents, health care, violent crimes, and fire losses—exceeds 100 billion dollars every year.[1] Alcohol is consistently linked to a high percentage of reported murders, assaults, and rapes, as well as to suicide, domestic violence, and child abuse. The role of social drinking as the starting point for much of this abuse can only be estimated.

Fetal Alcohol Syndrome (FAS) is one of the leading causes of mental retardation as a birth defect in the United States.[2] Whatever alcohol the pregnant mother consumes crosses the placenta and enters the bloodstream of the baby. The result too frequently is below-average birth weight and size, deformed and improperly formed joints and limbs, as well as heart defects. We should not be concerned only about the *life* of the unborn child; the *health* of the child is important too.

The consumption of alcohol has become a national crisis, tearing at the moral fabric of our nation. Christians cannot meet their moral responsibilities by a posture of neutrality about alcohol. The problem is not merely economic, cultural, or social. In the final analysis, the use of alcohol is a spiritual problem. Alcoholism is sin, not sickness. Its shocking increase is another manifestation of the permissive, lawless spirit produced by the spiritual degeneration so much in evidence today.

The Call to Abstinence

Alcoholic beverages should have no place in the life of the Christian. Let there be no doubt about the Assemblies of God stand on this critical issue. We declare unequivocally our conviction that total abstinence from alcoholic beverages is the only acceptable way of life for the Christian. We call upon every member and adherent in our Fellowship, including both the ministry and the laity, to teach by word and example a life-style that abstains totally from the consumption of alcoholic beverages.

1Statistics provided by the National Council on Alcoholism, Inc., 12 West 21st Street, New York, NY 10010. Up-to-date materials and statistics may be secured from the Council upon written request.

2National Council on Alcoholism, Inc.

16
The Kingdom of God as Described in Holy Scripture

The terms *kingdom of God* and *kingdom of heaven* are frequently found in Holy Scripture and in contemporary Christian usage. Yet there is widespread disagreement on the meaning and application of the terms. Some of this disagreement is a simple matter of interpretation on minor points, but some of it is crucial, challenging even the fundamental tenets of traditional evangelical and Pentecostal beliefs. For this reason it is appropriate to articulate those essential aspects of the kingdom of God that are commonly held by the Assemblies of God.

Linguistic Meaning of the Term *Kingdom*

The primary meaning of *malkuth* (Hebrew) and *basileia* (Greek) is the authority, reign, or rule of a king. The territory, subjects, and operations of the Kingdom are secondary meanings.

The kingdom of God is the sphere of God's rule (cf. Psalm 22:28). Yet fallen humanity participates in the universal rebellion against God and His authority (1 John 5:19; Revelation 11:17–18). By faith and obedience a person turns from this rebellion, is regenerated by the Holy Spirit, and becomes a part of the Kingdom and its operation. Though human participation in the Kingdom is voluntary, God's kingdom is present, whether or not people recognize and accept it.

There is only one kingdom of God, variously described in Scripture as the "kingdom of heaven," "kingdom of God," kingdom of "the Son of Man" (Matthew 13:41), "kingdom of the Son" (Luke 22:30), "kingdom of Jesus" (Revelation 1:9), "kingdom of the Lord Christ" (2 Timothy 4:1), "kingdom of Christ and of God" (Ephesians 5:5), and "kingdoms of our Lord and of His Christ" (Revelation 11:15).

The Kingdom of God in the Old Testament

"Kingdom of the Lord" occurs once in the Old Testament: *malkuth Yahweh* (1 Chronicles 28:5). There are of course many occurrences of "kingdom" for earthly territory or domain. "Dominion" or "rule" is occasionally the translation for the idea of God's authority and power (1 Chronicles 17:14; 29:11; Psalms 22:28; 45:6; 66:7; 103:19; 145:11–13). Throughout the Old Testament (but especially in the psalms and the prophets) the idea of God as King ruling over His creation and over Israel is clearly expressed. Although God's immediate kingship is evident in the Old Testament, there is also a strong emphasis on a future fulfillment of God's universal rule. This anticipation often coincides with messianic expectations associated with both the first and second advents (cf. Isaiah 9:6–7; 11:1–12; 24:21–23; 45:22–23; Zechariah 14:9). Daniel 4:34 describes God's rule as "an eternal dominion" and a "kingdom [that] endures from generation to generation."

The Kingdom in the New Testament

While the idea of the universal rule of God permeates the

Old Testament, the kingdom of God takes on additional meaning and importance in the teaching and ministry of Jesus. The ministry of Jesus begins with the proclamation, "the kingdom is near" (Matthew 3:2; 4:17; Mark 1:15). Although Jesus never specifically defined the Kingdom, He illustrated it through parables (Matthew 13; Mark 4) and demonstrated its power in His ministry. He instructed His disciples to proclaim the Kingdom as He sent them out in missionary ministry (Matthew 10:7; Luke 9:2; 10:9,11). Every description of Jesus Christ as *Lord* is a reminder that Christ is the ruler of the kingdom of God.

From the various contexts of the word *kingdom* in the Gospels, the rule of God is seen as (1) a present realm or sphere into which people are entering now and (2) a future apocalyptic order into which the righteous will enter at the end of the age.

Thus the kingdom of God is both a present reality and a promise of a future fulfillment. The Kingdom is already present on earth in the person and acts of Jesus, by the Holy Spirit. Yet the fullness of the Kingdom awaits a final apocalyptic arrival at the end of this age (Matthew 24:27,30–31; Luke 21:27–31).

The State of the Kingdom Now

Just as some who followed Jesus "thought that the kingdom of God was going to appear at once" (Luke 19:11), some today are expecting Christians to usher in the fullness of the Kingdom in an earthly rule. When the Pharisees asked Jesus at what time the kingdom of God would come, he answered, "The kingdom of God is within [among] you" (Luke 17:21). The restored reign of God was soon to be a reality, for the One who was to reclaim the usurped territory was on earth to accomplish His work of redemption. The overthrow of Satan's dominion had already begun.

Today, the redemptive work is complete, yet the reality of the ultimate Kingdom is qualified. In the present age, the power of the Kingdom does not halt the aging or death process. Though God does overrule natural laws by sovereign act or in response to the prayer and faith of believers, the Kingdom still works through fallible human beings. The Church will not finally change the world prior to the Second Coming. Righteous political and social actions are important, but the main thrust of the Kingdom is the spiritual transformation of individuals who make up the body of Christ. The millennium and the ultimate expression of the Kingdom will not come without the physical return of Jesus Christ to the earth (Luke 21:31). The Kingdom is already present, but not yet complete. It is both present and future.

The interim between the first and second advents of Christ (the present age) is marked by violent confrontation between the power of the Kingdom and the power that dominates the world in this present age. Divine conflict with the demonic characterizes the present era. It is the era of conflict as well as the era of the Spirit. Believers must engage the forces of darkness (Ephesians 6:12).

We are not guaranteed total, instant success in this conflict. Each victory over sickness, sin, oppression, or the demonic is a reminder of the present power of the Kingdom and of the final victory to come, a victory made sure by the Resurrection. We are called to wage war against sickness, but we face the reality that not everyone we pray for gets well. We are in harmony with the purposes of God in this age as we move against sickness in every way possible; we rejoice at notable victories but are not bewildered when some are not healed. We do not surrender to the evil and the struggles of the present order; but neither do we rage against God or blame others when every request is not granted.

The essence of the Spirit-energized life is to move against the forces of darkness, fully aware that total deliverance is always possible but does not come immediately in every instance (cf. Romans 8:18–23). Some of the heroes of faith (Acts 12:2; 2 Corinthians 11:23 to 12:10; Hebrews 11) suffered or died, having their deliverance deferred to a future time. We do not give in to the ravages of evil; we do not give up the fight. As instruments of the Kingdom in this present age, we faithfully battle against evil and suffering.

The Holy Spirit and the Kingdom of God

As Pentecostals we recognize the role of the Holy Spirit in the inauguration and ongoing ministry of the Kingdom. At His baptism, Jesus was anointed with the Spirit (Matthew 3:16; Mark 1:10; Luke 3:22). His acts of power, energized by God's Spirit, brought healing to the sick and spiritual restoration to sinful men and women. The descent of the Spirit at His baptism was a significant point in the ministry of Jesus. "Jesus, full of the Holy Spirit, returned from the Jordan and was led by the Spirit in the desert" (Luke 4:1). The working of the Spirit in the ministry of Jesus proved the presence of the Kingdom.

Jesus described the role of the Holy Spirit in the kingdom of God. As part of the fulfillment of Old Testament prophecy, He told His disciples, "You will be baptized with the Holy Spirit" (Acts 1:5). The power of the Kingdom, so manifest in the Cross, the Resurrection, and the Ascension, was passed on to all who would be filled with the Spirit. The age of the Spirit is the age of the Church, the community of the Spirit. Through the Church the Spirit continues the Kingdom ministry of Jesus himself.

The Kingdom as a Future Reality

Biblical charismata, anointed proclamation of the Word, and confirming signs and wonders are distinguishing marks of the kingdom of God at work now. The kingdom of Satan has already been invaded by Jesus in the power of the Spirit (John 16:11; Colossians 1:13; 2:15). Yet final destruction of Satan and complete victory over all evil is part of a future eschatological consummation (Revelation 20:10).

We believe in the premillennial return of Christ before the thousand-year period described in Revelation 20. We believe that we are living in the last days of the present age; the next major fulfillment of Bible prophecy will be the Rapture, or physical removal, of the Church from the earth (1 Corinthians 15:51–52). We believe that the rapture of the Church is imminent (Mark 13:32–37), that it will take place before the Great Tribulation (1 Thessalonians 4:17–18; 5:9), and that it is the "blessed hope" (Titus 2:13) to which we look even while signs in the heavens and on earth signal the approaching end of this age (Luke 21:25–28).

The second coming of Christ includes the physical rapture of the saints followed by the visible return of Christ with His saints to reign on the earth for one thousand years (Zechariah 14:5; Matthew 24:27,30; Revelation 1:7; 19:11–14; 20:16). Satan will be bound and inactive for the first time since his rebellion and fall (Revelation 20:2). This millennial reign will bring the salvation of Israel (Ezekiel 37:21–22; Zephaniah 3:19–20; Romans 11:26–27) and the establishment of universal peace (Isaiah 11:6–9; Psalm 72:3–8; Micah 4:3–4) for the first time since before humanity's fall. God's rejection of Israel is not permanent. After the age of the Gentiles, God will regraft Israel into His kingdom, and "so all Israel will be saved" (Romans 11:24–26).

The Kingdom and the Church

The kingdom of God is not the Church. Yet there is an inseparable relationship between the two. The invisible and true Church is the spiritual body of which Christ is the head (Ephesians 1:22–23; Colossians 1:18). It includes all who have believed, or will believe, in Christ as Savior from the Church's inception until the time God takes it out of the world.

The kingdom of God existed before the beginning of the Church and will continue after the work of the Church is complete. The Church is therefore part of the Kingdom, but not all of it. In the present age the kingdom of God is at work through the Church. When the Church has proclaimed the gospel of the Kingdom "in the whole world as a testimony to all nations" (Matthew 24:14), the drama of end-time events will begin. Finally, Christ will reign in majesty over His eternal kingdom, which will include the Church glorified.

The Kingdom of God and the Kingdoms of Earth

The kingdom of God and the kingdoms of this world exist side by side at the present time. However, these kingdoms will not be one and the same until Christ returns and the kingdoms of this world become "the kingdom of our Lord and of his Christ" (Revelation 11:15). The kingdom of God may operate within, but is not to be identified with, any present political system. Believers take the gospel of the Kingdom into the world so that individuals may voluntarily choose the lordship of Jesus Christ.

Although the kingdom of God is not a present political entity, the citizens of the Kingdom are responsible to exert a positive influence on their society. Though all human government is currently, to some extent, under the influence of the evil one

(Daniel 10:13,20; John 12:31; 14:30; Ephesians 6:12), the Bible teaches that government is ordained by God to maintain order and punish evildoers (Romans 13:1–7). Governmental authorities are God's servants (Romans 13:6) whether they recognize it or not. Ideals of justice and decency found in government and society are the legacy of God's grace in the world (Romans 1:20; 2:14). Though they may be in rebellion, the kingdoms of the world are yet responsible to God and must be called to account for injustice and wickedness.

While the Bible does not give clear guidelines for Christian action in combating the social evils embedded in the structures of our society, and sincere believers will differ on the means to be employed, Christians clearly are to be salt and light (Matthew 5:13,14). They are to be concerned about the needy (James 1:27; 2:16) and the oppressed (James 5:4–6). Filled with the Spirit, and given the opportunity to influence society, they are impelled to denounce unjust laws (Isaiah 10:1,2) and to seek justice and goodness (Micah 6:8; Amos 5:14,15).

The kingdoms of the earth are subject to the influence of Satan (John 12:31; 14:30). Christ alone will accomplish the supernatural and cataclysmic destruction of the powers of evil (cf. Daniel 2, Revelation 19). Even the good structures of the present social and political order must ultimately come to an end in order to bring in the better rule of the Kingdom. The kingdom of God is not the blueprint for a radical cultural change based on some carnal theocratic or revolutionary agenda. Instead, it radically changes human personalities and lives. Through men and women who recognize its authority and live by its standards, the kingdom of God invades the stream of history. This process began with the first advent of the Messiah, has been advanced through the Church Age, and will be completed with the Second Coming. God's children should be in the world, but not of it (John 17:11,14,16). Romans 14:17 shows that the kingdom of God (God's rule in our lives) is demonstrated in and through us by "righteousness, peace and joy in the Holy Spirit."

Erroneous Views of the Kingdom of God

Neither positive thinking nor positive confession will change the biblical realities concerning the kingdom of God. To claim that the glory of the Kingdom to come may be realized here and now misleads and confuses sincere Christians. To offer the health and prosperity of the Kingdom to come as a recompense for simply confessing that one has them is to violate the plain meaning of Scripture. The theological claim that believers are "little gods" who can have what they desire by claiming their "divine right" is clearly contrary to biblical truth. God has promised to supply all of our *needs* (Philippians 4:19), but not all our material *wants*. Any teaching that discounts or destroys the important biblical themes of suffering, cross-bearing, and self-denial, or assumes an elitist attitude toward Christians who suffer economic deprivation is not of divine origin.

Christ urged His followers to take no thought about their basic needs because they are already known to God and will be met by divine provision (Matthew 6:25). Preoccupation with life's basic necessities indicates little faith (Matthew 6:30). How must Christ feel about those who are preoccupied with the luxuries of life? If we focus attention on material possessions as we claim the promise of receiving that for which we ask, we place "all these things" before the Kingdom we are to seek *first* (Matthew 6:33).

Thy Kingdom Come

Christ taught His disciples to pray to the Father, "Your kingdom come" (Matthew 6:10). The Kingdom is already among us in that it has invaded Satan's domain and has assured final victory. The Kingdom comes in a measure whenever a person receives Christ as Savior, is healed or delivered, or is touched in any way by the divine. Yet the future consummation of the kingdom of God—the time when all evil and rebellion will be eliminated—is the fervent hope of the Christian. So with the disciples we pray, "Your kingdom come"—both now and when Christ returns.

The rapture of the Church, the coming of Christ for His own, will set in motion the consummation and reality of the eternal completed Kingdom. The angel will declare, "The kingdom of the world has become the kingdom of our Lord and of his Christ, and he will reign for ever and ever" (Revelation 11:15). With John the beloved revelator we say, "Amen. Come, Lord Jesus" (Revelation 22:20).

17
The Role of Women in Ministry as Described in Holy Scripture

Supernatural manifestations and gifts of the Holy Spirit have played a distinctive role in the origin, development, and growth of the Assemblies of God. From the earliest days of our organization, spiritual gifting has been evident in the ministries of many outstanding women. Divine enablement has also been seen in the spiritual leadership of women in other Pentecostal groups. The Pentecostal movement believes that the 20th-century outpouring of the Spirit is a true fulfillment of the scriptural prediction, "Your . . . daughters will prophesy. . . . Even on my servants, both men and women, I will pour out my Spirit in those days" (Joel 2:28,29).

The Bible as Final Authority

The history and current practice of the Assemblies of God give demonstration that God can and does bless the public ministry of women. Yet there is currently much debate concerning the proper role of women in spiritual leadership. So it is appropriate to ask if Scripture describes any limits to this public ministry.

We all agree that Scripture must be our final authority in settling questions of faith and practice. But when born again, Spirit-filled Christians, following proper hermeneutical principles, come to reasonable but differing interpretations, we do well not to become dogmatic in support of one position. We affirm the inerrancy and authority of Scripture. We desire to know for certain what God expects of us. When we come to a sure understanding of His divine Word, we are committed to declaring and obeying those clear instructions. But we also exercise caution in giving authoritative importance to interpretations that do not have indisputable support from the whole of Scripture. Although the Holy Spirit may be active in the work of translation and interpretation, we cannot claim inerrancy for interpretations (even of extant Hebrew or Greek texts).

Historical and Global Precedent

In the early days of most revivals, when spiritual fervor is high and the Lord's return is expected at any time, there is often a place for, and acceptance of, the anointed ministry of women. Over time, however, concerns about organization and lines of authority begin to emerge, and the group moves toward a more structured ministry. As institutional concerns come to the forefront, the spiritual leadership of women is accepted less readily, and church leadership becomes predominately male. The experience of the Assemblies of God has been no exception to this progression.

Twentieth-century practice among Pentecostals around the world reveals evidence of a genuine struggle to apply biblical truth in various cultural contexts. In some settings, female spiritual leadership is readily accepted; in others, though women may have limited ministry, leadership posts are withheld from them. At times there is inconsistency between the leadership a female missionary has at home and that which she has on the field, or between her opportunities and those of a national female. Indeed, culture has influenced the extent of leadership a woman has been allowed to share. The Church must always be sensitive to cultural concerns, but it must look to Scripture for the truth that applies to all times and cultures.

Biblical Examples of Women in Ministry

Old Testament history includes accounts of strong female leadership. Miriam was a prophet, one of the triumvirate of leaders God sent to Israel during the Exodus period (Exodus 15:20). Deborah, as prophet and judge, led the army of the Lord into successful combat (Judges 4 to 5). Huldah, also a prophet, authenticated the scroll of the Law found in the temple and helped spark the great religious reform in the days of Josiah (2 Kings 22; 2 Chronicles 34).

The New Testament also records ministering women in the Church Age. Tabitha (Dorcas) is called a disciple and had a ministry of helps (Acts 9:36). Philip had four virgin daughters who prophesied (Acts 21:8,9). Euodia and Syntyche were Paul's coworkers who shared in his struggle to spread the gospel (Philippians 4:2,3). Priscilla was another of Paul's exemplary "fellow workers in Christ Jesus" (Romans 16:3,4). In Romans 16, Paul greets a multitude of ministering persons, a large number of them women.

Phoebe, a leader in the church at Cenchrea, was highly commended to the church at Rome by Paul (Romans 16:1,2). Unfortunately, biases of modern English translators have sometimes obscured Phoebe's position of leadership, calling her a "servant" or "helper," etc. Yet Phoebe was a *diakonos* of the church at Cenchrea. Paul often used this term for a minister or leader of a congregation and applied it specifically to Jesus Christ, Tychicus, Epaphras, Timothy, and to his own ministry. Depending on the context, *diakonos* is usually translated "deacon" or "minister." Though some translators have chosen the word *deaconess* (because Phoebe was a woman), such a distinction is not in the original Greek. It seems likely that *diakonos* was the designation for an official leadership position in the Early Church.

Junia was identified by Paul as an apostle (Romans 16:7). But many translators and scholars, unwilling to admit there could have been a female apostle, have since the 13th century masculinized her name to Junias. The biblical record shows that Paul was a strong advocate of women's ministry.

The instances of women filling leadership roles in the Bible should be taken as a divinely approved pattern, not as exceptions to divine decrees. Even a limited number of women with scripturally commended leadership roles should affirm that God does indeed call women to spiritual leadership.

A Biblical Survey of the Role of Women in Ministry

Of primary importance in defining the scriptural role of women in ministry is the biblical meaning of "ministry." Of Christ our great model, it was said, "'Even the Son of Man did not come to be served, but to serve, and to give his life as a ransom for many'" (Mark 10:45). New Testament leadership, as modeled by Jesus, portrays the spiritual leader as a servant. The question of human authority is not of primary significance, though it naturally arises as organization and structure develop.

Genesis 2:18–25

Some expositors have taught that all women should be subordinate to adult men because Eve was created after Adam to be his helper ("help meet," KJV). Yet the word *ezer* ("helper") is never used in the Hebrew Bible with a subordinate meaning. Seventeen out of the twenty times it is used, it refers to God as the helper. Instead of being created as a subordinate, Eve was created to be a "suitable" *(kenegdo)* helper, or one "corresponding to" Adam.

Some argue that God created men and women with different characteristics and desires, and that these differences explain why leadership roles should be withheld from women. Others attribute these perceived differences to culture and social expectations imposed on children from birth to adulthood. Physical differences and distinctive biological functions are obvious; but it is only by implication that gender distinctives can be made to suggest leadership limitations.

Paul's Emphasis on Charismatic Ministry

Ministry in the New Testament is charismatic in nature. It is made possible and energized as the Holy Spirit sovereignly distributes spiritual gifts *(charismata)* to each member of the body of Christ (Romans 12:6–8; 1 Corinthians 12:7–11,27,28; Ephesians 4:7–12; 1 Peter 4:10,11). While some gifts are a spontaneous work of the Spirit and others are recognized ministry gifts to the Body, all are given for service without regard to gender differentiation. For example, the gift of prophecy is explicitly for both men and women: "Your sons and daughters will prophesy" (Acts 2:17). That women received and exercised this gift of the Spirit is well attested in the New Testament (Acts 21:9; 1 Corinthians 11:5).

If Peter found certain statements by Paul hard to understand (2 Peter 3:16), then it is no surprise that we, who are removed by 1900 additional years of history, would share his struggle in interpreting some Pauline passages. And we, like Peter (2 Peter 3:15), must respect and love our brothers and sisters who hold alternative interpretations on issues that are not critical to our salvation or standing before God. We only request that those interpretations be expressed and practiced in love and consideration for all of God's children, both men and women.

First Corinthians 11:3–12

The statement that "the man is the head of the woman" has for centuries been used to justify the practice of male superiority and to exclude women from spiritual leadership. Two alternative translations for *kephale* ("head"), debated widely by contemporary evangelical scholars, are (1) "authority over" and (2) "source" or "origin." Both meanings can be found in literature of Paul's time.

Taking the passage as a whole, the second meaning fits as well as or better than the first meaning, leading to the summary statement of verse 12: "For as woman came from man, so also man is born of woman. But everything comes from God." Even the relationship between the eternal Son and the Father—"the head of Christ is God" (11:3)—fits better as "source" than "authority over" (cf. John 8:42). Without attempting to resolve this debate, we do not find sufficient evidence in kephale to deny leadership roles to women (in light of biblical examples of women in positions of spiritual authority, and in light of the whole counsel of Scripture).

First Corinthians 14:34–36

There are only two passages in the entire New Testament

which might seem to contain a prohibition against the ministry of women (1 Corinthians 14:34; 1 Timothy 2:12). Since these must be placed alongside Paul's other statements and practices, they can hardly be absolute, unequivocal prohibitions of the ministry of women. Instead, they seem to be teachings dealing with specific, local problems that needed correction.

There are various interpretations of what Paul was limiting when he said, "Women should remain silent in the churches. They are not allowed to speak" (14:34). Options include (1) chatter in public services, (2) ecstatic disruptions, (3) certain authoritative ministries (such as judging prophecies), and (4) asking questions during the service. Yet, Paul does allow women to pray and prophesy in the corporate service (1 Corinthians 11:5).

Although we may not solve all the difficulties of this chapter, we do conclude that this passage does not prohibit female leadership, but like the rest of the chapter, it admonishes that "everything should be done in a fitting and orderly way" (1 Corinthians 14:40).

First Timothy 2:11–15

The meaning and application of Paul's statement "I do not permit a woman to teach or to have authority over a man" (1 Timothy 2:12) have puzzled interpreters and resulted in a variety of positions on the role of women in ministry and spiritual leadership. Is the prohibition of women teaching and exercising authority a universal truth, or was Paul reporting his application of divine truth for the society and Christian community to which he and Timothy ministered?

From the above survey of passages on exemplary women in ministry, it is clear that Paul recognized the ministry of women. Yet there were some obvious problems concerning women in

Ephesus. They were evidently given to immodest apparel and adornment (1 Timothy 2:9). The younger widows were getting into "the habit of being idle . . . And not only do they become idlers, but also gossips and busybodies, saying things they ought not to" (1 Timothy 5:13). In his second letter to Timothy, Paul warned against depraved persons (possibly including women) who manipulated "weak-willed," or "gullible," women (2 Timothy 3:6).

A reading of the entire passage of 1 Timothy 2:9–15 strongly suggests that Paul was giving Timothy advice about dealing with some heretical teachings and practices involving women in the church of Ephesus. The heresy may have been so serious that he had to say about the Ephesian women, "I am not allowing women to teach or have authority over a man." But we know from other passages that such an exclusion was not normative in Paul's ministry.

First Timothy 3:1–13

This entire passage has been held by some to confirm that all leaders and authorities in the Early Church were intended to be, indeed were, males. It is true that the passage deals primarily with male leadership, most likely because of majority practice and expectations. When there were women leaders, like Phoebe, they would be expected to meet the same standards of character and behavior.

Translations of verse 11 present evidence of the translator's choice based on personal expectations. The word *guniakas* can be translated as either "wives" or "women," depending on the translator's assumptions concerning the context. One rendering leaves the impression that these are qualifications for deacon's wives; the other suggests this exhortation is addressed to female spiritual leaders.

Although the first-century cultural milieu produced a primarily male church leadership, this passage along with other biblical evidence of female spiritual leadership (e.g., Acts 21:9; Romans 16:1–5; Philippians 4:2,3) demonstrates that female leadership was not prohibited, either for Paul's day or for today. Passages which imply that most leaders were male should not be made to say that women cannot be leaders.

Galatians 3:28

Those who oppose allowing women to hold positions of spiritual leadership must place contextual limitations on Galatians 3:28. "There is neither Jew nor Greek, there is neither bond nor free, there is neither male nor female: for ye are all one in Christ Jesus" (KJV).

Some interpreters restrict the meaning of the triad to salvation by faith or oneness in Christ. That truth is certainly articulated throughout Scripture. Yet the verse carries a ring of universal application for all our relationships, not just an assurance that anyone can come to Christ. "There is neither Jew nor Greek. . . slave nor free. . . male nor female"—these are basic relationship principles to which faithful followers of Christ must give highest priority.

The God of the Bible "does not show favoritism" (Romans 2:11; cf. also 2 Samuel 14:14; 2 Chronicles 19:7; Acts 10:34; Ephesians 6:9). He calls whom He will and gives gifts and ministries as He chooses; human beings must not put limitations on divine prerogatives. In Christ we are truly set free from sin and its curse, which separate from God and elevate or demean according to race, social standing, or gender.

Therefore We Conclude

After examining the various translations and interpretations of biblical passages relating to the role of women in the first-century church, and desiring to apply biblical principles to contemporary church practice, we conclude that we cannot find convincing evidence that the ministry of women is restricted according to some sacred or immutable principle.

We are aware that the ministry and leadership of women are not accepted by some individuals, both within and outside the Christian community. We condemn all prejudice and self-promotion, by men or women. The existence in the secular world of bigotry against women cannot be denied. But there is no place for such an attitude in the body of Christ. We acknowledge that attitudes of secular society, based on long-standing practice and tradition, have influenced the application of biblical principles to local circumstances. We desire wisely to respect yet help redeem cultures which are at variance with Kingdom principles. Like Paul, we affirm that the Great Commission takes priority over every other consideration. We must reach men and women for Christ, no matter what their cultural or ethnic customs may be. The message of redemption has been carried to remote parts of the world through the ministry of dedicated, Spirit-filled men *and* women. Believer's gifts and anointing should still today make a way for their ministry. The Pentecostal ministry is not a profession to which men or women merely aspire; it must always be a divine calling, confirmed by the Spirit with a special gifting.

The Assemblies of God has been blessed and must continue to be blessed by the ministry of God's gifted and commissioned daughters. To the degree that we are convinced of our Pentecostal distinctives—that it is *God* who divinely calls and supernaturally anoints for ministry—we must continue to be open to the full use of women's gifts in ministry and spiritual leadership.

As we look on the fields ripe for harvest, may we not be guilty of sending away any of the reapers God calls. Let us entrust to these women of God the sacred sickle, and with our sincerest blessings thrust them out into the whitened fields.

18
Theology of Ministry

Although the word "ministry" is often associated with the work of the clergy, in its biblical sense it properly denotes the work of the entire Church, the body of Christ in the world. Ministry is what the church does, or is supposed to do. However, the church's understanding of ministry has varied considerably over the centuries and must be restated for each generation on the basis of a fresh study of the Scriptures.

Our English word "ministry" is commonly used to translate several words in the New Testament, the most prominent being *diakonía* and its related forms.[1] This particular word group is rooted in the humble service one person renders to another. It is often the work of a servant who waits on tables.

Jesus—the Model for Our Ministry

Ministry in the New Testament is clearly and authoritatively taught in the words and deeds of Jesus Christ and can never be understood or realized apart from Him. Therefore, any theology of ministry must begin with the life and teachings of our Lord as presented in the New Testament.

His ministry was first of all *incarnational*. In Jesus of

Nazareth, God came to dwell among people. The Gospel of John sets out this truth in vivid terms: "The Word became flesh and made his dwelling among us" (John 1:14). Much the same understanding is found in Matthew's designation of the virgin-born Jesus as "Immanuel . . . 'God with us'" (Matthew 1:23). The Son of God took upon himself full humanity in order to draw near to humankind and win their redemption through an atoning sacrifice upon the cross. As Paul later expressed it, "God was in Christ reconciling the world to himself" (2 Corinthians 5:19, NASB).

Jesus strongly emphasized the *kerygmatic* nature of His ministry. Drawn from the noun *kērygma*, "preaching," this term highlights the central place of the proclamation of the gospel. Nowhere is this more evident than in Jesus' Scripture lesson in the Nazareth synagogue: "The Spirit of the Lord is on me because he has anointed me *to preach good news [euangelízomai]* to the poor. He has sent me to proclaim *[kērýsso]* freedom for the prisoners and recovery of sight for the blind, to release the oppressed, *to proclaim [kērýsso]* the year of the Lord's favor" (Luke 4:18,19).

Christ's ministry was carried out in the *power of the Holy Spirit*. The Gospels strikingly depict the descent of the Spirit upon Jesus at the outset of His ministry immediately after His baptism and before His public activity (Matthew 3:16; Mark 1:10; Luke 3:22; John 1:32). Peter referred to that coming of the Spirit as an "anointing" which empowered Jesus for His work: "After the baptism that John preached . . . God anointed Jesus of Nazareth with the Holy Spirit and power, and . . . he went around doing good and healing all who were under the power of the devil, because God was with him" (Acts 10:37,38). Not infrequently Jesus himself made reference to the power of the Spirit at work in His miracles (Matthew 12:28; Luke 4:14,18).

His ministry was also one of *humble service.* In counteracting the self-serving instincts of the disciples, Jesus pointed to His own costly service to humanity: "Even the Son of Man did not come to be served *[diakonēthēnai],* but to serve *[diakonēsai],* and to give his life as a ransom for many" (Mark 10:45). Luke's account reports Jesus' words, "I am among you as one who serves *[diakonéō]*" (Luke 22:27). Nowhere is Jesus' attitude more strikingly illustrated than at the Last Supper where He chastened His competitive followers: "Now that I, your Lord and Teacher, have washed your feet, you also should wash one another's feet" (John 13:14).

Finally, Jesus' ministry was one of *shepherding.* Jesus depicted himself as a faithful and caring shepherd who knows each of His sheep and leads them out for water and pasture (cf. John 10:1–18). As the Good Shepherd, He interposes His own body between the sheep and all dangers, whether thieves or wolves. Repeatedly Jesus made the point, "The good shepherd lays down his life for the sheep" (John 10:11,15,17,18). Elsewhere in the New Testament He is called the "great Shepherd" (Hebrews 13:20), "the Shepherd and Overseer of your souls" (1 Peter 2:25), and the "Chief Shepherd" (1 Peter 5:4).

The ministry of Jesus finally culminated in His death, which He clearly saw as a substitutionary offering for the sins of humanity (Matthew 26:28; Mark 10:45). He gave himself, in life and death, for others.

The Church As the Extension of Christ's Ministry

From the Gospels it is readily apparent that Jesus intended to extend His own ministry through the Church which He himself would found and build (Matthew 16:18). One of His earliest actions was calling designated apostles "that they might be with him and that he might send them out to preach" (Mark 3:14).

After His death and resurrection, Christ explicitly commissioned the apostles to carry on His ministry. In His final charge the risen Lord claimed all authority in heaven and on earth and in that divine authority commanded them, "Go and make disciples of all nations, baptizing them in the name of the Father and of the Son and of the Holy Spirit, and teaching them to obey everything I have commanded you" (Matthew 28:19,20).

The other Gospels emphasize the commission in other ways. Luke noted that Jesus predicted the preaching of repentance and forgiveness of sins in His name to all nations. The disciples were to be His witnesses, and for that purpose they would shortly receive the promised heavenly power (Luke 24:48,49). John recorded that before Jesus breathed on the disciples and said to them "Receive the Holy Spirit" (20:22), He told them, "As the Father has sent me, I am sending you" (v. 21).

An awareness of a derived and continuing ministry is present in the Acts narrative as the disciples sought a replacement for the reprobate Judas. Casting lots to distinguish between Barsabbas and Matthias, they prayed, "Lord, . . . show us which of these two you have chosen to take over this *apostolic ministry,* which Judas left to go where he belongs" (Acts 1:24,25, emphasis added). In selecting seven men to handle the social services of the Early Church, the apostles were conscious of the primacy of their "ministry of the Word" (Acts 6:4). The central task of leadership in the Early Church was the anointed proclamation *(kērygma)* of God's Word to His people.

This consciousness of ministry was not limited to the original disciples of Jesus or even to the larger group of apostles, which included Paul and James and perhaps others as well. A fellow worker of the apostles was readily called *diákonos,* i.e., "minister": Phoebe (Romans 16:1), Tychicus (Ephesians 6:21, KJV), Epaphras (Colossians 1:7), Timothy (1 Timothy 4:6).

Others are said to participate in *diakonía*, i.e., "ministry": the household of Stephanas (1 Corinthians 16:15, KJV), Archippus (Colossians 4:17, KJV), and Mark (2 Timothy 4:11). Qualified elders were soon chosen and prayerfully commissioned for ministry in each new missionary church (Acts 14:23). Ministry clearly was not the sole prerogative of an apostolic elite, to be passed down from generation to generation by a rite of apostolic succession. It was a pervasive and vibrant reality wherever the Church was to be found.

The Role of the Holy Spirit in Ministry

The necessity of a spiritual endowment for ministry may be seen in the lives of both Jesus and the apostles. The descent of the Spirit upon Jesus at His baptism was a prerequisite for His ministry. Similarly Jesus instructed the apostles to remain in Jerusalem until they had received the promised Holy Spirit (Luke 24:49; Acts 1:4,5). Only after the outpouring of the Spirit on the Day of Pentecost were they decisively impelled into active public ministry. Then their ministry was carried out with a striking sense of the Spirit's power and wisdom rather than with mere professionalism and administrative skill. Therefore, a Pentecostal baptism in the Holy Spirit and a subsequent Spirit-filled life are essential to the most effective Christian ministry.

Paul's understanding of his own induction into ministry is highly significant. "I became a servant *[diákonos]* of this gospel by the gift *[dōreá]* of God's grace *[cháris]* given me through the working *[enérgeia]* of his power *[dýnamis]*" (Ephesians 3:7). Paul was certainly conscious of being "called" (Romans 1:1). He also possessed excellent theological training (Acts 22:3). But in addressing the essential nature of his ministry, it was far more natural for him to speak of an inner work of the Spirit that in a supernatural way had gifted him to be a minister of the gospel of Christ.

That same sense of sovereign supernatural action in the preparation of ministers is present in Paul's exhortations to the Ephesian elders, "Keep watch over yourselves and all the flock of which *the Holy Spirit has made you overseers*" (Acts 20:28, emphasis added). While in all probability Paul had been instrumental in the public ordination of these elders, he was deeply aware of a powerful prior work of the Spirit which their public ordination merely facilitated.

Historically the church has commonly spoken of the divine summons to ministry as a *call* to the ministry. Indeed the Scriptures frequently indicate that God does summon individuals to His service. Abraham (Genesis 12:1), Moses (Exodus 3:6,10), and Isaiah (Isaiah 6:8,9) are good Old Testament examples. In the New Testament, Jesus personally called the Twelve (Mark 3:13,14), and the Holy Spirit prophetically separated Paul and Barnabas for their missionary assignment (Acts 13:2).

The Scriptures also support the church's traditional concept of an *inward call* to describe the individual's personal awareness of a divine summons to ministry and an *outward call* which attests to everyone that the Holy Spirit has filled a chosen vessel. It must always be remembered, however, that those who are called to the ministry are supernaturally gifted by the Spirit to fulfill that call. Like Paul, they become ministers "by the gift of God's grace . . . through the working of his power" (Ephesians 3:7).

Spiritual Gifts for Ministry

A primary function of the Spirit is the provision of specific gifts for ministry. The New Testament refers to these as "spiritual gifts" (Romans 1:11). These gifts are most commonly identified by the Greek term *chárisma,* which in the majority of its occurrences denotes "spiritual gift." "Spiritual gift" is also occasionally denoted by the terms *pneumatikós* (1 Corinthians 12:1,28; 14:1) and *dóma* (Ephesians 4:7).

A wide range of spiritual gifts accompanies and effects the broad diffusion of ministry that has already been observed in the New Testament. In fact, a special touch of the Spirit has qualified every single Christian for one or more special ministries: "To *each one of us grace [cháris]* was given according to the measure of *Christ's gift [dōreá]*" (Ephesians 4:7, NASB).

This revolutionary concept of every-member gifting is found in other passages dealing with spiritual gifts. "We have different gifts *[chárisma],* according to the grace *[cháris]* given us" (Romans 12:6). "Now to each one the manifestation of the Spirit is given for the common good" (1 Corinthians 12:7). There is a similar emphasis in 1 Peter 4:10: "*Each one* should use whatever gift *[chárisma]* he has received to serve *[diakonéō]* others, faithfully administering God's grace *[cháris]* in its various forms."

Several important lists of spiritual gifts, identified as such by the word *chárisma, pneumatikós,* or *dóma,* are included in the New Testament. There are the familiar nine gifts of the Spirit in 1 Corinthians 12:8–10: the word of wisdom, the word of knowledge, faith, gifts of healing, working of miracles, prophecy, discerning of spirits, kinds of tongues, and interpretation of tongues. Several of these gifts are also found in the lists of Romans 12:6–8, 1 Corinthians 12:28–30, and Ephesians 4:11.

These nine gifts may readily be recognized as supernatural and spontaneous, always under the immediate control of the Spirit who will use obedient and spiritually sensitive believers, often on a regular basis. But sprinkled among the gift lists, and equally identified as *chárisma, pneumatikós,* or *dóma,* are other very important spiritual gifts for carrying on the work of the church. They are serving (Romans 12:7), teaching (Romans 12:7), encouraging (Romans 12:8), giving (Romans 12:8), leadership (Romans 12:8), showing mercy (Romans 12:8), helping others (1 Corinthians 12:28), and administration (1 Corinthians 12:28). These gifts are not so readily recognized as being supernatural but nonetheless clearly have their origin in the action of the Holy Spirit. The Holy Spirit makes them available to believers to be used regularly, energetically, and conscientiously as they depend on Him in the service of the Church.

Although the gifts that are listed probably cover most of the ministry needs of the church, there is no reason to think that the New Testament writers intended to be comprehensive. For example, there is no reference to gifts of music, though the New Testament does mention "spiritual [*pneumatikós*] songs" (Ephesians 5:19). The Old Testament ascribes gifts of craftsmanship to the Holy Spirit (Exodus 31:2,3). It is entirely reasonable to think there are other gifts granted to the church by the Spirit to meet specific needs. In fact, Paul seemed at great pains to show a variety of gifts: "There are different kinds of gifts . . . different kinds of service [*diakonía*] . . . different kinds of working [*enérgēma*]" (1 Corinthians 12:4–6).

In every case these gifts are set within the context of the church and are designed for ministry to and through the body of Christ. Before noting the "different gifts" of Romans 12:6, Paul stressed the church's interdependence, "We who are many form one body, and each member belongs to all the others" (Romans 12:5). The gift list of 1 Corinthians 12:28–30 is prefaced by a similar statement, "Now you are the body of Christ, and each one of you is a part of it" (1 Corinthians 12:27). The rationale for the gifts of Ephesians 4:11 is "to prepare God's people for works of service, so that the body of

Christ may be built up" (Ephesians 4:12).

The purpose of spiritual gifts is most clearly expressed in 1 Corinthians 12:7, "Now to each one the manifestation of the Spirit is given *for the common good*" (emphasis added). Spiritual gifts are intended for the upbuilding of the congregation at large. Their only justification is to serve the purposes of Christ in His church, a lesson that was lost on the immature Corinthians who demeaned the gifts by their own proud exhibitionism.

Ministry Belongs to the Entire Church

An examination of the concepts of ministry and spiritual gifts makes it abundantly clear that ministry is the work of the entire body of Christ, not just of a special priestly or clerical caste. Even the ministries of apostle, prophet, evangelist, and pastor-teacher do not exist as ends in themselves, or as rewards for a special elite. They are expressly given "to prepare God's people for works of service [*diakonía*, "ministry"], so that the body of Christ may be built up" (Ephesians 4:12).

A part of the ministry of the church is given to every single member of the body of Christ. All are called in some way to be ministers. To be baptized into Christ is to be baptized into the ministry of His church. No group of leaders alone can embody the full spectrum of spiritual gifts and provide all the wisdom and energy required to do the work of the church. Therefore, the ministry of the laity is integral to the accomplishment of the mission of the church.

Spiritual gifting for ministry is also without regard to race or sex. Wherever the Church exists, the Holy Spirit pours out His gifts, "and he gives them *to each one*, just as *he determines*" (1 Corinthians 12:11, emphasis added). They are bestowed as widely as the blessing of salvation, in which "there is neither

Jew nor Greek, slave nor free, male nor female, for you are all one in Christ Jesus" (Galatians 3:28).

Consequently there is no scriptural basis for excluding any believer from the gifting of the Holy Spirit. "In the last days, God says, I will pour out my Spirit on all people. Your sons and daughters will prophesy. . . . Even on my servants, both men and women, I will pour out my Spirit in those days, and they will prophesy" (Acts 2:17,18, from Joel 2:28,29). Both the didactic teachings and the historical examples of the New Testament show that women and men of various ethnic backgrounds were granted spiritual gifts for the ministry of the church.

Ordination as Recognition of Spiritual Leadership

A strong biblical doctrine of the ministry of the laity may at first appear to diminish the necessity and importance of an ordained clergy, those who are specially set apart for the leadership of the church. But to the contrary it actually heightens the need, for the laity must be trained and led on a massive scale if the work of the church is to be accomplished. Ministerial leaders are Christ's gifts [dóma] for the explicit purpose of preparing the people of God for their ministries of building up the Church (Ephesians 4:7–12).

Spiritual leadership is a crucial issue throughout the New Testament. Jesus' appointment and nurture of the apostles was clearly to provide servant-leaders who proclaimed and modeled the faith. The apostles exercised a vital leadership role in the early Christian church. They were aided by men like Stephen (Acts 6), Philip (Acts 8), and Barnabas (Acts 13), whom the Spirit singularly marked out for ministry. These and others are to be found among an expanding leadership group in the New Testament.

Paul and Barnabas were very careful to appoint elders for

leadership in each new church. These appointments were made with prayer, fasting, and some kind of public ordination service (Acts 14:23). The congregations may well have had a part in the selection, as in the choice of the "seven" in the Jerusalem church (Acts 6:1–6). Paul's letters to Timothy certainly reflect a formal ordination, for both Paul and a body of elders laid hands on Timothy to set him apart for the ministry (1 Timothy 4:14; 2 Timothy 1:6).

Ordination was done with great care. "Do not be hasty in the laying on of hands," Paul commanded Timothy, who was responsible to oversee the appointment of elders (1 Timothy 5:22). Titus was specifically commanded to "appoint elders in every town" (Titus 1:5).

Both Timothy and Titus were given basic qualifications for the elders/overseers to be appointed. The stated qualifications have to do with spiritual maturity and godliness, public credibility, a faithful marriage,[2] a well-managed and respectful family, personal temperance and discipline, hospitality, and teaching ability (1 Timothy 3:1–7; Titus 1:6–9). Elders and overseers were to be godly leaders to whom others could look for examples. Clearly the Scriptures show that certain people were marked out by the Spirit to be set apart, or ordained, for the leadership of the whole people of God in their ministry.

Ministerial Leadership

The New Testament makes very clear that ministerial leadership is of divine origin. Thus Paul noted in 1 Corinthians 12:28, "In the church *God has appointed* first of all apostles, second prophets, third teachers, then workers of miracles, also those having gifts of healing, those able to help others, those with gifts of administration, and those speaking in different kinds of tongues." A similar order exists in the gifts Christ gave to the Church: "It was he who gave some to be apostles, some to be prophets, some to be evangelists, and some to be pastors and teachers" (Ephesians 4:11). These ministries are not provided by human initiative but by a gracious act of the Lord Jesus Christ who works through His Spirit in the Church.

Apostles. The foundational importance of the apostles *(apóstoloi)* is reflected in Ephesians 2:20, where the Church is said to be "built on the foundation of the apostles and prophets, with Christ Jesus himself as the chief cornerstone." The New Testament does not directly answer the question of whether the apostolic office survives today.

Contemporary discussions should note that scriptural qualifications for the office of apostle were (1) personal training with Jesus during the whole of His earthly ministry (Acts 1:22), and/or (2) a personal appearance of the risen Christ to them and a summons from Him, as in the cases of Paul and James, the Lord's brother (1 Corinthians 15:3–7; cf. 1 Corinthians 9:1).

The apostles were to be personal witnesses of the life and teachings of the historical Jesus and especially of His death and resurrection (Luke 24:48; Acts 2:32). To fulfill this important function, they were given a special promise: "The Counselor, the Holy Spirit, . . . will remind you of everything I have said to you" (John 14:26). Quite understandably the apostles became the authoritative teachers of the Early Church, conveying and safeguarding divine revelation, which came to be written down as the New Testament canon. If apostles were to be named in the church today, their similarity with the first apostles would lie in their specially gifted leadership among the people of God. Unlike their biblical forebears, they would neither have seen the risen Christ nor written Scripture.

Prophets. The prophet *(prophētēs)* also had a very important foundational role in the Early Church (Ephesians 2:20). Some, if not all, of the apostles were numbered among the prophets (cf. Saul in Acts 13:1). So were Judas and Silas who "said much to encourage and strengthen the brothers" (Acts 15:32), indicating a ministry that was positive, upbuilding, and encouraging. The writer of the Revelation, traditionally understood to be the apostle John, identified himself only as a prophet (Revelation 1:3; 22:9, etc.). Barnabas, Simeon, and Manaen were also among the prophets (Acts 13:1). But the gift of prophecy (1 Corinthians 12:10) was much more broadly diffused in the Early Church, including Philip's four unmarried daughters and Agabus (Acts 21:9,10). As a gift of the Spirit, prophecy was apparently a common experience of laypersons within the early congregations (1 Corinthians 14:1,5,39), and should continue, with proper biblical guidelines (1 Corinthians 14:29–33), in the modern era.

Evangelists. The ministry of the evangelist (*evangelistēs,* Ephesians 4:11) as mentioned in the New Testament is not well defined. Philip was known as "the evangelist" (Acts 21:8), and Paul commanded Timothy, clearly an elder and pastor, to do the work of an evangelist (2 Timothy 4:5) as one of the duties of his ministry. The term itself implies the proclamation of the *evangélion,* the good news of the saving acts of God in Christ for the benefit of sinful humanity. The New Testament evangelist was probably more akin to a missionary who preaches regularly among unreached peoples than to an itinerant minister who preaches regularly to the converted.

Teachers. The ministry of the teacher *(didáskalos)* is listed as third in importance in 1 Corinthians 12:28, superseded only by apostles and prophets, who certainly themselves were teachers (Acts 2:42). *Teaching* is first of all a spiritual gift *(chárisma,* Romans 12:7) granted to ministers and laypersons, the Holy Spirit himself being the divine teacher who anoints the people of God to comprehend the truth (1 John 2:20,27). So teachers were those uniquely equipped by knowledge and spiritual charisma to instruct the congregation in doctrine, ethics, and Christian experience. Elders, whose work was teaching as well as preaching, were especially highly esteemed (1 Timothy 5:17). In Ephesians 4:11 pastors and teachers are linked together, many scholars referring to them as "pastor-teacher." New Testament teachers were not mere purveyors of ideas. They taught with pastoral needs in view.

Pastors, Overseers, and Elders. The term "pastor," found only in Ephesians 4:11 in the English translation, is the Greek *poimēn* and means "shepherd." The shepherding role (verb *poimaínō*) is often attributed to ministers (Acts 20:28; 1 Peter 5:2), following the model of Christ himself (John 10:14; Hebrews 13:20; 1 Peter 5:4).

Two somewhat interchangeable terms used for pastoral leadership roles in the Early Church are "overseer" *(epískopos)* and "elder" *(presbýteros)*. Note that the "elders" of Ephesus (Acts 20:17ff.) were told that the Holy Spirit had made them "overseers" *(epískopoi)* to "shepherd," i.e., "pastor" *(poimaínō)*, the church of God. The two terms appear to be synonymous also in Titus 1:5–7 where Paul spoke of the appointment of "elders" and gave the qualifications of "overseers." Elders, overseers, and pastors, then, appear to be essentially equivalent terms, with each term stressing some unique aspect of the leader's role. In every case, however, the terms apply to those set apart as leaders of the church, not to laypersons.

As to derivation, "overseer" *(epískopos)* emphasizes the function of leadership or supervision. The verb is commonly rendered by such terms as "see to it," "care for," "oversee," "see after." "Elder" *(presbýteros)* signifies greater age, hence greater wisdom and more extensive experience, and was a common title for Jewish civil and religious leaders. Ministries encompassed by these terms may well include the spiritual gifts of "leadership" *(proístēmi)* (Romans 12:8) and "administration" *(kybérnēsis)* (1 Corinthians 12:28).

Deacons. The word "deacon" *(diákonos)* is used widely in the New Testament to denote the ministries of leaders and laypersons alike. Therefore, the special role of the deacon as implied in the qualifications of 1 Timothy 3:8–10 is somewhat difficult to identify. This ministry is often traced to Acts 6:1–6, though the seven appointed there are never called deacons and at least two of them quickly assumed major roles in teaching and preaching. However, their task was "to wait [*diakonéō,* the verb form of "deacon"] on tables," a work of practical administration in dispensing the charitable gifts of the church. The word "deacon" *(diákonos)* was also used for a woman, Phoebe, who was well known for her service to the church in Cenchrea (Romans 16:1). Our modern application of the term to laypersons serving with pastors in local churches may not be far from the New Testament usage.

In making an application of biblical leadership roles to the modern era, we conclude that pastors carry out the functions of elders and overseers in the local congregations. The teaching and preaching of the Word lie at the heart of their ministry of building up the body of Christ.

In view of the wide-ranging administrative and spiritual oversight of the early apostles and their associates, it also seems legitimate to extend these ministry functions of elders *(presbýteroi)* and overseers *(epískopoi)* to district and General Council levels. Yet we must acknowledge that in the providence of God there are many unanswered questions about the polity of the Early Church, and it is unwise to assume that any modern system of church government perfectly replicates it. If a single system were necessary, surely the divine revelation would have been more extensive, and we would have little difficulty understanding the details of New Testament church government.

A Word to Credentialed and Prospective Clergy

You have been called! And if you have been called, you have been gifted. Use those gifts for the upbuilding and edification of the church, not for personal gain or acclaim. The ministry in which you are or will be engaged is God's ministry, not yours. You will be held accountable for the integrity with which you fulfill *your* great commission. Your call is a great privilege and honor. But never forget, "From everyone who has been given much, much will be demanded; and from the one who has been entrusted with much, much more will be asked" (Luke 12:48). Integrity, morality, and holiness are not faces that are worn in public. They are character traits that must permeate the private and personal life of the spiritual leader.

While every believer should be a minister in the broadest sense—for we all belong to a holy and royal priesthood (1 Peter 2:5,9)—you have been set apart for a special ministry among the many ministries that edify the Church. Your communion with Your Lord and Master must be frequent and regular; you will lead others into deeper commitments and devotion by your example. Though every believer has direct access to God, in a special way you must be God's voice speaking His Word with conviction and anointed power.

Do not despise the gifts and ministry you have been given. But just as important, do not despise the gifts and ministry God has given those you serve. Let there be no competition to prove that one ministry is more significant than another. If God has given gifts to all believers for the edification of the entire Body, He must intend those gifts to be used for His glory. A jealous competition that treats gifts and ministry as evidence of honor rather than as opportunities for humble service cannot bring glory to our Lord. In a growing, evangelistic church the many gifts and ministries, of both clergy and laity, flow together under the impulse of the Holy Spirit.

If you have heard God's call to full-time ministry and are now preparing to fulfill that call, learn these lessons early and learn them well. You can be God's vessel and an anointed catalyst to revive fainting hearts, to inspire ministry in those you serve, and to reach a lost world through the convicting power of the Holy Spirit. Like Timothy, serve a faithful apprenticeship to a spiritual leader who embodies the high standards of God's most holy calling. Immerse yourself in the Word, spend time at the feet of our Master, and join the ranks of those committed to fulfilling the charge of the Great Commission.

We All Have a Ministry

Having seen the importance and necessity of an ordained clergy, set apart for leadership in the church, we return to the biblical truth that all believers are called to ministry. This is not a time for laity to sit back and watch leadership perform. We are all called to use our gift(s) in the fulfillment of the Great Commission. Paul's testimony must be the witness of every believer/minister: "Therefore, since through God's mercy we have this ministry, we do not lose heart. Rather, we have renounced secret and shameful ways; we do not use deception, nor do we distort the word of God. On the contrary, by setting forth the truth plainly we commend ourselves to every man's conscience in the sight of God" (2 Corinthians 4:1,2).

We call on every believer to expect and then cultivate a ministry of edification and service for the glory of God and the extension of His kingdom. He who is faithful in the exercise of a few gifts will be made custodian of greater gifts and greater service.

Rise up, O [Church] of God! Have done with lesser things;
   Give heart, and soul, and mind, and strength to serve the King of kings.
   Lift high the cross of Christ! Tread where His feet have trod:
   As brothers [and sisters] of the Son of Man, Rise up, O [Church] of God!
   —William P. Merrill

Biblical Terms for Ministry

The noun *diakonía*, "ministry" or "service," is used over 30 times (Luke 10:40; Acts 1:17; 6:4; Romans 12:7; 1 Corinthians 16:15; Ephesians 4:12; Colossians 4:17; 2 Timothy 4:5, etc.). The verb *diakonéō*, "to minister" or "to serve," is also used over 30 times (Matthew 4:11; 8:15; Mark 10:45; John 12:26; Romans 15:25; 2 Corinthians 3:3; 1 Timothy 3:10; 1 Peter 1:12, etc.). *Diákonos*, "minister," "servant," or "deacon," is used nearly as often (Matthew 20:26; John 12:26; Romans 13:4; 1 Corinthians 3:5; 2 Corinthians 3:6; Ephesians 3:7; 6:21; Philippians 1:1, etc.).

The ministry concept is also present in the verb *leitourgéō* (Luke 1:23; 2 Corinthians 9:12; Philippians 2:17,30; Hebrews 8:6; 9:21) and the noun *leitourgós* (Romans 13:6; 15:16; Philippians 2:25; Hebrews 1:7; 8:2). In early Greek thought these terms had to do with service rendered for the public good. Significantly they were used almost exclusively in the Septuagint (the Greek translation of the Old Testament widely used in the New Testament era) for the service of priests and Levites in the Old Testament tabernacle and temple. The New Testament uses the word group with both its public and priestly sense.

The third important word group comes from the verb *hypēretéō* (Acts 13:36; 20:34; 24:23). The *hypērétēs* (Matthew 5:25; Luke 1:2; 4:20; Acts 13:5; 1 Corinthians 4:1) is a free person who willingly accepts a subordinate role to serve a superior, the key thought apparently being that of willing subordination.

The work of the ministry is often graphically depicted in the verb *poimaínō* (Matthew 2:6; John 21:16; Acts 20:28; 1 Peter 5:2; Jude 12), which means to do the work of a shepherd. Here the idea is that of feeding, watering, and protecting the flock.

Another important word for ministry is the verb *oikodoméō* (Matthew 16:18; Acts 9:31; Romans 15:20; 1 Corinthians 14:4; 1 Thessalonians 5:11; 1 Peter 2:5) which means literally "to build a house" but is usually used metaphorically in the New Testament in the sense of "upbuilding" or "edification." The noun *oikodomē* frequently appears in that sense also (Romans 14:19; 15:2; 1 Corinthians 14:3,26; 2 Corinthians 10:8; Ephesians 4:12,16).

Summary: *Diakonía* and its related forms make up the single most important word group having to do with ministry and is rooted in humble service for others. The *leitourgía* grouping draws from both Greek public life and Old Testament temple service and thus stresses both the public and priestly aspects of ministry. The *hypērétēs* is one who willingly accepts a subordinate role to serve someone else. The *poimēn* is a shepherd willing to give his life for the nurture of the sheep. All ministries effectively build up the body of Christ.

---

[1]A brief overview of *diakonía* and other biblical words related to "ministry" can be found under "Biblical Terms for Ministry," beginning on the previous page.

[2]Not all early ministers were married, e.g., the apostle Paul.

19
A Biblical Perspective On Assisted Suicide

A Biblical Perspective on Assisted Suicide

The Supreme Court's landmark decision legalizing abortion, Roe v. Wade, introduced a sustained and divisive public debate over the value of human life. By lifting protections for the unborn, the Court retreated from a sacred view of life and recognized instead a woman's personal autonomy in the decision to abort her child, the popularly expressed "right to choose." Not unexpectedly, this retreat has recently extended to end-of-life decisions, with efforts to sanction euthanasia and physician-assisted suicide under the principle of an individual's "right to die."

The seriousness of this new threat to the sacredness of human life is evident in its growing practice and perceived legitimacy. In 1996, six percent of surveyed physicians indicated they had actually complied with a request for physician-assisted suicide or euthanasia.[1] In 1998, the first legally sanctioned assisted suicides occurred under Oregon's assisted-suicide law.[2] Assisted suicide is openly endorsed in public opinion polls, medical journals, court opinions, and legislative debates. As Francis Schaeffer and C. Everett Koop predicted in 1979, "With arbitrary abortion already declared legal, the speed with which the other forms of killing are being accepted must take even their advocates by surprise."[3]

Many factors have energized the right-to-die movement, including sincere concerns over excessive reliance on life-sustaining technologies and inadequate pain-relief care for the terminally ill. Its driving force, however, is a mistaken, deceptive, and frankly evil philosophy that devalues suffering people. Consequently, our opposition to physician-assisted suicide must be understood in spiritual terms and must be guided by biblical principles. Specifically, the church must (1) proclaim humankind's dignity as God's sovereign creation, (2) reassert God's authority over life from conception to death, and (3) affirm meaning and hope for suffering humanity.

Understanding the Issues

We must first clarify the terminology used in discussions of end-of-life ethical issues. Physician-assisted suicide and euthanasia may be differentiated as follows: "Physician-assisted suicide occurs when a physician provides a medical means for death, usually a prescription for a lethal amount of medication that the patient takes on his or her own. In euthanasia, the physician directly and intentionally administers a substance to cause death."[4] Both are acts of killing, distinguished by the agent (self versus other) who administers the life-ending medication or substance. Euphemistic expressions for physician-assisted suicide, such as "assistance in dying," are specifically used to mask the true content of these actions and should be rejected.

Further, physician-assisted suicide must be distinguished

from informed decisions by patients to refuse life-sustaining treatment. Such decisions are supportable by the highest moral and ethical standards and should be respected.

In His Image

The claim that human life is valuable, even sacred, has its foundation in God's creation of humankind: "God created man in his own image, in the image of God he created him" (Genesis 1:27). This truth imparts extraordinary value to every life, independent of gender, race, socioeconomic position, age, or health status. Those who hold to biblical creation attach great worth to human life and will stand in its defense. Those who hold to the prevailing materialist model, which explains our existence as the chance outcome of impersonal physical forces, find the value of life to be relative and incidental.

Our creation in God's image is at the heart of the biblical injunction against murder: "'Whoever sheds the blood of man, by man shall his blood be shed; for in the image of God has God made man'" (Genesis 9:6). By placing His mark upon humankind, God clearly established His own authority over human life and holds accountable those who would usurp that authority.

A person's intrinsic value is confirmed by God's expression of love in the sacrifice of His Son who paid the price for human sin and transgression. God rightly claims ownership of those He has purchased:

"Do you not know that your body is a temple of the Holy Spirit, who is in you, whom you have received from God? You are not your own; you were bought at a price" (1 Corinthians 6:19,20).

Not only does God forbid the claims of others against our lives, but He also forbids our own claims against our lives. Both homicide and suicide run contrary to God's clearly articulated standard.

Advocates of physician-assisted suicide are compelled to deny these standards and reject this valuation of human life. Specifically, they contend for personal autonomy over one's own existence. The argument is as follows:

"I am my own;

The time and means of my dying lie at the heart of my private life;

I therefore retain the 'right to die,' and no one may take it from me."[5]

This assertion of personal sovereignty holds the promise of freedom but delivers self-destruction. It resonates with the falsity of Satan's reasoning with Eve: "'You will not surely die. . . . For God knows that when you eat of it your eyes will be opened, and you will be like God, knowing good and evil'" (Genesis 3:4,5). As with any exercise of personal choice outside the parameters of God's law—abortion, euthanasia, drug abuse, homosexual practices, and heterosexual promiscuity— the invariable consequence is physical and spiritual death.

Conversely, the righteous decision to obey God's commands brings true freedom. Within the parameters of His law, the individual may anticipate the joy of His blessing. God confronts each of us with the stark alternatives: "This day I call heaven and earth as witnesses against you that I have set before you life and death, blessings and curses. Now choose life, so that you and your children may live and that you may love the LORD your God, listen to his voice, and hold fast to him" (Deuteronomy 30:19,20).

The Boundaries of Life

God determines the boundaries of life and holds in His

hands the two fragile ends of human experience. He is active in the conception of life and the conclusion of life, in birth and in death.

Of his beginning, the Psalmist writes, "You created my inmost being; you knit me together in my mother's womb. . . . My frame was not hidden from you when I was made in the secret place" (Psalm 139:13,15). The womb is the place of God's creative handiwork. It is there each life is endowed with unique personality, unique physical traits, and a unique spiritual nature. The glimpses we have seen of this work through the eyes of biomedical advance only intensify our awe at God's techniques. We may be less discerning, on the other hand, of God's activity in the final moments of death. We naturally shrink from death and view it as an adversary, reluctantly yielding in the end to its inexorable demand upon us.

Of course, death was not God's ideal. Death was introduced by rebellion and subsequently spread from one man to the entire race: "Just as sin entered the world through one man, and death through sin . . . in this way death came to all men, because all sinned" (Romans 5:12). God's plan is to deliver us from this last enemy. "'Where, O death, is your victory? Where, O death, is your sting?' The sting of death is sin, and the power of sin is the law. But thanks be to God! He gives us the victory through our Lord Jesus Christ" (1 Corinthians 15:55–57).

For the believer, death is not a final defeat but a transition in which the perishable is exchanged for the imperishable, the temporal for the eternal, the imperfect for the perfect. The believer experiences assurance even when facing death. Job concludes, "You will call and I will answer you; you will long for the creature your hands have made" (Job 14:15). The Psalmist implies the symmetry of God's activity in his birth and death when he writes, "All the days ordained for me were written in your book before one of them came to be" (Psalm 139:16).

If life's beginning at conception and life's end at death are in God's hands, abortion and assisted suicide represent the supreme violations of His prerogative. Abortion steals from the womb a life yet to be started; assisted suicide hastens to the grave a life yet to be completed.

The argument for assisted suicide also ignores the profound spiritual implications of the transition from life to death. Its proponents and practitioners offer no insights into the spiritual reality beyond the grave. There is no acknowledgment of mortality or final judgment. This apparent naiveté is indicative of the spiritual deception underlying the right-to-die philosophy.

As Nigel Cameron concludes, "The abdication of conscious acknowledgment of mortality has greatly diminished the capacity of the West to address any real questions concerning human identity, especially at its fragile margins. The ambiguities of unborn human life remain unresolved; and the uncertainties of the processes of degeneration and, finally, dying itself continue unabated."[6]

The Meaning of Suffering

Our difficulty in understanding God's activity in death is matched only by our difficulty understanding His activity in human suffering. From the biblical perspective, however, suffering is potentially purposeful and refining. From the perspective of the proponents of assisted suicide, suffering is meaningless and degrading; it is to be avoided and, if possible, eliminated.

Job offers the prototype of meaningful suffering. He endured pain and disfigurement. "Satan went out from the presence of the LORD and afflicted Job with painful sores from the soles of his feet to the top of his head" (Job 2:7). His wife's callous response is curiously contemporary: "'Are you still holding on to your integrity? Curse God and die!'" (Job 2:9). Rejecting her advice, Job held to his integrity, affirming his ultimate confidence in God, saying, "'I know that my Redeemer lives, and that in the end he will stand upon the earth. And after my skin has been destroyed, yet in my flesh I will see God'" (Job 19:25,26).

Suffering becomes comprehensible when we look upon the One who "was despised and rejected by men, a man of sorrows, and familiar with suffering" and who "took up our infirmities and carried our sorrows" (Isaiah 53:3,4). Jesus' Passion assures us of His identity with our suffering and His faithfulness to preserve us through the inevitable tests and trials of life. This is the hope of all who suffer and the only true consolation in the face of unrelenting pain. Christ identifies with suffering humanity, affirms suffering humanity, and heals suffering humanity.

This biblical perspective suggests a life-affirming alternative to assisted suicide for the terminally ill. It acknowledges that fear, helplessness, pain, depression, and isolation are real factors. It also provides, in the person of Christ, a worthy example of compassionate involvement in the suffering of others, which may lessen the very pain and distress that motivate death wishes.

Combining effective medical care with emotional and spiritual help, the hospice movement has demonstrated that few individuals request assisted suicide once their pain and symptoms are addressed. A hospice president has observed, "The public perception is that people are (choosing suicide) every day. But these are people in their own homes, they have the means, they have lots of medication, and they don't choose death."[7] Of 50,000 patients under this group's care, as few as 6 have committed suicide. Suffering people want their existence and meaning affirmed, not a convenient escape into the nothingness offered by assisted suicide.

A biblical view of suffering also resists the slippery logic of the right-to-die philosophy, a logic which argues that the value of life is in some way or another conditional. For the terminally ill, the value is conditioned upon quality of life. But what of other categories of people that are not healthy, young, and vigorous? Assisting in the suicide of the terminally ill sets an ominous precedent that opens the door to a more general devaluation of life and the broader practice of euthanasia. Even the American College of Physicians has expressed concern that assisted suicide may lead to actions against the poor, the chronically ill, the demented, the disabled, and the very young.[8]

History justifies this concern. German physicians in the 1920s began to entertain the notion that "there is such a thing as a life not worthy to be lived" and to embrace the practice of euthanasia for the chronically ill, later acquiescing to ever broader categorizations of "unfit" persons.[9] More recently, the Netherlands has legalized voluntary euthanasia, only to open the door permissively to the practice of involuntary euthanasia, where the elderly and chronically ill may be terminated against their wishes.

At this critical juncture in our own history as a nation, it is imperative that we return to an absolute, timeless standard of human value rooted in biblical truth. We must return to the divine appraisal of the worth and dignity of life, whether born or unborn, young or old, healthy or suffering. We must recognize once again the One in whose image we are made, the One who determines the time of our beginning and the time of our end, and the One who provides meaning and hope to suffering people through the redemptive work of the Cross.

A Christian Response

Having developed a biblical perspective on the practice of assisted suicide, it is important to translate our ethical concerns into corresponding action. To that end, the following suggestions are offered for Christians individually and for the church corporately toward the objective of eliminating the demand for and practice of assisted suicide.

Seek First His Kingdom

The battle in our day is not between those for and those against assisted suicide. The real battle is being waged between the kingdom of heaven and the kingdom of this world. Any fundamental change in society will result not from social or political activism; people will be won over to a pro-life perspective through the changing of hearts. Christians must be salt and light; the Church must be the clear expression of Jesus' ministry to the world. After Jesus' example, we pray, "'Your kingdom come, your will be done on earth as it is in heaven'" (Matthew 6:10).

Love With Actions

Arguably the strongest public statements in favor of the unborn and against abortion are made each and every day by countless individuals who staff pregnancy care centers, show hospitality to unwed mothers, or support friends in crisis. Likewise, the strongest statements in favor of the terminally ill and against assisted suicide are made by those who provide spiritual support in hospice facilities, serve as hospital chaplains, render loving care in nursing homes, and otherwise minister to the suffering and dying. As the apostle John urges us,

"Let us not love with words or tongue but with actions and in truth" (1 John 3:18). Let us affirm our high valuation of suffering people by loving suffering people. Visit the friend who has cancer; give time as a volunteer to a nursing home; support a hospice program. Such actions will make the difference for someone who is terminally ill and also set a forceful example of Christian love.

Contend for Truth

It is also necessary that we publicly acknowledge biblical truth as it pertains to the critical issues of our day, including assisted suicide. The church must express in uncompromising terms its core moral values and spiritual convictions as they pertain to abortion and euthanasia. We must hold elected officials accountable for voting records, support pro-life legislation, oppose referendums in favor of assisted suicide, challenge our physicians, and articulate our opinions in public forums. The evangelical community was strangely silent in 1973 when Roe v. Wade was announced. We dare not remain silent as new threats to life emerge.

---

[1]D. E. Meier, C. A. Emmons, S. Wallenstein,T. Quill, R. S. Morrison, C. K. Cassel, "A National Survey of Physician-Assisted Suicide and Euthanasia in the United States," *New England Journal of Medicine* (1998), 338:1193–1201.

[2]"Assisted Suicide: When Physicians Hasten Death," *US News & World Report*, 6 April 1998.

[3]Francis A. Schaeffer and C. Everett Koop, *Whatever Happened to the Human Race?* in *The Complete Works of Francis A. Schaeffer*, vol. v.

(Westchester, Ill: Crossway Books, 1984), 337.

[4]*American College of Physicians Ethics Manual* (4th edition). Annals of Internal Medicine (1998), 128:576–594.

[5]Nigel Cameron, "Autonomy and the 'Right to Die,'" in *Dignity and Dying: A Christian Appraisal* (Grand Rapids: Eerdmans Publishing Co., 1996), 23.

[6]Cameron, 29.

[7]J. Loconte, "Hospice, Not Hemlock," Policy Review (1998), 44.

[8]*American College of Physicians Ethics Manual.*

[9]L. Alexander, "Medical Science Under Dictatorship," *New England Journal of Medicine* (1949), 241:44.

20

The Baptism In The Holy Spirit: The Initial Experience And Continuing Evidences of the Spirit-Filled Life

On the Day of Pentecost visitors to Jerusalem witnessed the unbelievable sight of Spirit-filled believers declaring the glory of God in languages they had never learned. Their response to the supernatural was natural: "What does this mean?"[1] (Acts 2:12).

Twenty centuries later the same question is being asked as the Holy Spirit is doing spectacular things all around the world, not just in one location. Tongues-speaking Pentecostals have become the second largest family of Christians in the world, surpassed only by the Roman Catholic Church. Convincing statistics exist on the explosion of church growth around the world in the Pentecostal and charismatic groups that teach the necessity of speaking in tongues as the initial physical evidence of being filled with the Holy Spirit.[2]

Biblical and Historical Background

The emphasis on the person and work of the Holy Spirit, which Pentecostals promote, is not new to the Church. The outpouring of the Spirit on the Day of Pentecost was the logical culmination of revealed truth about the Holy Spirit as found throughout Old Testament Scriptures.

The usual reference in the Old Testament to the Holy Spirit is "the Spirit of God" or "his Spirit." At creation, "the Spirit of God was hovering over the waters" (Genesis 1:2). Artisans at the building of the tabernacle were "filled with the Spirit of God" (Exodus 31 and 35). Prophets and national leaders ministered supernaturally when prompted by the Spirit of God (Numbers 24:2; 1 Samuel 10:10; 11:6; 2 Chronicles 15:1; 24:20; Isaiah 48:16; Ezekiel 11:24; Zechariah 7:12).

Prophecy, or speaking in behalf of God, is evident throughout the Old Testament. Sometimes the message came almost silently, in thoughts, dreams, or visions. At other times it came with significant emotion (cf. Numbers 11:24–29). In each case, however, prophetic speech is the unique sign of the Spirit's coming to anoint particular persons for divinely given ministries.[3]

In Acts 2:17 Peter decisively connects the Pentecost event with the fulfillment of Old Testament prophecy, "I will pour out my Spirit on all people. Your sons and daughters will prophesy, your old men will dream dreams, your young men will see visions. Even on my servants, both men and women, I will pour out my Spirit in those days" (Joel 2:28,29). In fact, lest we miss the point, Peter repeats Joel's prophecy in a way not found in the Hebrew text, saying a second time, "I will pour out my Spirit in those days and they will prophesy" (v. 18). The viewpoint of both the Old and New Testaments is that the coming of the Spirit is indicated by prophetic speech. The initial prophetic speech in Acts is speaking in tongues.

The Israelites were unaccustomed to such a universal move of the Spirit in the lives of sons and daughters, old and young, men and women. Only a select few charismatic prophets, kings, and judges were moved by the Holy Spirit to minister supernaturally and experience the presence of the Spirit, as David demonstrates in the Psalms. Peter put the Day of Pentecost visitation into perspective as fulfillment of Old Testament prophecy and a divinely ordered gift of the Spirit for all believers, not just for leadership offices.

Biblical theology is a unity based on the entire Bible. It is both progressive and unified because God reveals cumulative truth from Genesis to Revelation. The Old Testament prophesied a coming age of the Spirit. The theme is enlarged in the Spirit-empowered ministry of Jesus. At Pentecost the Spirit comes in power to all God's people. Yet individual writers emphasize special aspects of the doctrine of the Holy Spirit. The writings of Paul emphasize the Spirit-filled life subsequent to the baptism in the Holy Spirit. Luke's writings place more emphasis on the coming of the Spirit to empower and ministry through the Spirit-filled life. There is no contradiction between Paul's writings and Luke's writings. They are complementary.

Baptism in the Spirit as the Distinctive Message of Pentecostals

The very essence of Pentecostalism is the recognition that the experience of conversion, while supremely precious, does not exhaust God's supply of what is available to the believer. Scripture makes it clear that all believers have the Holy Spirit (Romans 8:9,16). However, the constant hunger for "more of God" is the heartbeat of Pentecostalism. This is particularly true when, within Scripture, we recognize another life-changing experience available to every believer.

The baptism in the Spirit is not an end in itself, but a means to an end. The scriptural ideal for the believer is to be continually filled with the Spirit (Ephesians 5:18).[4] Baptism in the Holy Spirit is the specific event that introduces the believer to the ongoing process of living a Spirit-empowered life. Although speaking in tongues is the outward sign of Spirit baptism, it is designed by God to be much more than evidence. Subsequent speaking in tongues brings enrichment to the individual believer when employed in private prayer (1 Corinthians 14:4) and to the congregation when accompanied by the interpretation (1 Corinthians 14:6,25).

From its founding, The General Council of the Assemblies of God has recognized the baptism in the Holy Spirit as an experience distinct from and subsequent to the experience of the new birth. It has also recognized that the initial physical evidence of the baptism in the Spirit is speaking in tongues.[5] The church's Statement of Fundamental Truths contains the following statements:

Fundamental Truth 7: All believers are entitled to and should ardently expect and earnestly seek the promise of the Father, the baptism in the Holy Ghost and fire, according to the command of our Lord Jesus Christ. This was the normal experience of all in the early Christian church. With it comes the enduement of power for life and service, the bestowment of the gifts and their uses in the work of the ministry (Luke 24:49; Acts 1:4,8; 1 Corinthians 12:1–31). This experience is distinct from and subsequent to the experience of the new birth (Acts 8:12–17; 10:44–46; 11:14–16; 15:7–9). With the baptism in the Holy Ghost come such experiences as an overflowing fullness of the Spirit (John 7:37–39; Acts 4:8), a deepened reverence for God (Acts 2:43; Hebrews 12:28), an intensified consecration to Him and a dedication to His work (Acts 2:42), and a more active love for Christ, for His Word, and for the lost (Mark 16:20).

Fundamental Truth 8: The baptism of believers in the Holy Ghost is witnessed by the initial physical sign of speaking with other tongues as the Spirit of God gives them utterance (Acts 2:4). The speaking in tongues in this instance is the same in essence as the gift of tongues (1 Corinthians 12:4–10,28), but different in purpose and use.

The Assemblies of God has consistently taught the importance of the Baptism and the Spirit-filled life for both the individual believer and the entire Church.

While the exact phrase "baptism in the Holy Spirit" never occurs in Scripture,[6] it is closely related to the biblical expression "baptize(d) in [or with] the Holy Spirit" (cf. Matthew 3:11; Acts 1:5; 11:16). John the Baptist, the first to use the expression shortly before Jesus began His public ministry, said, "He [Jesus] will baptize you with the Holy Spirit" (Matthew 3:11; Mark 1:8; Luke 3:16; cf. also John 1:33). At the conclusion of His earthly ministry, Jesus referred to John's statement (Acts 1:5); and Peter, in reporting on the events in the home of Cornelius, also repeated the statement (Acts 11:16).

Several other terms express essentially the same idea as the expression "baptized in the Holy Spirit." Acts 1:8 promises the reception of power when "the Holy Spirit comes on you" (cf. also 19:6). Acts 2:4 states, "All of them were filled with the Holy Spirit," on the Day of Pentecost (see also Acts 9:17). In Acts 2:17 Peter describes this filling with the Holy Spirit as a fulfillment of the prophet Joel's prophecy that God will "pour out [his] Spirit on all people" (cf. 10:45). According to Acts 8:16, prior to the ministry of Peter and John in Samaria, the Holy Spirit "had not yet come" on any of the Samaritans (cf. 10:44; 11:15). After the laying on of the apostles' hands, the Samaritans "received the Holy Spirit" (cf. 10:47).

The word *baptism* refers literally to a "dipping" or "immersing" in water. When one uses the term *baptism in the Holy Spirit*, it is analogous to what is being described by the term *baptism in water*. Christian water baptism is an initiatory rite, acknowledging conversion and the indwelling presence of the Spirit.[7] The baptism in the Holy Spirit is a subsequent, powerful, overwhelming immersion in the Holy Spirit. While New Testament believers sometimes received later infillings of the Spirit (Acts 4:31), "baptism" in the Holy Spirit in all the biblical examples happens only once to an individual.

A Gift With Rich Benefits

Modern evangelical Christians place great stress on being "born again" (John 3:3,5–8; 1 Peter 1:3), which is rightly understood to be the work of the Holy Spirit in regeneration (John 3:6; Titus 3:5). As He comes in regenerating power, the Spirit makes His presence known as an inner witness to the believer's new status as a child of God. The new believer can now pray "*Abba,* Father," expressing the intimate and confident relationship of children to their Heavenly Father (Romans 8:15,16). Having taken up residence within, the Spirit also guides and enables the new believer in a transforming life of progressive sanctification and spiritual maturity (Romans 8:13; 1 Corinthians 6:11; Galatians 5:16,22–24).

The work of the Spirit, however, is not just an inner transformation of new birth and sanctification; it is also a work of empowering believers as witnesses for Christ, thus fulfilling the mission of the Church (Matthew 28:18–20; Acts 1:8).[8] Peter presented the initial descent of the Spirit on the Day of

Pentecost as a mighty inauguration of the last days in which all of God's people will be baptized, or filled, with the Spirit (Joel 2:28,29; Acts 2:17,18). The final words of his sermon are, "Repent, and be baptized. . . . And you will receive the gift of the Holy Spirit. The promise is for you and your children and for all who are far off—for all whom the Lord our God will call" (Acts 2:38,39). Far from being a one-time event on the Day of Pentecost, the Spirit is noted to have baptized, or filled, believer after believer. Both the Book of Acts and the Pauline epistles show repeated and continuing empowerment by the Holy Spirit and the impartation of powerful gifts for ministry (Acts 8:17; 9:17; 10:44–46; 19:4–7; Romans 1:11; 1 Corinthians 12–14; Ephesians 5:18–21; 1 Thessalonians 5:19,20; Hebrews 2:4). Any understanding of the Spirit's work that is limited to regeneration is not representative of the biblical record.

Fidelity to Scripture, therefore, indicates that men and women ought to seek not only the transformational work of the Spirit in regeneration and sanctification, but also the empowering work of the Spirit in the Baptism promised by Jesus and repeatedly witnessed in the Book of Acts and the Epistles. Lives are to be changed by the Spirit in regeneration and then set ablaze and gifted by the same Spirit for a lifetime of service. Seeking the baptism in the Spirit is strategic for effective Christian living and ministry.

An Experience Subsequent to Regeneration

The baptism in the Spirit is subsequent to and distinct from the new birth. Scripture clearly describes a conversion experience in which the Holy Spirit baptizes believers into the body of Christ (1 Corinthians 12:13). Scripture just as clearly describes an experience in which Christ baptizes believers in the Holy Spirit (Matthew 3:11). These cannot refer to the same experience since the agent who does the baptizing and the element into which the candidate is baptized are different in each case.[9]

Luke, author of both the Gospel of Luke and the Acts of the Apostles, generally presents the baptism or infilling of the Spirit as something which occurs to *disciples,* or *believers,* his characteristic terms for those who have already been converted or saved. For Luke, baptism in the Holy Spirit is an experience distinct from and logically subsequent to personal salvation. Moreover, Luke presents baptism in the Spirit and its accompanying power as the normal expectation of believers.

Subsequent usually means a time separation, but not always. The Gentiles who had gathered at the house of Cornelius (Acts 10) seemingly experienced both regeneration and baptism in the Holy Spirit at the same time. While a theological description of what happened would require regeneration as a prerequisite for baptism in the Spirit, everything happened so quickly that two separate works of God were experienced as one event. In this case, Spirit baptism was logically subsequent to regeneration, although it may not have been subsequent in time to any perceptible degree.[10]

Every believer has the privilege of being baptized in the Spirit and should then expect to speak in tongues. The obvious starting point for such a declaration is the account of the initial outpouring of the Spirit on the Day of Pentecost (Acts 2). On that day all the believers were gathered together in one place (Acts 2:1); their number was apparently about 120 (Acts 1:15). For roughly 10 days they had been waiting for "the promise of the Father," as Jesus had charged them to do prior to His ascension (Acts 1:4). Then according to Acts 2:4, "all of them were filled with the Holy Spirit and began to speak in other tongues as the Spirit enabled them."[11] As Peter explained to the crowd witnessing the marvelous event, this outpouring of the Spirit fulfilled the ancient prophecy of Joel for the last days (Acts 2:17). No longer would God's Spirit be restricted to a few prophets, but in the new age initiated by the death and resurrection of Jesus Christ, the work of the Spirit would now be available to all (cf. also Acts 2:39).

Acts 8:4–13 describes Philip's effective ministry in Samaria. Verse 12 summarizes, "But when they believed Philip as he preached the good news of the kingdom of God and the name of Jesus Christ, they were baptized, both men and women." Acts 8:14–24 then reports about additional ministry among the Samaritans by the apostles Peter and John. In particular, verses 15–17 say:

> When they [Peter and John] arrived, they prayed for them that they might receive the Holy Spirit, because the Holy Spirit had not yet come upon any of them; they had simply been baptized into the name of the Lord Jesus. Then Peter and John placed their hands on them, and they received the Holy Spirit (Acts 8:15–17).

The dramatic account of the conversion of Saul of Tarsus on the road to Damascus is recounted in Acts 9. Saul is knocked down and blinded by the light of Christ's presence. After being led on to Damascus, still without sight, Saul is visited by a believer named Ananias, who says to him, "Brother Saul, the Lord—Jesus, who appeared to you on the road as you were coming here—has sent me so that you may see again and be filled with the Holy Spirit." Ananias regards Saul's conversion as having already occurred, apparently at the time of his encounter with the risen Christ. Nevertheless, Saul still needed to be filled with the Holy Spirit and Ananias prayed for him to that end. Clearly Saul (also called Paul) was filled with the

Spirit some 3 days after his conversion.

Years later Paul came to the great city of Ephesus on his third missionary journey. According to Acts 19:7 there were about 12 believers, described as "disciples" in Acts 19:1. The dialogue recorded between Paul and the Ephesus disciples is instructive:

> And [Paul] asked them, "Did you receive the Holy Spirit when[12] you believed?" They answered, "No, we have not even heard that there is a Holy Spirit." So Paul asked, "Then what baptism did you receive?" "John's baptism," they replied. Paul said, "John's baptism was a baptism of repentance. He told the people to believe in the one coming after him, that is, in Jesus" (Acts 19:2–4).

Clearly, at the time of this conversation these believers had not yet been baptized in the Holy Spirit, for they had not heard of the experience. The context presumes that something was lacking. They also had not been instructed about Christian water baptism; although, once Paul explained it to them, they were quickly baptized (19:5). Following their water baptism, "When Paul placed his hands on them, the Holy Spirit came on them, and they spoke in tongues and prophesied" (19:6). The narrative could not be clearer in its emphasis that the fullness of the Spirit was received following both the Christian belief of the Ephesian "disciples" and their Christian water baptism (19:5).

In the Acts 2, Acts 9, and Acts 19 accounts, the reception of the Spirit occurs following conversion. According to Luke's inspired record, baptism in the Spirit is not an aspect of conversion but rather a separate and distinct experience. It is also logically subsequent to conversion, although as the experience of the Gentiles at the house of Cornelius makes clear, conversion and baptism in the Spirit can occur in such swift succession that they seem to take place simultaneously.

Tongues as Initial Physical Evidence

The Holy Spirit can inspire people to speak in languages which they have not learned, as was demonstrated conclusively on the Day of Pentecost (see Acts 2) when people from all over the world heard *Galileans* speaking foreign languages which they could not have known. In the modern era similar episodes have occurred many times.[13]

The expression "initial physical evidence of the baptism in the Holy Spirit" refers to the first outward, observable sign that the Holy Spirit has come in filling power. The repeated testimony of Scripture is that this physical sign occurred at the time the Spirit was poured out on individuals. When the 120 disciples were filled with the Spirit, they spoke in tongues (Acts 2:4). They spoke then, not a day, week, or year later. When Cornelius's household was baptized in the Spirit, members spoke in tongues, and the believing Jews were amazed (Acts 10:44–48). Again, they spoke in tongues at the same time they were baptized, not at some later time. When the Ephesian believers were baptized in the Spirit, they spoke in tongues and prophesied (Acts 19:1–6). There is no statement or implication of a delay between the event of the baptism in the Spirit and the evidence of speaking in tongues. Those who teach there can be a delay in speaking in tongues draw their conclusions from personal experience or the testimony of others, not from a clear statement of Scripture. Scripture nowhere teaches, implies, or gives an example of a delay occurring between the baptism in the Spirit and the evidence of speaking in tongues; therefore we must adhere to the testimony of Scripture.

Prior to the Day of Pentecost, many within Israel had concluded that after God spoke to and through the last of the Old

Testament prophets, He was speaking directly to Israel no more. Only after Messiah was to arrive, along with the anticipated Age to Come, would God again speak to His people through the inspiration of the Holy Spirit.

Suddenly, in this spiritually lifeless context, the Spirit is poured out, not just on selected individuals as in the Old Testament, but upon masses of people, essentially everyone in the fledgling Church. It was as if the cry of Moses' heart had been fulfilled: "I wish that all the LORD's people were prophets and that the LORD would put his Spirit on them!" (Numbers 11:29). In some marvelous sense the Age to Come had begun, and a church filled with people who spoke in tongues was a sign signifying the dawn of a new period in God's eternal plan for humankind.

Luke understands speaking in tongues to demonstrate the infilling presence of the Holy Spirit; this is clearly indicated by an examination of Acts 10:44–48.

"While Peter was still speaking these words, the Holy Spirit came on all who heard the message. The circumcised believers who had come with Peter were astonished that the gift of the Holy Spirit had been poured out even on the Gentiles. For they heard them speaking in tongues and praising God" (Acts 10:44–46).

The conclusion is clear: If someone, even someone unexpected, hears the Word and speaks in divinely inspired tongues, that person has received the Holy Spirit. This was the reasoning of Peter and the other Jewish Christians present. Speaking in tongues is clear evidence someone has received the gift of the Holy Spirit (or been baptized in the Holy Spirit). The evidence was so clear for Peter he insisted Cornelius and his Gentile friends be baptized in water (10:48).

Later, as Peter discussed the Cornelius incident with the

apostles and believers in Jerusalem, he again referred to the phenomenon he had witnessed: "So if God gave them the same gift as he gave us, who believed in the Lord Jesus Christ, who was I to think that I could oppose God?" (Acts 11:17). The next verse confirms the apostles and believers accepted tongues as convincing evidence of the baptism in the Spirit: "When they heard this, they had no further objections and praised God" (11:18).

While Acts 10:45,46 establishes that speaking in tongues is clear evidence of Spirit baptism, evidence supporting this doctrine is also provided by the overall pattern of Acts associating speaking in tongues with baptism in the Spirit. Acts describes five occasions on which people received an empowering of the Spirit for the first time (i.e., baptism in the Spirit). In none of these accounts are all of the details given, but four of these occasions include significant detail. (For Paul's reception of the Spirit recorded in Acts 9:17,19, hardly any detail is recorded.) As previously noted, supernatural phenomena are a sign of the coming of the Spirit. The New Testament simply picks up on a very important Old Testament motif.

In Acts 2, 10, and 19 various phenomena are indicated, such as the sound of wind, tongues of fire, prophecy, and speaking in tongues.[14] The only phenomenon occurring in each case, however, is speaking in tongues.

In the Acts 8 account of Peter and John's ministry among the Samaritans, speaking in tongues is not specifically mentioned but it is strongly implied. After the apostles had laid their hands on the Samaritans, some visible and extraordinary manifestation accompanied the reception of the Spirit. This is evident for, after seeing something remarkable, the magician Simon wanted to buy the ability to confer the Holy Spirit. Acts 8:18 notes explicitly, "When Simon saw that the Spirit was given at the laying on of the apostles' hands, he offered them money." Based on the pattern found in Acts 2, 10, and 19 it seems most likely that what Simon saw was the Samaritan believers speaking in tongues. Had the experience been only by faith without any accompanying sign, Simon would not have known whether the Samaritan believers actually received the Holy Spirit.

Acts 9:17–19 suggests that Saul of Tarsus (i.e., the apostle Paul) was filled with the Holy Spirit through the ministry of Ananias. Though no details of this filling are given, we know from 1 Corinthians 14:18 that Paul prayed in tongues regularly and often. It would hardly be surprising if that pattern was begun at the time he was filled with the Spirit.

Despite the sketchiness of the report about Paul's baptism in the Spirit, and despite the fact tongues are not explicitly mentioned in Acts 8, the evidence of chapters 2, 10, and 19 demonstrates an overall pattern of speaking in tongues as regularly accompanying the baptism in the Holy Spirit. When these three witnesses are linked with (1) Luke's underlying awareness of the Spirit's presence in divinely inspired speech and (2) the strong inference of Acts 10:45,46 connecting speaking in tongues with the gift of the Spirit, the Pentecostal doctrine that speaking in tongues constitutes evidence of Spirit baptism is clearly established.[15]

The Baptism—Entry Into the Spirit-Filled Life

The baptism in the Holy Spirit is just the open door leading into a Spirit-filled life—a fact that can be easily overlooked, even by Pentecostals. Though we believe speaking in tongues is the unmistakable initial evidence of the baptism in the Holy Spirit, we do not believe it signifies instant maturity. *There are many other evidences that a life continues to be filled with the Spirit and is growing and maturing spiritually.*

Having spoken in tongues upon being baptized in the Spirit, the believer must continue to respond to the supernatural promptings of the Holy Spirit. For example, praying in the Spirit (intercessory and worship expressions in tongues) should be a continuing part of the new Spirit-filled life. Though not all Spirit-filled believers are given the gift of tongues which through interpretation edifies the church congregation (1 Corinthians 12:30), they all have the privilege of praying in the Spirit, especially at times when the human intellect does not know how to pray. Likewise, every Spirit-filled believer can and should expect to be used in supernatural ways in some, though not all, of the gifts of the Spirit.

We cannot agree with those who teach that the fruit of the Spirit (Galatians 5:22,23) alone are sufficient evidence a believer has been baptized in the Holy Spirit.[16] But we do affirm such character qualities (love, joy, peace, patience, kindness, goodness, faith and faithfulness, gentleness, and self-control) should be seen in the lives of those who have been baptized in the Holy Spirit. After baptism in the Spirit, the fruit of the Spirit should develop alongside a growing ministry empowered by the gifts of the Holy Spirit. We urge all believers to pursue these character qualities with the same zeal they pursue the gifts of the Spirit.[17]

A Promise for All Believers

We are fully aware that within the Christian community there are various interpretations of the biblical description and universal availability of the baptism in the Holy Spirit with the initial evidence of speaking in tongues. This paper has attempted to deal with the biblical texts relating to the subject in as open and careful a manner as possible. Though some critics have accused Pentecostals of making theology subservient to individual experience, we feel that the studied conclusions presented above are both taught in Scripture and confirmed by experience, not unjustifiably based on experience alone. Could it be that those who seek to refute the baptism in the Spirit on the ground that it is based on experience rather than on Scripture may indeed be arguing from their own experience of not having received the Baptism with the initial biblical evidence? We appeal to all believers to study the biblical passages prayerfully, and with open mind and heart seek the fullness of the Spirit for today's challenges, just as that same Spirit moved upon a unified body of believers in the Early Church.

The overwhelmingly godless condition of society today, with evil becoming increasingly rampant, calls for a Spirit-filled church that can meet the challenges of Satan with a supernatural demonstration of Holy Spirit power. If there is fear of an experience that seems beyond one's rational control, let the personal love of a benevolent Heavenly Father give assurance to both heart and mind. "Which of you fathers, if your son asks for a fish, will give him a snake instead? Or if he asks for an egg, will give him a scorpion? If you then, though you are evil, know how to give good gifts to your children, how much more will your Father in heaven give the Holy Spirit to those who ask him!" (Luke 11:11–13).

We appeal to our fellow believers who may in complete sincerity disagree with Pentecostal theology and practice. Rather than engaging in attacks on fellow believers who likewise base their spiritual experience on Scripture, please follow the example of Gamaliel (Acts 5:34–39). "For if their purpose or activity is of human origin, it will fail. But if it is from God, you will not be able to stop these men; you will only find yourselves fighting against God" (5:38,39). We believe this last-days outpouring of the Holy Spirit is God's sovereign move to meet the satanic challenges of the day and to prepare Christ's bride for His soon return. Around the world, God is moving by His Spirit in powerful and dynamic ways.

We are not more loved because we have received the baptism in the Holy Spirit, but we have become better equipped to witness with boldness to God's abundant grace. Empowered service and holy living accompany the Spirit-filled life after the Baptism initiation. In believing, expecting faith, ask Jesus to baptize you in the Holy Spirit.

Frequently Asked Questions

Questions are often raised about the doctrine of baptism in the Holy Spirit. The following are a few of the more frequently asked questions.

1. Is the Book of Acts intended to be history or theology, and can doctrine be based on less than declarative statements?

The Bible itself responds to this question. The Holy Spirit inspired Paul to write, "All Scripture is given by inspiration of God, and is profitable for doctrine" (2 Timothy 3:16, KJV). Again Paul wrote, "Whatsoever things were written aforetime were written for our learning" (Romans 15:4, KJV). After recounting Old Testament events that happened to the Israelites, Paul says, "These things happened to them as examples and were written down as warnings for us, on whom the fulfillment of the ages has come" (1 Corinthians 10:11).

While doctrine should not be based on isolated fragments of Scripture, it can be based on substantial, implied truth. The doctrine of the Trinity is based not on declarative statement, but on a comparison of Scripture passages relating to the Godhead. Like the doctrine of the Trinity, the doctrine of tongues as evidence of the baptism in the Holy Spirit is based on substantial portions of Scripture relating to this subject. It is evident Peter and the church leaders in Jerusalem established doctrine based on repeated experiences of the Spirit understood to be the fulfillment of Old Testament prophecy. They recognized tongues as evidence of people being filled with the Spirit (Acts 10,11). The weight of the biblical text, both in quantity and frequency, provides a solid base for doctrinal formulation.

Luke's writings (Luke and Acts) clearly present more than just history. While Luke describes his Gospel as a "narrative" (Greek *diegesis*—Luke 1:1) written to be "accurate" and "orderly" (1:3), the way he selects items to include and his editorial and narrative comments reveal an author with an agenda to advance the cause of Christ. Luke is clearly a Christian. In fact, today there is an overwhelming consensus among New Testament scholars that Luke is a theologian, not just a historian. For those interested in learning more about Luke and Acts as inspired historical narratives that also teach theology, we recommend Roger Stronstad's *Charismatic Theology of St. Luke* (Hendrickson, 1984).

2. Isn't baptism in the Holy Spirit connected with water baptism in some special way? Since water baptism is a witness to one's faith in Christ and the reception of God's saving grace, isn't Spirit baptism also associated with salvation?

The answer to both questions is no. The theology of the Spirit presented in Acts emphasizes the empowering of believers by the Spirit for effective witness and the utterance of inspired speech. Only by wrongly imposing Paul's theology of the Spirit (never intended to stand apart from the remainder of biblical revelation) upon Luke's Gospel and Acts can baptism in the Holy Spirit be associated with personal conversion, spiritual renewal, or ethical transformation. In short, baptism in the Holy Spirit is a gift given to those who are already Christians. It does not make people Christians.

3. Isn't speaking in tongues a phenomenon that belonged only to the apostolic period? Did not Paul say that tongues "shall cease" (1 Corinthians 13:8)?

First Corinthians 13:10 says, "When that which is perfect has come, then that which is in part will be done away" (NKJV). This does not imply, however, that speaking in tongues would be in effect only during the apostolic period or until the New Testament canon had been completed, as some have suggested. Clearly the arrival of "the perfect" is connected in some way with the second coming of Christ and the perfect establishment of God's kingdom in which God's will shall "be done on earth as it is in heaven." Paul also indicated that at the time when tongues shall cease, knowledge shall also vanish away and prophecies shall fail (1 Corinthians 13:8). If knowledge and prophecy are necessary and available to the Church today, then speaking in tongues is as well.

4. When Paul wrote, "Not all speak with tongues, do they?" (1 Corinthians 12:30), does this not contradict the teaching that all should expect to speak in tongues as evidence of baptism in the Holy Spirit?

To understand 1 Corinthians 12:30 one must recognize the various functions of speaking with tongues. Speaking with tongues serves as the initial physical evidence of the baptism in the Spirit (Acts 2:4; 10:46). Speaking or praying with tongues in private is for personal edification (1 Corinthians 14:4). And speaking with tongues in the congregation, accompanied by interpretation of tongues, is for the edification of the Church

(1 Corinthians 12:4–11, 14:5).

There is no contradiction between Paul's desire that all speak with tongues (1 Corinthians 14:5) and the implication of his rhetorical question in 1 Corinthians 12:30, since different contexts are in view. These contrasting contexts are highlighted in 1 Corinthians 14:18,19: "I thank God that I speak in tongues more than all of you. But in the church . . ." Here private tongues are contrasted with public tongues (that is, in a worship service).

Paul recognizes that the Corinthian believers prayed quite frequently in tongues, so frequently in fact that congregational meetings had been disrupted because the distinction between tongues appropriate in public and tongues appropriate only in private prayer had not been observed. To address the potential for disruption, Paul limits the public exercise of tongues while encouraging private prayer in tongues (1 Corinthians 14:18, 19,27,28). Thus private prayer in tongues is encouraged for "all" (1 Corinthians 14:5), with Paul's own practice as a model (1 Corinthians 14:18), but "not all" pray publicly in tongues in church meetings (1 Corinthians 12:30; 14:27,28). Only those to whom the gift of tongues has been apportioned by the Spirit are to speak in tongues publicly (1 Corinthians 12:10,11) and such tongues must always be interpreted (1 Corinthians 14:27). Private tongues, on the other hand, do not require interpretation, for even without interpretation the one who prays in tongues privately is edified (1 Corinthians 14:4).

When examined in context, any apparent contradiction between Paul's teaching in 1 Corinthians 12:30 and the Pentecostal expectation that all Spirit-baptized believers will speak in tongues quickly evaporates. Instead of contradiction, we find complementary truth.

5. If speaking with tongues either as evidence or gift is scriptural, why were there periods in church history when the phenomenon seemed to be absent?

The possibility exists that any biblical doctrine can suffer from neglect. In fact, great spiritual renewals have often been accompanied by the revival of doctrine. For example, the doctrine of justification by faith was almost completely lost until the time of the Reformation, when Martin Luther and others reemphasized this biblical truth. The doctrine of sanctification had suffered neglect until the time of the Wesleyan Revival, when it was again brought to the attention of the Church. While the truth of the baptism in the Holy Spirit and speaking with tongues has appeared in revivals throughout Church history, it did not have the emphasis it has received in the present revival.

Just as there were those who opposed the revival of the doctrines of justification by faith and sanctification, there are those who oppose the revival of the doctrine of the baptism in the Holy Spirit with the initial physical evidence of speaking in tongues. The fact some refuse to accept a doctrine, however, does not make it unscriptural. The instruction for believers is to "prove all things; hold fast that which is good" (1 Thessalonians 5:21, KJV). The basis of the testing is not human opinion but the Word of God (Acts 17:11).

6. In teaching the doctrine of tongues as evidence of the baptism in the Holy Spirit is there a danger that people will seek for tongues rather than the actual baptism in the Holy Spirit?

Unfortunately this is a possibility, but the abuse of a doctrine does not invalidate the doctrine. Abuses and counterfeits, rather than disproving a doctrine, help to establish the importance of the genuine. While speaking in tongues accompanies the baptism in the Holy Spirit, it is important to remember

Jesus' command to the disciples was to wait until they were filled with the Spirit. The emphasis must always be on seeking to be filled with the Spirit. Tongues will naturally accompany the experience.

7. If people speak in tongues, will there not be a temptation to spiritual pride?

When people truly understand the baptism in the Holy Spirit, it will result in humility instead of pride. Believers are baptized in the Spirit not because of personal worthiness, but to empower them for service and a more meaningful life. The baptism in the Spirit is received by faith and not because of meritorious works. It cannot be earned or bought. Like all gifts of God it is by grace through faith. Baptism in the Spirit does not guarantee spiritual maturity. Paul's need to rebuke the Christians at Corinth provides clear evidence of that. The cultivation of fruit of the Spirit and a sanctified life are the real indicators of spiritual maturity.

8. What about truly born-again people who have accomplished great things for the Lord but do not speak in tongues?

Without question, some believers who do not speak in tongues have accomplished great things for God. However, every student of Scripture must determine whether to base doctrine on God's Word or on experiences of even the most devout believers. Because the Bible indicates that all may speak with tongues in private prayer, if not in the congregation, every believer must determine whether to accept or reject this provision of God's grace.

Scripture makes clear that believers must recognize their accountability to God and not evaluate Christian experience on the basis of human comparison. Paul wrote: "We do not dare to classify or compare ourselves with some who commend themselves. When they measure themselves by themselves and compare themselves with themselves, they are not wise" (2 Corinthians 10:12). Doctrine must always be based on the Word of God, not on personal experience.

9. What is the relationship between the baptism in the Holy Spirit and the experiences of regeneration and sanctification?

Spiritual life is composed of specific experiences or events, ongoing processes, and occasional unique experiences. Conversion is a specific experience, or event. At a certain moment a person believes in Christ, is forgiven of sin, and is converted or justified. However, after that, there is a lifelong process of sanctification, of conforming to the image of Christ. In the same way, the baptism in the Holy Spirit is a specific event. After it, however, there is a lifelong development of Spirit-filled life and ministry. The person matures in the Spirit-filled life, is more responsive to the leading of the Spirit, and is more fruitful in the ministry of the Spirit. In the same way that salvation is an initiation experience leading to Christlikeness, the baptism in the Holy Spirit marks a supernatural enduement leading to Christlike ministry in the power of the Spirit. For example, children or teenagers may be baptized in the Holy Spirit at a young age. Their baptism is real and valid, but as they mature they will grow in their ability to be used by the Spirit in various supernatural ministries. What they receive at the moment of their baptism is not all they will ever receive, nor is it the fullness of the expression of the power of the Spirit that will flow through their lives.

10. What is the relationship of the baptism in the Holy Spirit to other spiritual experiences such as weeping, falling, shaking, etc.?

Periods of renewal and revival have historically included physical manifestations not described in Scripture.[18] The writings of Jonathan Edwards and John Wesley contain many such references.

As one's spiritual life develops, one may experience a variety of spiritual responses. For example, during periods of revival, including both personal and corporate revival, it is not unusual for people to be overcome by compulsive weeping. They may fall or shake, or quake, when influenced by the power of the Spirit, or they may run, jump, and shout. In short, when people feel the power of God they may respond in a number of ways. These are, or can be, very legitimate and fruitful encounters with the power of God. However, it is a mistake to confuse these responses with the experience of salvation or the baptism in the Holy Spirit.

11. What is the "anointing" and how does it relate to the baptism in the Holy Spirit?

Old Testament kings and priests were anointed with oil to symbolize the power of God in their lives to fulfill their calling. Jesus used this imagery when He said that the Spirit of the Lord was on Him, for He was anointed to minister in a number of ways (Luke 4:18). Therefore, anointing is a declaration that the power of God rests on a person's life enabling one to fulfill the ministry God has given.

The baptism in the Holy Spirit fits this imagery perfectly. This is the thrust of Peter's words at the household of Cornelius when, in explaining the baptism in the Holy Spirit, he indicates that Jesus was anointed with the Spirit and went about doing good and performing miracles (Acts 10:38).

Some, however, when they experience the presence of God in a significant way or when they respond to the power of God in an unusual way (falling, etc.) report that they have received an anointing. Further, some teach, or at least imply, that certain individuals possess a unique "anointing" and are able to minister it (pass it along) to others when they pray for them. We believe that this is an unwarranted confusion of (1) the anointing that comes from God in the form of the baptism in the Holy Spirit with (2) other legitimate spiritual experiences a person may have when sensing the power and presence of God. If people come to believe that the unusual spiritual experiences they have (falling, etc.) are the anointing, then the biblical doctrine of the baptism in the Holy Spirit could easily be replaced by other experiences. We can acknowledge and rejoice in these other experiences that contribute to a person's spiritual life. Nonetheless, people should not be led into confusing these experiences with the baptism in the Holy Spirit. It is the baptism in the Holy Spirit that endues a person with power for ministry. Nothing else can take its place.

12. Is speaking in tongues the only evidence of the baptism in the Holy Spirit and a Spirit-filled life?

Tongues are not the only evidence of a Spirit-filled life, but they are always the initial, or first, evidence that one has been baptized in the Holy Spirit as the entrance into a Spirit-filled life. One purpose of baptism in the Spirit is to empower the believer for witness; therefore, enthusiasm and boldness in witnessing, divine guidance and enabling in the presentation of the gospel, and miraculous manifestations of God's power before unbelievers all may serve as additional evidences of baptism in the Holy Spirit, though not as substitutions for speaking in tongues.

The Spirit-filled life should also demonstrate progressive development toward a complete Christlike character. The fruit of the Spirit (Galatians 5:22,23) should be developing in the life of every believer. It has been observed that some who have received the baptism in the Holy Spirit and claim to be living Spirit-filled lives demonstrate less evidence of the fruit of the Spirit than some who have not received the Baptism experience. Such a fact does not destroy the truth that the Spirit takes raw material and, if given the opportunity, helps develop Christlike character traits in every believer. Yet development of the fruit of the Spirit can, and should, be enhanced in those who have been filled with the Spirit.

Other supernatural gifts of the Spirit (besides speaking in tongues), though sometimes seemingly evident in the lives of believers who have not been baptized in the Spirit, do not in themselves give evidence of having been baptized in the Spirit. The manifestation of supernatural gifts in the life of a believer who has not been baptized in the Holy Spirit is possible, but being baptized opens the door to a more dynamic, more effective manifestation. See Question 13 and its response.

13. Can believers who have not experienced the baptism in the Holy Spirit minister with supernatural signs following?

As the question is stated, the answer must be yes. Mark 16:17 speaks of signs following "those who believe." Yet the promise to believers before the outpouring of the Spirit on the Day of Pentecost was, "You will receive power when the Holy Spirit comes on you" (Acts 1:8). The power is a supernatural, divine power consistently doing supernatural things through Spirit-filled believers.

The question might better be, "Is there any difference between the frequency and effectiveness of the supernatural gifts of the Spirit in the life of a believer after being baptized in the Holy Spirit?" The Bible records many miraculous demonstrations of the supernatural in the lives of Old Testament individuals, and in the lives of New Testament believers both before and after their Baptism experience. When Jesus sent out the pre-Pentecost 70, they returned reporting with joy, "Lord, even the demons submit to us in your name" (Luke 10:17).

But there was definitely a higher incidence of spiritual gifts operating through Spirit-filled members of the Early Church than there was prior to the outpouring of the Holy Spirit upon yielded believers. Miracles were wrought through people like Stephen and Philip who did not have apostolic positions (Acts 6:8 and 8:6,7). The full range of gifts was everywhere seen after the Day of Pentecost. It was as if a high-octane fuel additive propelled the Church to incredible growth and outreach. Activity after the Day of Pentecost was not just an extension of activity before the great outpouring. The Church had experienced a major empowerment for more effective ministry. The baptism in the Holy Spirit, with the initial physical evidence of speaking in tongues, is the doorway leading to a greatly empowered church of Jesus Christ.

14. What about persons who are convinced they were baptized in the Holy Spirit in a definite encounter with God, but did not speak in tongues until some time later?

Since the Bible teaches and demonstrates that tongues are the initial evidence of receiving the baptism in the Holy Spirit, the Church cannot confirm the opinion of individuals until they actually speak in tongues. But neither can we depreciate a person's special experience of the presence of the Holy Spirit of God. Such an in-between time might be described as involving a process that is completed only when the person speaks in tongues. To take any other position on the question would open the door to individuals claiming to be baptized in the Holy

Spirit without having received the biblical evidence of speaking in tongues as the Spirit gives utterance, and feeling content with what they already have experienced spiritually.

15. What is the relationship of John 20:22 with Acts 1:8 and Acts 2:4?

John 20:22 is important to understanding the full ministry of the Holy Spirit. This verse records the disciples' receiving the regenerating work of the Holy Spirit before the Day of Pentecost (under the New Covenant founded on the resurrection of the crucified Jesus). The Acts 2:4 experience occurred after the disciples' regeneration by the Holy Spirit, as a separate and distinct work of the Spirit. The regeneration and the Spirit baptism experiences are normative for all believers. Thus all believers receive the Holy Spirit at salvation, or regeneration. After this regenerating work of the Holy Spirit, every believer can experience the baptism in the Holy Spirit, the enduement of power to be more effective witnesses (Acts 1:8; 2:4; 2:39).

Some have suggested that John 20:22 was merely a symbolic promise of the Holy Spirit's descent at Pentecost. But the Greek aorist imperative for "receive" indicates that an action took place at that time, not sometime later. John recorded a historical event which had its own significance for the normative experiences of every believer today.

---

[1]All Scripture quotations are from the New International Version.

[2]Vinson Synan, "Policy Decisions on Tongues as an Indicator of Future Church Growth," Address to the Evangelical Theological Society meeting in Orlando, Florida, November 20, 1998.

[3]Throughout Scripture, some kind of supernaturally inspired speech accompanies the giving of the Spirit. For example, it is said of the elders of Israel, "When the Spirit rested on them, they prophesied, but they did

not do so again" (Numbers 11:25). The prophet Samuel told Saul, "The Spirit of the LORD will come upon you in power and you will prophesy . . . " (1 Samuel 10:6,10). When God gave the promise to Joel, "And afterward, I will pour out my Spirit on all people," He added, "Your sons and daughters will prophesy . . . " (Joel 2:28). In the Old Testament, the Holy Spirit is most often active in prophesying through specially selected human beings. The Spirit is quite literally the Spirit of prophecy, and some form of verbal proclamation, perhaps along with other power phenomena, is the special sign of His coming.

In the New Testament, the Pentecost phenomena are consistent with this promise, "All of them were filled with the Holy Spirit and began to speak in other tongues as the Spirit enabled them" (Acts 2:4). The word "enabled" is from the Greek verb *apophthengomai,* which means "to speak" usually in connection with an inspired utterance, e.g., "to speak as a prophet." The same word is found in Acts 2:14 where Peter "addressed" the crowd. Luke understood Peter's address to be prophetic, a sign that the Spirit had come in power as prophesied by Joel.

[4]"Being continually filled with the Spirit" is the meaning of the tense of the Greek word.

[5]"Speaking in tongues" refers to the ability the Holy Spirit gives believers to speak in languages they have not learned. Like our English word *tongue,* the Greek word *glossa* of the New Testament era meant both the physical organ and the language it produces. The technical term for this usage of one word (tongue) to indicate a related concept (language) is *metonymy.*

[6]Neither are such widely accepted theological terms as *Trinity* and *Incarnation* found in Scripture.

[7]I.e., people are baptized only once as a first-time expression of faith in Christ and entry into the community of the Church.

[8]At the very outset of Jesus' ministry, each one of the Gospel writers emphasizes John the Baptist's prophecy "He will baptize you with the Holy Spirit and with fire" (Matthew 3:11; see also Mark 1:8; Luke 3:16; John 1:33). Jesus himself reiterated the prophecy to His disciples just before His ascension: "In a few days you will be baptized with the Holy Spirit" (Acts 1:5). Jesus also explicitly commanded the disciples to "wait" for the promised gift of the Spirit (Acts 1:4; cf. Luke 24:49), described by Him as being "clothed with power from on high" (Luke

24:49) and "power . . . [to] be my witnesses" (Acts 1:8). For the disciples, the promise was fulfilled on the Day of Pentecost when the Spirit came in dynamic and powerful ways, filling them with His presence and enabling them to speak prophetically in other tongues (Acts 2:1–4). True to the baptismal language of the biblical promise, Pentecostal believers have referred to the Spirit's coming in power as "the baptism in the Holy Spirit."

[9]The Holy Spirit baptizes *into the body of Christ* at conversion; Christ baptizes *in the Spirit* at Spirit baptism.

[10]Though conversion and Spirit baptism appear in this instance to be simultaneous because Baptism with the evidence of speaking in tongues follows conversion so quickly, there is still a chronological distinction in the two experiences.

[11]"As the Spirit gave them utterance" (KJV) does not mean that some who were baptized spoke in tongues while others did not. It simply means that all spoke in tongues prompted by the Holy Spirit. Speaking with other tongues as the Holy Spirit gives utterance is not achieved through a heightened emotional state or through the repetition of words and phrases. It is not the result of imitating the sounds made by others. To the contrary, human attempts to speak with tongues only stand in the way of the utterance the Holy Spirit gives. The believer speaks by the supernatural, *motivating* power of the Spirit, although cooperation is required. One needs only to respond in faith and speak out as the Spirit gives utterance. Any manipulative technique for receiving the baptism in the Holy Spirit is without biblical pattern or propriety.

[12]The King James translation *"since* ye believed" is more accurate than "when." The Greek *pisteusantes* is an aorist active participle more accurately translated as "having believed," indicating that the believing took place prior to the action Paul is asking about.

[13]See Ralph W. Harris, *Acts Today: Signs and Wonders of the Holy Spirit* (Springfield, MO: Gospel Publishing House, 1995). Includes documented instances of individuals speaking in French, Croatian, Chinese, Ukrainian, and Aramaic-Hebrew, despite a lack of any training in those languages.

[14]The sound of wind and the sight of tongues of fire preceded and were external to the disciples' personal experience.

[15]For all its importance as initial evidence, speaking in tongues is not

the only purpose of the baptism in the Holy Spirit. Another purpose of the baptism in the Holy Spirit, according to Jesus' words in Acts 1:8, is to empower believers to be witnesses. The Greek word translated "power" is *dynamis*, or the power and ability to get things done. God's Great Commission is the evangelization of the world. As the Book of Acts clearly shows, evangelizing the world is to be done in the power of the Spirit. The powerful proclamation of the gospel, healings, casting out of demons, raising the dead are all clearly seen in the Book of Acts as Spirit-empowered believers, after being baptized in the Holy Spirit, bear witness to the saving power of Jesus. All of these powerful signs of God's presence are available to the Church today. When believers are baptized in the Holy Spirit with the evidence of speaking in tongues, they should expect to become agents of God's power in this world.

[16]The fruit of the Spirit result from the sanctification process, which must take place continually after conversion.

[17]For a complete biblical description of the gifts of the Spirit, see Romans 12:4–8; 1 Corinthians 12:1–11,27–30; Ephesians 4:11.

[18]See *Christian History,* Issue 58 (Spring 1998).

21
Ministry to People With Disabilities:
A Biblical Perspective

Pentecostal evangelicals, believing that miracles still happen today, sometimes have difficulty dealing with people with permanent disabilities and with those who are not healed after much prayer. But does our theology include, along with our belief in supernatural miracles today, a biblical explanation for those who are not immediately healed or made whole? We accept death by old age, and even by accident; but constant reminders of many with mental and physical disabilities, who are not restored to full health and activity, seem to suggest that our belief or our faith is faulty.

Our theology makes place for pain and suffering, because we have hope for healing and an end to pain. But how does our theology, our faith, and our practice handle the person who may never walk again or the mentally challenged child who may never participate in normal social interaction? A proper understanding of the gospel must boldly proclaim, even though we do not have all the answers, that the God who created the universe and all human life in it is aware of the tension His children feel. He expects us to be people of compassion as well as people of power.

God Still Heals and Works Miracles

We affirm that "Jesus Christ is the same yesterday and today and forever" (Hebrews 13:8).[1] He heals today. His miracles confirm His deity, omnipotence, and faithfulness to His promises. We preach the biblical truth of His healing power, even though divine power does not respond immediately to every human plea and desire. Though His ways are beyond our understanding (Romans 11:33), we trust His decisions in response to *all* our prayers.

The New Testament records many miracles and healings wrought by Jesus. Yet not every disease and infirmity in His immediate proximity was removed. Scripture records that upon returning to His hometown, "he did not do many miracles there because of their lack of faith" (Matthew 13:58). In John 5, Jesus healed only one of many gathered at the pool of Bethesda for a superstitious expectation of physical healing. So if prayer for healing is not immediately answered, we do not change our theology to say God no longer heals. We continue to trust Him in anticipation of the day when the infirmities of earthly existence drop away in the perfect light of His eternal presence.[2]

A Biblical Attitude Toward Disabilities[3]

Some speculate that God does not value persons with physical or mental defects or disabilities, and He particularly does not want such persons in spiritual leadership. This erroneous interpretation of God's impartial love and compassion is drawn by some from Leviticus 21:17–23: "'For the generations to come none of your [Aaron's] descendants who has a defect may come near to offer the food of his God. No man who has any defect may come near: no man who is blind or lame, disfigured or deformed; no man with a crippled foot or hand, or who is hunchbacked or dwarfed, or who has any eye defect, or who has festering or running sores or damaged testicles. No descendant of Aaron the priest who has any defect is to come near to present the offerings made to the LORD by fire. He has a defect; he must not come near to offer the food of his God. He may eat the most holy food of his God, as well as the holy food; yet because of his defect, he must not go near the curtain or approach the altar, and so desecrate my sanctuary. I am the LORD, who makes them holy.'"

The Aaronic priesthood as a group anticipated the perfect, sinless High Priest. "Because Jesus lives forever, he has a permanent priesthood. Therefore he is able to save completely those who come to God through him, because he always lives to intercede for them. Such a high priest meets our need—one who is holy, blameless, pure, set apart from sinners, exalted above the heavens. Unlike the other high priests, he does not need to offer sacrifices day after day, first for his own sins, and then for the sins of the people. He sacrificed for their sins once for all when he offered himself" (Hebrews 7:24–27).

Now that the perfect High Priest has come to die for us, there is no longer need for physically perfect priests who foreshadowed the coming of the great High Priest. Yet even apart from the restriction on impaired priests participating in ceremonies that looked toward the future, the priests with disabilities were still priests whose every need was taken care of by divine command: "'He may eat the most holy food of his God, as well as the holy food'" (Leviticus 21:22).

After Moses met with God at the burning bush, the call to leadership followed immediately: "'So now, go. I am sending you to Pharaoh to bring my people the Israelites out of Egypt'" (Exodus 3:10). Moses, after giving several reasons why he was not the man for the job, complained, "'O Lord, I have never been eloquent, neither in the past nor since you have spoken to your servant. I am slow of speech and tongue'" (Exodus 4:10).

Stephen, New Testament martyr, referred to Moses as being "'powerful in speech'" (Acts 7:22). So Moses was either unaware of his strength of speech, or he was downplaying his abilities. Through a series of questions, God reminded Moses that He determines human abilities and disabilities. Was Moses' claim to be "'slow of speech and tongue'" a disability or a lack of confidence in his God-given ability? Either way, God had the answer: "'Who gave man his mouth? Who makes him deaf or mute? Who gives him sight or makes him blind? Is it not I, the Lord?'" (Exodus 4:11).

Some say that God is responsible for sin in the world and for the physical defects and disabilities humans have. But the suffering Job spoke truth, "'Far be it from God to do evil, from the Almighty to do wrong'" (Job 34:10). God neither creates evil nor sends it on anyone. When He has to punish, it is loving correction (Hebrews 12:5,6). God was saying to Moses, "As Creator of all life, even in a fallen world of sin and disabilities, I take loving responsibility for everyone. So, Moses, if you have a disability, I can take care of that too."

God imparts *ability*, and He knows about *disability* because He at least allows it. God could have said to Moses what He later said to Paul: "'My grace is sufficient for you, for my power is made perfect in weakness'" (2 Corinthians 12:9).

We find additional confirmation in other Scripture passages. The Israelites were admonished to show kindness to those who were deaf and blind (Leviticus 19:14; Deuteronomy 27:18). Those who minister to the weak and helpless are blessed (Psalm 41:1). Jesus welcomed people with all manner of disabilities into the kingdom of God, even though they would have been excluded from service under the Old Testament (Matthew 4:23ff; 15:30). He instructed us how to treat people with disabilities: "Then Jesus said to his host, 'When you give a luncheon or dinner, do not invite your friends, your brothers or relatives, or your rich neighbors; if you do, they may invite you back and so you will be repaid. But when you give a banquet, *invite the poor, the crippled, the lame, the blind, and you will be blessed.* Although they cannot repay you, you will be repaid at the resurrection of the righteous'" (Luke 14:12–14, italics added). Countless healings in the Old and New Testaments provide proof of the compassionate nature of God, in spite of the fact that not all illnesses, diseases, or disabilities were removed.

Mental Disabilities

Secular society has found ways to accommodate those with physical disabilities better than those who are mentally impaired. The church of Jesus Christ, the earthly representative of spiritual reality, should be the leader in providing opportunity for all people to connect with the Spirit of God. We do not fully understand the age of accountability and its application to persons with mental disabilities. We do not understand how those with a mental disability relate to God. But we must give opportunity for the Spirit of God to speak to them at their level of comprehension.

Recent special-education approaches indicate that individuals with moderate levels of mental disabilities can be mainstreamed in traditional schools and can participate in emotional and social experiences with their peers. Some demonstrate an unusual level of creativity in artistic expression. Many grasp spiritual realities and participate in worship and other church activities, especially in smaller groups. The church should provide such activities for those who can be introduced to genuine encounters with God's presence.[4]

The primary key to understanding and working with people with mental disabilities is building relationships with them. Developing friendship and trust encourages them to open up to the love of God. Such ministry fulfills the words of Jesus: "'I was hungry and you gave me something to eat, I was thirsty and you gave me something to drink, I was a stranger and you invited me in, I needed clothes and you clothed me, I was sick and you looked after me, I was in prison and you came to visit me'" (Matthew 25:35,36). He could well have added, "I was different, yet you loved me."

A Call to a Compassionate Church

Ministry to people with disabilities. The biblical command to "serve one another in love" (Galatians 5:13) includes everyone. To view people with disabilities as flawed and defective, and possibly a divine mistake, is wrong for a church with Christlike compassion. People with disabilities are platforms for the demonstration of His power to heal or His power to use weakness to display His strength. The church often ministers well to persons with acute illnesses and injuries, where the natural healing process and/or the miracle of divine healing seems a possibility. But in situations where disability is long-term or permanent, faith is challenged. Our faith and practice must include a compassionate hand extended to those with disabilities.

The challenges to church leadership are: (1) affirming and

ministering to those with disabilities, while (2) encouraging congregational acceptance of them into church life and activity. If we are to fulfill the Great Commission to preach the gospel to "'every creature'" (Mark 16:15, NKJV), we cannot overlook this segment of society.

Ministry to people with disabilities is challenging. Volunteers grow weary when there are limited positive responses. Medication, therapy, pain, and slow deterioration may persist. Yet, we must remember that God's love for us persists even though *our* failures and disobedience keep recurring. When His love consumes and motivates us, our ministry to people with disabilities is ministry as to Christ himself.

The church's compassion may cost money to modify physical facilities. Federal, state, and local governments have standards that allow the physically handicapped access to public facilities. Such requirements should be considered minimal. Our responsibility, as representatives of the kingdom of God, is to include those with disabilities in church functions and worship. Reserving easily accessible pews or aisle seats for people with physical limitations will say, "We want you to worship with us." Ushers trained to show kindness to worshipers with physical and mental disabilities and to their caregivers demonstrates the seriousness of the church's concern.

Though salvation is the greatest need of every person, the Great Commission includes more than evangelizing. Discipling and equipping people with disabilities to use their gifts to build up the body of Christ is also a response to the church's commission.

Ministry of caregiving. Caregivers need our thanks. Sometimes those they care for don't have the ability to say thank you. It is easy to become weary serving a family member who has a terminal illness or a permanent disability.

Knowing that God is all-powerful, caregivers may be tempted to blame the One who can make that person well, but doesn't. Yet until He answers, they must trust the God who compassionately loves both the caregiver and the one with a disability.

Word to caregivers. Be proud to be seen in public and in a worship service with your family member or friend with a disability. Scripture commands us, "Carry each other's burdens" (Galatians 6:2). You do that when you give love and compassionate care to one who cannot return the kindness. Others may not be quick to help you bear your burden of caring for one of God's special people, but our Heavenly Father, who shows compassion for them, understands and will bless your ministry.

A Word to People With Disabilities

You may have asked, "Why me, Lord?" Students of the Scriptures have searched the Bible for the answer to that question. And since the Bible does not give a final answer, neither can we. Some have tried to penetrate the mystery of suffering, but in doing so have gone beyond God's Word. There are examples in Scripture of people suffering because of sin in their lives. But righteous people suffer too. Others have suggested that God has a special love for those with long-term pain and suffering, knowing they can handle what others could not. But the love of God to every person is beyond comprehension or deserving.

A mother with disabilities, whose children are serving God, said, "My greatest desire of seeing my entire family following Jesus has been answered, even though my prayer for physical healing has not yet been answered. It may be that their commitment has in some way been linked with my suffering and how I have handled it. God has given me the first desire of my heart."

The answer the Bible gives concerning your pain and suffering is that we all live in a fallen, sin-cursed world. God did not make it that way. We have made it that way, from Adam and Eve to the present, "for all have sinned and fall short of the glory of God" (Romans 3:23). The bigger question is, "Why do we not all suffer more than we do?"

God calls you to come to Him with your disability, just as He invites everyone to come to Him. He says to each of us, "'Come to me, all you who are weary and burdened, and I will give you rest. Take my yoke upon you and learn from me, for I am gentle and humble in heart, and you will find rest for your souls'" (Matthew 11:28,29). His first concern for every person is the soul: Is it right with God in preparation for eternal wholeness in His presence? A lifetime with a disability followed by an eternity with God is to be preferred to a lifetime with health and wealth followed by an eternity separated from God. Seek to know God intimately until He speaks peace to your heart. As you seek God, invest your time, talents, and energies in serving others. Jesus said, "'Freely you have received, freely give'" (Matthew 10:8).

Conclusion

People with disabilities are essential to the wholeness of the Christian community. In a culture that worships physical perfection, devalues human life, and takes pride in disposability, the church must protect the helpless, vulnerable, disenfranchised, including people with disabilities. They are people created in God's image, possessing dignity, value, and purpose.

The church must extend open arms of invitation and fellowship. Those with mental disabilities can respond to the presence of the Holy Spirit. Paul reported the answer he received when he asked that his thorn in the flesh be removed: "[The Lord] said to me, 'My grace is sufficient for you, for my power is made perfect in weakness'"(2 Corinthians 12:9). We can trust God to reveal His power through the weakness of those with disabilities.

Frequently Asked Questions About Ministry to People With Disabilities

1. What is a disability?

A disability is a physical or mental impairment that substantially limits one or more of the major life activities of an individual. Disabling conditions come in countless forms and have many causes. Those causes include, but are not restricted to: birth, sickness and disease, the violence of others, accidents, sin and satanic activity, and the infirmities of advancing age. Disability is distinct from sickness and disease. Sickness and disease can often result in disabilities, but not all disabilities are caused by sickness and disease.

2. How did disability originate?

God established His authority over Adam and the rest of the human family by giving Adam one restriction: "'You must not eat from the tree of the knowledge of good and evil, for when you eat of it you will surely die'" (Genesis 2:17). Imperfection, pain, sorrow, and suffering came when Adam and Eve became subject to death (Genesis 3:7–24).

Prior to the disobedience of Adam and Eve, God had declared His entire creation to be very good—exceedingly suitable (Genesis 1:31). That divine declaration not only described the status of His creation, but serves also as an indicator of His benevolent intent for His children. It was never God's original purpose to fill the days of His children with difficult circumstances, including disabilities.

3. Why does God allow suffering?

Pain, suffering, and death are more than simply penalty for the sinful acts of Adam and Eve. The presence of suffering in the world is a witness to the integrity and holiness of God. He is indeed not a man that He should lie (Numbers 23:19). Suffering is essential so we may understand that the world we live in is not the same one that God declared to be perfect in Genesis 1:31. It has been violated and violently altered as a result of the sin of humankind (Genesis 3:17–19). The healthiest human being lives in a marred body. The healthiest human being is still appointed once to die (Hebrews 9:27). Death is the ultimate universal disability, and its presence in the world points us to the Cross. Living in marred bodies in a marred creation declares sinful humankind's need for God's plan of redemption through Jesus Christ (Romans 8:20–22). The good news is that God promises us that earthly suffering is temporary (2 Corinthians 4:17,18; Romans 8:18).

4. How does God view people with disabilities?

God determines both ability and disability. Exodus 4:11 states: "The Lord said to him, 'Who gave man his mouth? Who makes him deaf or mute? Who gives him sight or makes him blind? Is it not I, the Lord?'" The word picture of God as a potter and people as the workmanship of His hands is used in both the Old and New Testaments. It implies personal involvement and attention to detail, deliberate intent, and the specific design and purpose of the potter for each individual vessel. The potter forms the clay in a way that pleases Him. People with disabilities are not damaged goods. God takes full responsibility for their existence.

5. *What is the purpose of suffering and trials?*

Trials keep us dependent on God. They drive us to pray and cause us to seek His face and His help (Hebrews 4:14–16; 1 Peter 5:6,7). Trials help our faith develop endurance and patience (James 1:2,3), and they allow God to establish a track record of His faithfulness in our lives (Psalm 37:25). They remind us that the love of Christ is constant and far greater than any problem or pain: "Who shall separate us from the love of Christ? Shall trouble or hardship or persecution or famine or nakedness or danger or sword? As it is written: 'For your sake we face death all day long; we are considered as sheep to be slaughtered.' No, in all these things we are more than conquerors through him who loved us. For I am convinced that neither death nor life, neither angels nor demons, neither the present nor the future, nor any powers, neither height nor depth, nor anything else in all creation, will be able to separate us from the love of God that is in Christ Jesus our Lord" (Romans 8:35–39).

6. *What part does sin in a person's life or a lack of faith play in the healing process?*

John 9 indicates there are times when God allows a person to have a disability so the power of God can be displayed at some point. In John 9 and Acts 3 that power came in the form of divine healing. There are other Scripture passages where God chose to display His power *through* a person's weaknesses (1 Corinthians 1:27–29; 2 Corinthians 12:9). People with the disability are the best judges of their own spiritual condition, because they are the ones the Holy Spirit will convict, if need be (John 16:8).

7. *Why doesn't God heal everyone?*

Ultimately, every Christian will experience a permanent release from all sickness, pain, and disability (1 Corinthians 15:43,54). Because of this certainty of ultimate healing, every Christian who suffers can live with hope. We know God does heal today. We serve a God who does things when the time is right (see Daniel 9:24; Galatians 4:4) and in perfect season (Ecclesiastes 3:1–8; Psalm 30:5). The timing of an individual's healing and the means of that healing are subject to God. Healing is not at the whim of individual believers. The apostle Paul wrote to the Philippians about Epaphroditus who nearly died before he was healed (Philippians 2:27). Paul wrote to Timothy about taking a little wine medicinally for his stomach and other chronic ailments (1 Timothy 5:23). The apostle Paul could not heal people at will. The Old and New Testaments show that the timing of divine healing rests with God and usually occurs as people of His choosing can be impacted for His glory, or when He deems that the purpose for the affliction or disability is fulfilled. Therefore, it is best to view healing as a divine appointment with the divine Physician.

8. What if a person is prayed for but doesn't get healed?

The physical or spiritual condition of people with disabilities should not be judged only on what our physical eyes observe. It is imperative that spiritual leaders exercise discernment when praying for people with disabilities, and not simply assume that their most pressing need is for physical healing. Likewise, those who pray should not judge the results of their prayer by what they see. They can never know, without asking, how a person has been ministered to by the Spirit of God. Remember, people with disabilities often have internal physical disorders and dysfunction. People with disabilities often experience the healing power of God, without being healed of their physical disability. For example, a young man with cerebral palsy was hit by a bus and was close to death. God healed his injuries, but not his disability. The Holy Spirit may heal spiritual or emotional problems rather than physical ones.

9. What is the most critical need in the life of a person with a disability?

Salvation from sin is the greatest need every person has. Some people with disabilities become consumed with regaining what they have lost. They equate attaining physical and mental wholeness with attaining peace and contentment. Jesus understood that soul salvation was a higher priority than physical healing or wholeness. Moments before healing a paralytic, Jesus said, "'Take heart, son; your sins are forgiven'" (Matthew 9:2).

10. What is the biblical model for reaching people with disabilities?

Christ provided an example of servanthood that took ministry beyond miracles. People with disabilities are painfully aware that their condition and circumstances often make others uncomfortable, and that their lifestyle and behavior are sometimes interpreted as being weird, abnormal, or bizarre. They are also painfully aware that, as a result, people around them are often uncomfortable. Christ's example of humility, empathy, and servanthood teaches us that the compassion of the Body must be greater than its need for comfort. Jesus took the dirt-encrusted feet of His disciples in His holy hands and washed them. The best analogy in the Bible for reaching out and touching the lives of people with disabilities is washing feet. "You call me 'Teacher' and 'Lord,' and rightly so, for that is what I am. Now that I, your Lord and Teacher, have washed your feet, you also should wash one another's feet. I have set you an example that you should do as I have done for you. I tell you the truth, no servant is greater than his master, nor is a messenger greater than the one who sent him. Now that you know these things, you will be blessed if you do them" (John 13:13–17).

---

[1]Scripture references are from the New International Version, unless otherwise noted.

[2]For a biblically based affirmation of the Assemblies of God belief in divine healing and miracles today, see position paper, "Divine Healing: an Integral Part of the Gospel."

[3]The term *disability* is sometimes used interchangeably with *handicap.* Both words refer to something that hampers, hinders, or prevents one's ability to perform a task because of mental or physical impairment through natural deterioration, chronic disease, birth defect, or traumatic injury.

[4]For further assistance in conducting ministry to people with mental and physical disabilities, contact Special Touch Ministry, Inc., P.O. Box 25, Waupaca, Wisconsin 54981. For assistance in ministry to the blind, contact the Assemblies of God National Center for the Blind, 1445 N. Boonville Ave, Springfield, MO 65802.

22
Homosexuality And The Bible

Increasing political and religious advocacy for homosexuality[1] has prompted us to restate our position on this critical issue.[2] We believe that all matters of faith and conduct must be evaluated on the basis of Holy Scripture, which is our infallible guide (2 Timothy 3:16,17). Since the Bible does speak on the subject of homosexuality, it is imperative that the Church correctly understands and articulates the truth on this important contemporary issue.

This reaffirmation of truth has become all the more urgent because writers sympathetic to the homosexual community have advanced revisionist interpretations of relevant biblical texts that are based upon biased exegesis and mistranslation. In effect, they seek to set aside almost 2,000 years of Christian biblical interpretation and ethical teachings. We believe these efforts are reflective of the conditions described in 2 Timothy 4:3, "For the time will come when men will not put up with sound doctrine. Instead, to suit their own desires, they will gather around them a great number of teachers to say what their itching ears want to hear."[3] (See also v. 4.)

It should be noted at the outset that there is absolutely no affirmation of homosexual activity found anywhere in Scripture. Rather, the consistent sexual ideal in the Bible is chastity[4] for those outside a monogamous heterosexual marriage and fidelity[5] for those inside such a marriage. There is also abundant evidence that homosexual behavior, along with illicit heterosexual behavior, is immoral and comes under the judgment of God.

We believe, in the light of biblical revelation, that the growing cultural acceptance of homosexual identity and behavior, male and female, is symptomatic of a broader spiritual disorder that threatens the family, the government, and the church. This paper is a brief exposition of salient biblical teachings on this subject.

I. Homosexual Behavior Is Sin.

Historically, homosexuality often has been defined as an emotional (psychological) or organic (physiological) problem. In recent years, some have lobbied mental health organizations to have homosexuality removed from the list of classified diagnostic pathologies, and many have come to see it as nothing more than a morally neutral personal preference or a naturally occurring aspect of human biological diversity. In making moral judgments, we must remember scriptural warnings against depending on our own reasoning or even personal experience to discern truth (Proverbs 3:5,6).

A. Homosexual behavior is sin because it is disobedient to scriptural teachings.

When God called Israel to be His people in a distinctive sense, He miraculously delivered them from Egyptian bondage. But God did more. He entered into a covenant relationship with them and provided the Law, predicated on love for God and neighbor, by which they could order their lives as a holy people. That law included specific prohibitions of homosexual practice, such as that of Leviticus 18:22: "Do not lie with a man as one lies with a woman; that is detestable." Lest the previous injunction be misunderstood, Leviticus 20:13 provides a restatement, "If a man lies with a man as one lies with a woman, both of them have done what is detestable." "Detestable," used in both verses, is a strong word that indicates divine displeasure with sin.[6]

The Christian church has historically understood that although the ceremonial provisions of the Old Testament law were no longer in effect after the atoning death of Christ, the New Testament interpretation and restatement of its moral law was. On the subject of homosexuality, both the Old and New Testaments speak with one voice. The moral prohibitions against homosexual behavior in the Old Testament are pointedly repeated in the New Testament.

To those who witnessed on a daily basis the sexual license of imperial Rome, Paul depicted the results that followed in the lives of those who rejected God and "worshiped and served created things rather than the Creator. . . . Because of this God gave them over to shameful lusts. Even their women exchanged natural relations[7] for unnatural ones. In the same way men also abandoned natural relations[8] with women and were inflamed with lust for one another. Men committed indecent acts[9] with other men, and received in themselves the due penalty for their perversion" (Romans 1:25–27). Paul is referring to both male homosexuality and lesbianism.

In Paul's day, the city of Corinth was especially notorious for sexual immorality. It was not only a crossroads of commerce, but of all kinds of vice. Because the church was being established in this city, it was important that new Christians come to understand God's moral order. The record is explicit. Paul wrote, "Do you not know that the wicked will not inherit the kingdom of God?" Then he continued, "Do not be deceived: Neither the sexually immoral[10] nor idolaters nor adulterers nor male prostitutes nor homosexual offenders . . . will inherit the kingdom of God" (1 Corinthians 6:9,10). In this case, Paul is understood to identify male homosexuals in both active and passive homosexual behavioral roles.[11]

Paul wrote, "Law is not made for a righteous man, but for those who are lawless and rebellious, for the ungodly and sinners, for the unholy and profane, for those who kill their fathers or mothers, for murderers and immoral men and homosexuals[12] . . . " (1 Timothy 1:9,10, NASB[13]).

An unbiased study of these passages makes it clear that Scripture consistently identifies homosexual behavior as sin. Not only do the Scriptures condemn more flagrant examples of homosexual violence and promiscuity, they also provide no support for the popular modern idea that loving and committed homosexual relationships between two long-term partners are morally acceptable. Homosexual activities of every kind are contrary to the moral commandments God has given us.

B. Homosexual behavior is sin because it is contrary to God's created order for the family and human relationships.

The first chapter of the Bible says, "So God created man in his own image, in the image of God he created him; male and female he created them" (Genesis 1:27). After God had created the male, He indicated it was not good for him to live alone (Genesis 2:18). So God created a companion for him (Genesis 2:18). It should be noted that the male's aloneness was not to be remedied by the creation of another male but by the creation of a female. God created two sexes, not just one, and each for the other.

When God brought the woman to Adam, he said, "This is now bone of my bones and flesh of my flesh; she shall be called 'woman,' for she was taken out of man." Scripture then states, "For this reason a man will leave his father and mother and be united to his wife, and they will become one flesh" (Genesis 2:23,24).

In creating humankind God established the order of sexuality by which the race was to develop. Psychologically, the relationship is sound. Physically, the relationship is natural. Sociologically, it establishes the foundation for the family. The biblical order for human sexual expression is that of an intimate physical relationship to be shared exclusively within a lifelong marriage covenant—a heterosexual and monogamous relationship.

When people choose to engage in homosexual behavior, they depart from the God-given nature of sexuality. Their unnatural sexual behavior is a sin against God, who established the order of sexuality (Romans 1:27). And the social unit they seek to establish is contrary to the divine instruction for the man to leave father and mother and be "united to his wife" (Genesis 2:24).

In Jesus' discussion with the Pharisees, He reiterated the order of sexuality that God established in the beginning: "Haven't you read . . . that at the beginning the Creator 'made them male and female,' and said, 'For this reason a man will leave his father and mother and be united to his wife, and the two will become one flesh'?" (Matthew 19:4,5). He pointed out that the only alternative to heterosexual marriage is celibacy for the kingdom of heaven's sake (Matthew 19:10–12).

C. Homosexual behavior is sin that comes under divine judgment.

The name of the ancient city of Sodom[14] has become a synonym for homosexual behavior. While other evils existed in this community, sodomy was prominent. The homosexuals of Sodom were so depraved that they threatened homosexual rape of Lot's guests. "Bring them ["the men who came to you"] out to us so that we can have sex[15] with them," Lot was told (Genesis 19:5). The biblical record indicates that the mob became violent and tried to break down the door of Lot's house. Only divine intervention spared Lot and his household from their evil intentions, and God subsequently destroyed both Sodom and the neighboring city of Gomorrah (Genesis 19:4–11,24,25).

God's punishment of these cities was of such severity that it is used as an illustration of divine judgment by both Peter (2 Peter 2:6) and Jude (7). Jude's commentary is particularly apt, "In a similar way, Sodom and Gomorrah and the surrounding towns gave themselves up to sexual immorality and perversion. They serve as an example of those who suffer the punishment of eternal fire."

The Book of Judges (19:1–30) records an incident in the ancient Benjamite city of Gibeah that has many similarities to the sin of Sodom. Certain "wicked men of the city" (19:22) sought to force a visiting Levite male into homosexual acts[16] with them. Denied their insistent requests, the attackers finally settled for vicious sexual abuse and gang-rape[17] of the Levite's concubine that resulted in her death (19:25–30). The other tribes of Israel found the crime so repugnant that when the tribe of Benjamin refused to surrender the offenders, they eventually went to war—decimating the Benjamites (20:1-48).

These are particularly notorious examples of homosexual expression that undoubtedly most homosexual persons today would repudiate. It should be understood that while expressing abhorrence at such rapacious perversion, the biblical writers do not imply that heterosexuals are not capable of sexual atrocities nor that every homosexual is as depraved as the residents of those ancient cities. Nor should modern Christians draw those implications. It is important to note, however, that wherever homosexuality occurs in the biblical record it is an occasion of scandal and judgment. Homosexuality is never viewed in a positive light.

The biblical writers make it clear that practicing homosexuals, along with sexually immoral heterosexuals and all other unrepentant sinners, will not inherit the kingdom of God (1 Corinthians 6:9,10). Paul also described homosexual conduct as one evidence of God's judgment for humankind's corporate rebellion against Him (Romans 1:26,27). Jesus himself was explicit that at the end of the age "the Son of Man will send out his angels, and they will weed out of his kingdom everything that causes sin and all who do evil. They will throw them into the fiery furnace, where there will be weeping and gnashing of teeth" (Matthew 13:40–42).

II. Homosexual Behavior Is Sin For Which Reconciliation Is Possible.

While Scripture makes it clear homosexual behavior is sin and comes under the judgment of God, it also indicates that those who are guilty of homosexual behavior or any other sin can be reconciled to God (2 Corinthians 5:17–21).

In the church at Corinth were former homosexuals who had been delivered from the power of sin by the grace of God. In 1 Corinthians 6:9, Paul listed homosexuals along with immoral heterosexuals as those who cannot inherit the kingdom of God. His grammar implies continuing sexually immoral activity until their conversion. Verse 11 follows with a powerful contrast, "And that is what some of you were. But you were washed, you were sanctified, you were justified in the name of the Lord Jesus Christ and by the Spirit of our God." They had been homosexuals in orientation and behavior, but now through the power of God's Spirit their lives were radically transformed.

Scripture makes clear that the efficacy of the death and resurrection of Christ is unlimited for those who accept it. There is no stain of sin so dark that it cannot be cleansed. John the Baptist announced, "Look, the Lamb of God, who takes away the sin of the world!" (John 1:29).

The apostle Paul wrote, "God made him who had no sin to be sin for us, so that in him we might become the righteousness of God." (2 Corinthians 5:21).

The apostle John wrote, "If we confess our sins, he is faithful and just and will forgive us our sins and purify us from all unrighteousness" (1 John 1:9).

Through the regenerating power of the Holy Spirit, people, regardless of the nature of their sin, can be made new creations in Christ Jesus (2 Corinthians 5:17). God's plan of salvation is the same for all. The homosexual who wants to be delivered from the penalty and power of sin must come to God in the same way all sinners must come to God, in the same way all who are now His children have come for deliverance from their sins.

The act of turning to God for salvation includes both repentance and faith. Jesus is both Savior and Lord. He is the one who forgives our sin as we believe in Him and repent. Repentance represents a change of mind in which there is a turning from sin in both attitude and behavior.

Jesus is also the One whose lordship we affirm in holy living. "It is God's will that you should be sanctified: that you should avoid sexual immorality; that each of you should learn to control his own body in a way that is holy and honorable, not in passionate lust like the heathen, who do not know God" (1 Thessalonians 4:3-5).

Like the Philippian jailer who asked what he had to do to be saved, those desiring salvation must believe in the Lord Jesus Christ (Acts 16:30,31)—believe that He can save from the power as well as the penalty of sin. Obedient faith, like repentance, is a condition of salvation.

III. A Word to the Church.

Of fundamental importance for every individual, including those who struggle with homosexual temptation or behavior, is the need for reconciliation with God through His Son Jesus Christ.

Believers who struggle with homosexual temptations must be encouraged and strengthened by fellow Christians (Galatians 6:1,2). Likewise, they should be taught that temptation is universal, that temptation itself is not sin, and that temptation can be resisted and overcome (1 Corinthians 10:13; Hebrews 12:1–6).

The moral imperatives of Scripture are incumbent upon all persons. However, believers should not be surprised that unbelievers do not honor God and do not recognize the Bible as a rightful claim on their lives and conduct (1 Corinthians 1:18). Peter writes clearly of the conflict and contrast between believer and unbeliever in his first letter:

> Therefore, since Christ suffered in his body, arm yourselves also with the same attitude, because he who has suffered in his body is done with sin. As a result, he does not live the rest of his earthly life for evil human desires, but rather for the will of God. For you have spent enough time in the past doing what pagans choose to do—living in debauchery, lust, drunkenness, orgies, carousing and

detestable idolatry. They think it strange that you do not plunge with them into the same flood of dissipation, and they heap abuse on you. But they will have to give account to him who is ready to judge the living and the dead (1 Peter 4:1–5).

As Christians we must both exhort believers to live in moral purity and express in word and deed Christ's love for the lost. Aware of the claims of God on every aspect of our lives, we must emphasize that we are called to holiness. To unbelievers we must reach out with compassion and humility. We must hold no malice toward, or fear of, homosexuals—such attitudes are not of Christ. At the same time we must not condone sexual behavior God has defined as sinful.

Christians should also do all they can to assist the person who has struggled with homosexual behaviors to find deliverance. Change is not always easy but it is possible. It may require the help of others in the body of Christ, such as counselors and pastors, as well as a supportive church fellowship. Christian organizations are also available to help those who seek to change their lifestyles.

We desire all to be reconciled to God—to experience the peace and joy that stems from the forgiveness of sin through a personal relationship with Jesus Christ. God does not want any to perish in their sins; He invites all to accept His offer of eternal life (John 3:16). As part of His church, we issue that invitation to life in Christ to everyone.

---

[1]The term *homosexuality* is frequently used to describe both *orientation* and *behavior.* In this paper, homosexual *orientation* is understood to mean sexual attraction to other members of the same sex. Homosexual *behavior* is understood to mean participation in same-sex genital acts. Homosexual orientation may pose temptations to lustful thinking and behavior, like heterosexual temptations, that are not necessarily acted

upon and that may be resisted and overcome in the power of the Holy Spirit. Only homosexual lust and homosexual behaviors are understood in this study to be sinful.

[2]This paper is a revision of a position paper issued in 1979. Since that time revisionist interpretations of crucial biblical passages bearing on this subject have been widely circulated and debated.

[3]All biblical citations are from the New International Version unless otherwise noted.

[4]Here meaning to refrain from illicit sexual activity.

[5]Here meaning sexual faithfulness and exclusivity in marriage.

[6]The Hebrew word found here, *to'ebah,* is also used in this chapter of Leviticus for various abominable sexual practices of Israel's pagan neighbors (18:26,27,29,30). Elsewhere in the Old Testament it denotes such repugnant practices as idolatry, human sacrifice, and witchcraft. See R. Laird Harris, Gleason L. Archer, and Bruce K. Waltke, eds., *Theological Wordbook of the Old Testament* (Chicago, Moody Press, 1980), 2:976–77. It is not uncommon for revisionists to attempt to explain away the plain meaning of the text by assuming the homosexual acts to be judged wrong only because they were associated with pagan religious practices forbidden to Israel. However, nothing in the passages cited supports this interpretation and the fact that homosexual practice is implicitly or explicitly condemned wherever it appears in the biblical text negates this interpretation.

[7]"[N]atural intercourse," New Revised Standard Version (NRSV); Greek *chresis* has to do with sexual intercourse in such contexts. See *A Greek-English Lexicon of the New Testament and other Early Christian Literature,* 3rd edition, revised and edited by Frederick William Danker (Chicago: University of Chicago Press, 2000), 1089.

[8]Ibid.

[9]Greek *aschemosyne,* "shameless deed." See *A Greek-English Lexicon of the New Testament and Other Early Christian Literature,* 147.

[10]It is important to note that Scripture is even-handed in condemning heterosexual sins as well. Along with homosexuality, the apostle Paul includes such heterosexual sins as adultery, fornication, and prostitution. (See also such passages as Gal. 5:19–21 and 1 Tim. 1:10.) The Assemblies of God stands against all sexual immorality, heterosexual or

homosexual, and calls all participants to repentance.

[11]"[M]ale prostitutes" is translated from the Greek plural of *malakos;* "homosexual offenders" is translated from the plural of *arsenokoites.* The terms are defined respectively as "the passive male partner in sexual intercourse" and "the male partner in sexual intercourse" in Johannes P. Louw and Eugene A. Nida, eds., *Greek-English Lexicon of the New Testament Based on Semantic Domains.* Second Edition (New York: United Bible Societies; 1988, 1989) 1:772. See also the respective entries in *A Greek-English Lexicon of the New Testament and Other Early Christian Literature.*

[12]Plural of *arsenokoites.*

[13]New American Standard Bible.

[14]Some modern interpreters claim that Sodom was condemned in Scripture only for its general wickedness, not for a reputation of pervasive homosexual behavior. They also conclude from Heb. 13:2 ("some people have entertained angels without knowing it") and Matt. 10:14,15 ("shake the dust off your feet when you leave that home or town") that the sin of Sodom was nothing more than inhospitality. It is further claimed that even if the references to Sodom describe homosexual behavior, it is actually male rape, not consensual homosexual relations, that are denounced. While the Genesis account does not answer all our questions, it is clear from the story itself and the many references in both Testaments that promiscuous and violent homosexuality is in view.

[15]"[H]ave sex" is in this context an accurate translation of the Hebrew *yada',* which means "to know" but is frequently used as a euphemism for sexual intercourse (see Genesis 4:1, NRSV). The word is also used to denote sodomy (Gen. 19:5; Judg. 19:22) and rape (Judg. 19:25). See *Theological Wordbook of the Old Testament,* 1:366.

[16]Hebrew *yada'.* See previous note.

[17]Hebrew *yada'.* See previous notes.

23
Apostles And Prophets

Modern church statisticians cite the phenomenal growth of the Pentecostal movement and report that Pentecostals and charismatics now make up the second largest Christian group in the world. Pentecostals stand in awe of what God has done and attribute such amazing expansion to their simple trust in the supernatural power of the Holy Spirit, which continues to be at work in the church today.

The rapid advance of the Pentecostal revival has also been accompanied by a new openness to the gifts of the Spirit. The evangelical world increasingly has turned from cessationism, the belief gifts of the Spirit ceased at the end of the New Testament era, to an understanding that New Testament gifts of the Holy Spirit are vital for ministry today.

With the restoration of the miraculous gifts to the Church has also come the question of whether God is restoring the five-fold ministry of Ephesians 4:11: "It was he who gave some to be apostles, some to be prophets, some to be evangelists, and some to be pastors and teachers."[1] Bible scholars differ on whether the gifts of pastor and teacher are separate in Ephesians 4 (yielding a total of five), or whether a better translation might be " . . . and some to be pastor-teachers" (yielding a total of four). Greek grammar would seem to dictate four, but the New Testament often discusses pastoral and teaching roles separately. However, the best designation for ministry is neither fivefold nor fourfold but manifold. Ephesians 4:12 gives to all saints the work of ministry, while 1 Corinthians 12:28–30 and Romans 12:6–8 provide aspects of ministry beyond the designations in Ephesians 4:11,12.

Relatively few questions are raised about the validity of contemporary evangelists, pastors, and teachers. However, there are a number of voices in the church today calling for the restoration of apostles and prophets, thinking these offices are the key to continued growth and vitality. The issue is important, and this paper is an effort to seek scriptural guidance.

The Apostolic Church

Some advocate the recognition of contemporary apostles and use the term *apostolic*. They believe church bodies that do so have moved closer to the New Testament ideal of ministry.

Historically, the adjective *apostolic* has been used to signify (1) church bodies that attempt to trace a succession of their clergy back to the original 12 apostles, as do the Catholic and Episcopal churches; (2) Oneness, or Jesus-Only, Pentecostal churches, who since the early 20th century have used the description "Apostolic Faith" (previously used by Trinitarian Pentecostals such as Charles F. Parham and William J. Seymour) to designate their distinctive doctrines; (3) churches that claim God has raised up present-day apostles in their midst ("New Apostolic" and "Fivefold" churches); or (4) churches, including most Protestant groups, that claim to be apostolic because they teach what the apostles taught; that is, New Testament doctrine. Therefore, most Christian denominations think of themselves, in one sense or another, as apostolic.

Pentecostal churches believe they are apostolic because they teach what the apostles taught, and (2) they share in the power of the apostles through the baptism in and fullness of the Holy Spirit, who empowers their lives and ministries. They believe what matters is not a contemporary apostolic office but apostolic doctrine and power.

The New Testament Apostles

The origin of the apostolic office is traced in the Gospels to Jesus. The Gospel of Mark reads, "[Jesus] appointed twelve—designating them apostles—that they might be with him and that he might send them out to preach and to have authority to drive out demons" (Mark 3:14,15). Matthew and Luke contain similar attributions (cf. Matthew 10:2; Luke 6:13). The number 12 seems to have had significance, so the most common title for this group in the Gospels is "the Twelve" rather than "the Apostles" (cf. Matthew 26:14,20,47; Mark 4:10; 6:7; 9:35; Luke 8:1; 9:1; 18:31; John 6:67; 20:24). The designation "the Twelve" also continued in the life of the Early Church through the writings of Luke (Acts 6:2) and the apostle Paul (1 Corinthians 15:5). In addition, Jesus himself is called by the writer to the Hebrews "the apostle and high priest whom we confess" (Hebrews 3:1).

The word *apostle* comes from the Greek *apostolos*[2] and may be translated by such terms as *delegate, envoy, messenger,* or *agent*.[3] Since Jesus probably spoke Hebrew or Aramaic rather than Greek, it is possible the Hebrew/Aramaic *shaliach* also means much the same as *apostolos*. This is the actual word used by Jesus and His earliest followers and provides much of the conceptual background. The rabbis of Jesus' day regarded it as an important legal principle: "A man's agent *(shaliach)* is like unto himself."[4] This meant if a man's agent made a deal, it was the same as the man himself making the deal. The modern concept of power of attorney is very similar.

When it comes to apostles or other kinds of agents, it is of crucial importance whom the agent represents. The Gospels make it clear the apostles were appointed by Jesus to act on His behalf. Mark's tersely stated record of their initial commission is "that they might be with him and that he might send them out to preach and to have authority to drive out demons" (Mark 3:14,15). It has to do with personal fellowship with Jesus, preaching the good news of the kingdom of God on Jesus' behalf, and participation in the power of Jesus to cast out demons. Jesus apparently sent them out early in the Galilean ministry with instructions to preach and heal the sick (cf. Matthew 10:5–14; Mark 6:7–11; Luke 9:1–5). Like the Seventy dispatched later, their immediate scope of ministry was to "the lost sheep of Israel" (Matthew 10:6).

The Apostles and Pentecost

The commission of the Twelve was dramatically expanded following the death and resurrection of Jesus. In John's Gospel, Jesus anticipated that those who had faith in Him would do "greater things" than He had done by asking in His name (John 14:12–14). The Counselor, identified as the Holy Spirit and the Spirit of truth, who was "with" them during the time of His earthly ministry, would soon be "in" them (14:16,17). The Spirit would also teach them all things and remind them of everything He had said to them (14:26). John noted that Jesus appeared to the "disciples" after His resurrection and said, "'As the Father has sent me, I am sending you.' And with that he breathed on them and said, 'Receive the Holy Spirit. If you forgive anyone his sins, they are forgiven; if you do not forgive them, they are not forgiven'" (John 20:21–23). Luke makes it clear Jesus "opened" the minds of "the Eleven and those with them" (24:33) to "understand the Scriptures" to the end that "the Christ [would] suffer and rise from the dead on the third day, and repentance and forgiveness of sins [would] be preached in his name to all nations, beginning at Jerusalem" (Luke 24:45–47). Jesus then reminded the disciples they were "to stay in the city [i.e., Jerusalem] until [they had] been clothed with power from on high" (24:49).

This promise was so important that Luke recorded it again in Acts 1:4 with an explanatory word from Jesus: "For John baptized with water, but in a few days you will be baptized with the Holy Spirit" (1:5). The reason for the promise is couched in Jesus' words, "But you will receive power when the Holy Spirit comes on you; and you will be my witnesses in Jerusalem, and in all Judea and Samaria, and to the ends of the earth" (Acts 1:8). The promise was fulfilled in the descent of the Spirit at Pentecost (Acts 2:4) and identified in Peter's prophetic message as the "last days" gift of God's Spirit enabling all his "sons," "daughters," and "servants, both men and women" to "prophesy" (Acts 2:14–17).

Although earlier trained, called, and commissioned by the Lord Jesus, the apostles needed the baptism in the Holy Spirit as the final preparation for their mission. They were granted spiritual giftings and empowerment required for the apostolic office. Previously anxious and insecure, they were transformed and energized by the Holy Spirit.[5]

The apostles began to speak as those who were "filled with the Holy Spirit" (Acts 4:8) and were instrumental in others receiving the gift of the Spirit (8:14–17; 10:44–46; 19:6). When Paul was converted and called to apostolic ministry, he also received the gift of the Spirit and was similarly transformed (9:17). Barnabas was said to be "full of the Holy Spirit and faith" (11:24). The Holy Spirit guided the mission activities of the apostles, sovereignly selecting Paul and Barnabas (13:2) and sending them on their way (13:4). Later the Spirit prevented Paul and his companions from entering the province of Asia and Bythinia but directed them toward Troas and Macedonia (16:6–10). Paul was the recipient of prophetic guidance by Spirit-directed prophets as to his fate upon his return to Jerusalem (20:22,23). Whatever the natural ability of these early apostles, the genius of their ministry is found in the power and wisdom of the Spirit given to them.

The Place of the Twelve

The opening chapter of Acts reflects a concern to maintain the number of the Twelve. Peter and the other members of the original Twelve, with the 120, looked to the Scriptures and determined that the vacancy created by the defection and death of Judas should be filled. It was important that the full complement of 12 be maintained for the effusion of the Spirit. Luke had previously recorded the promise of Jesus to the Twelve: "I confer on you a kingdom, just as my Father conferred one on me, so that you may eat and drink at my table in my kingdom and sit on thrones, judging the twelve tribes of Israel" (Luke 22:29,30). The importance of maintaining 12 apostles as a symbol of the 12 tribes of Israel is unmistakable. The apostolate was to be intact for the coming of the Spirit and the launching of a fully equipped church on its worldwide mission.

The way the vacancy was filled is highly instructive. Jesus had personally appeared and given "instructions through the Holy Spirit to the apostles he had chosen" (Acts 1:2). Two qualifying issues stand out: (1) personal commissioning by the Lord, and (2) thorough familiarity with the teachings of Jesus. Careful attention was given to both in Peter's proposal. Any candidate had to have been with them for Jesus' entire ministry, "beginning from John's baptism" (Acts 1:22). Two qualified candidates, "Joseph called Barsabbas (also known as Justus) and Matthias," were presented and prayer was offered. "Then they cast lots, and the lot fell to Matthias; so he was added to the eleven apostles" (Acts 1:26).[6] After Pentecost, however, there was no effort to replace any of the original 12 apostles nor to perpetuate the number 12 (cf. Acts 12:2).

The Special Case of the Apostle Paul

Paul's status as an apostle is unique. He was neither a member of the Twelve nor present for Christ's post-Resurrection appearances; his calling as an apostle came in a later and separate vision of the risen Lord. Recorded three times in Acts (9:1–19; 22:4–16; 26:9–18) and often intimated in his letters (Galatians 1:12), the account of Paul's conversion demonstrates the authenticity and power of his call to be an apostle of Jesus Christ. Like the Twelve, he recognized the apostolic office was conferred in the personal call of Christ through post-Resurrection appearances (1 Corinthians 15:5–7). Paul acknowledged he was "as . . . one abnormally born [*ektroma*[7]]" (1 Corinthians 15:8). The word is usually used for miscarriages. But rather than Paul saying he was "born" unnaturally early, he is saying that as a witness to the Resurrection and as an apostle he was "born" unnaturally late. His apostolic calling was thus without parallel and made his credentials vulnerable to attack from enemies who sought to discredit him (1 Corinthians 9:1,2; 2 Corinthians 12:11,12).

Despite the unusual nature of his encounter with Christ, Paul did not consider his apostolic status to be less than that of the other apostles. They had seen the resurrected Lord; so had he. He regularly appealed to his having seen "Jesus our Lord" (1 Corinthians 9:1). While he referred to himself as "the least of the apostles," apparently because of his earlier persecution of the Church, he "worked harder than all of them" (1 Corinthians 15:9,10). Though insisting on a continuity of the message (cf. 1 Corinthians 15:3), he nonetheless distinguished his apostolic authority from the other apostles, even to the point of a public rebuke to Peter (Galatians 1:11 to 2:21). To his critics at Corinth he pointed out, "I do not think I am in the least inferior to those 'super-apostles'"[8] (2 Corinthians 11:5; 12:11) and rehearsed his Jewish heritage (11:22), hardships (11:23–33), and his "surpassingly great revelations" (12:1–7). He reminded the Corinthians, "[T]he things that mark an apostle—signs, wonders and miracles—were done among you with great perseverance" (2 Corinthians 12:12).

Apostles of Christ

Paul's sense of his own calling is reflected in the introduction to most of his letters: "Paul . . . an apostle of Christ Jesus" (1 Corinthians 1:1; cf. 2 Corinthians 1:1; Galatians 1:1; Ephesians 1:1; Colossians 1:1, et al.). The letters of Peter begin similarly: "Peter, an apostle of Jesus Christ" (1 Peter 1:1; cf. 2 Peter 1:1). Paul used this designation in the text of 1 Thessalonians: "As apostles of Christ we could have been a burden to you . . . " (2:6). Jude 17 refers to what "the apostles of our Lord Jesus Christ foretold." These references make it appear that the title "apostle of Christ (Jesus Christ/Lord Jesus Christ/Christ Jesus)" was standard nomenclature for all the apostles Christ had personally appeared to and appointed. It is almost always this group to whom the title "apostle" is applied in the New Testament.

Apostles of the Churches

Scholars occasionally point out a distinction between the

"Apostles of Christ" and the "Apostles of the Churches."[9] Paul spoke of unnamed "brothers" who are "representatives *[apostoloi]* of the churches and an honor to Christ" (2 Corinthians 8:23). He also wrote to the Philippians about "Epaphroditus . . . who is also your messenger *[apostolon],* whom you sent to take care of my needs" (2:25). These references provide ample evidence the early churches did use the word *apostle* from time to time for other than those who had witnessed the Resurrection. However, the term is used in these cases in its generic sense of dispatching representatives on an official mission on behalf of the senders. For that reason, English translations of the Bible normally render the word *apostolos* in the two instances above as "messenger" or "representative."[10]

False Apostles

Not all persons in the New Testament era who called themselves apostles or were accorded that status by star-struck followers were, in fact, apostles. Just as the Old Testament had its false prophets, so the New Testament had its false apostles. Much of Paul's second letter to the Corinthians reflects this very issue. Teachers, possibly itinerant Hellenistic Jews from the church at Jerusalem, had come to Corinth apparently with letters of commendation. They seem to have boasted of equality with, or even superiority to, Paul in an effort to wrest the leadership of the church away from him. Thus his references to such issues as "letters of recommendation" (2 Corinthians 3:1), his appearance and speech (10:10), "the one who commends himself" (10:18), his Jewish heritage (11:22), his extensive suffering on behalf of the church (11:23–33), and his visions and revelations (12:7)—all seem to have been an effort to deal with the threat.

Paul identified such people as "false apostles, deceitful

workmen, masquerading as apostles of Christ" (2 Corinthians 11:13). Jesus himself commended the church in Ephesus because they "tested those who claim to be apostles but are not, and have found them false" (Revelation 2:2). These references and others make it clear that many who either claimed for themselves the title of "apostle" or had the title wrongly conferred upon them by others were circulating among the early Christian churches. Discernment was necessary. Paul called for careful evaluation of spiritual phenomena: "Do not put out the Spirit's fire; do not treat prophecies with contempt. Test everything. Hold on to the good" (1 Thessalonians 5:19–21).

Apostolic Succession

A crucial issue is whether the apostolic office is to be passed on as an institutionalized office of the church. It is clear from both Acts and the letters of the New Testament that certain offices were instituted and maintained. For example, the apostles led the church in the selection of seven men, often called "deacons" though that noun is not in the text, to administer the charitable ministries of the church (Acts 6:3). Early in the Acts record the Church, probably operating with familiar Jewish models, is observed to have elders who are functioning in leadership roles along with the apostles (Acts 11:30; 15:2; 16:4). As Paul and Silas established missionary churches, they were careful to appoint "elders" *(presbyteros)* for the leadership of those churches (Acts 14:23). Paul also summoned "elders" *(presbyteros)* of the church at Ephesus and then addressed them as "overseers" *(episkopos)* who were also to be "shepherds" *(poimaino)*, or "pastors," of the church of God (Acts 20:17,28).

The letter to the church at Philippi indicates the presence of "overseers" *(episkopos)* and "deacons" *(diakonos)* among them. The pastoral letters, usually assumed to have been written somewhat later, reveal great concern for the appointment of carefully qualified elders/overseers and deacons (1 Timothy 3:1–12; Titus 1:3–9). As can be seen, the names for the office are somewhat flexible and interchangeable. Nevertheless, it is certainly accurate to say the New Testament provides—by such names, qualifications, and selection—for the careful appointment and continuation in office of such leaders as overseers, elders, and deacons.

It is also clear that while the apostles (with the elders) were established leaders in the Early Church, there was no provision for their replacement or continuation. To be sure, with the defection of Judas from his apostolic office, the Eleven sought divine guidance to fill the gap. Other apostles also emerged, including Paul who in his first letter to the Corinthians gave insight into their selection. After Christ's resurrection He appeared to the Twelve and later appeared to more than "five hundred of the brothers at the same time. . . . Then he appeared to James, then to *all the apostles,* and last of all he appeared to me also, as to one abnormally born" (1 Corinthians 15:6–8, emphasis added). Thus Paul seems to limit the office of apostle to those who had actually seen the risen Lord in the 40 days after His resurrection and to himself as having seen Him in a dramatic vision on the road to Damascus (Acts 9:1–9). There is some uncertainty about the exact number and identity of the apostles. However, besides the Twelve, the New Testament text appears to clearly designate such persons as Paul, James the brother of Jesus (1 Corinthians 15:7; Galatians 1:19), Barnabas (Acts 14:14), Andronicus and Junias (probably a woman) who were "outstanding among the apostles" (Romans 16:7).

It is instructive, however, that nowhere in the New Testament after the replacement of Judas is any attention given to a so-called apostolic succession. No attempt was made to replace James son of Zebedee (John's brother), executed by Herod (Acts 12:2). Other than the original appointments by Christ himself, there is nothing concerning the appointment of apostles. And apart from the criteria set for the selection of Matthias (Acts 1:21–26) and the criteria implied in the actions of Jesus and the account of Paul (1 Corinthians 15:3–11), there are no directions for making such an appointment. By contrast, there are clear qualifications and instructions for the appointment of elders/overseers and deacons (1 Timothy 3:1–13; Titus 1:5–9). It seems strange that apostles of Jesus Christ, concerned about faithful preservation of their message (cf. 2 Timothy 2:2), would provide for the appointment of overseers/elders while ignoring their own succession if such were indeed to be maintained.

In fact, there are certain exegetical hints the apostles of Jesus Christ are not to have successors. In 1 Corinthians 15:8, Paul listed all the Resurrection and post-Resurrection appearances of Christ and noted "last of all he appeared to me." While some disagree, the statement is most commonly understood to mean Paul looked upon himself as the last apostle to whom Christ appeared.[11] If this is the correct understanding, only the Twelve whom Jesus personally called and those He commissioned in His post-Resurrection appearances made up His original apostles. Apostles are named first among the offices of the church (1 Corinthians 12:28) and the ministry gifts of Ephesians 4:11 because they are foundational, not necessarily because they are continuous leaders in the church. The Ephesians 4:11 passage must be interpreted in the context of the Ephesians letter itself, wherein Paul had already described the church as "built on the foundation of the apostles and prophets, with Christ Jesus himself as the chief cornerstone" (Ephesians 2:20), and the form of leadership instituted by Paul in the Ephesian church itself and the other churches he founded (Acts 14:23). Writing to Timothy at Ephesus, Paul entrusts the oversight of the church to "elders" (synonymous with *bishop* or *pastor* or *overseer*) and deacons, not apostles and prophets. When he bids an emotional farewell to the leaders of the Ephesian church, which he himself had established, his meeting is with the elders (not apostles or prophets), to whom he entrusts the responsibility of bishop (or overseer) and pastor (or shepherd) (Acts 20:28).

It is difficult to escape the conclusion of Dietrich Müller: "One thing is certain. The N[ew] T[estament] never betrays any understanding of the apostolate as an institutionalized church office, capable of being passed on."[12]

The Authority of the Apostles

The authority of the apostles was modeled by the chief Apostle, the Lord Jesus Christ, who taught them that "the Son of Man did not come to be served, but to serve" (Mark 10:45). Jesus, on occasion, acted sharply and decisively against certain sins, such as the desecration of His Father's house (Mark 11:15–17; John 2:13–16) and the exploitative hypocrisy of the teachers of the Law and Pharisees (Matthew 23). However, He carefully avoided the trappings of political and institutional power and modeled extraordinary humility and patience for His apostles. His divine attributes were cloaked in human flesh and He was the exposition and example of His Father's word and work.

Even a cursory reading of the New Testament demonstrates the apostles of Christ possessed authority. The Early Church was formed around their teaching, which was in turn confirmed by the "wonders and miraculous signs" they did (Acts 2:42,43). They were the recognized spokesmen before the rulers (Acts 4:8ff.), and their authority was demonstrated in such events as the death of Ananias and Sapphira (Acts 5:1–11). In writing to the Corinthians, a church he founded, Paul threatened to come to them "with a whip" (1 Corinthians 4:21) and did not hesitate to give stern directions for discipline in a case of incest (1 Corinthians 5:1–5). Writing to the church in Rome, which he did not found, he stated his apostolic credentials (Romans 1:1), assumed the prerogative of imparting to them spiritual gifts (1:11), and planned to "come in the full measure of the blessing of Christ" (15:29). He laid out for their belief and practice the most systematic exposition of doctrinal and ethical truth in all of Scripture. He did not hesitate to give directions for their local ethical dilemmas such as relations between the weak and the strong (chapters 14,15). Peter also, claiming apostolic standing, wrote authoritatively to apparently Gentile churches that he did not pioneer (1 Peter 1:1).

Some modern interpreters insist apostolic authority was merely local, not universal, and exercised only in churches the apostles founded.[13] To be sure, apostles seem to have been aware of certain protocol in churches they did not pioneer (Romans 15:20; 1 Corinthians 3:10). However, they did cross geographical boundaries. The pattern of evidence throughout the New Testament indicates their authority was universal in doctrinal and ethical matters, binding in some sense upon all the churches. However, that authority must not be construed in political or bureaucratic terms. There is little evidence of their involvement in local administrative matters.

When they worked together, one of the apostles usually took the lead, as in Peter's early activity in Jerusalem and Paul's direction of his missionary teams. However, in dealing with the practical and doctrinal problems of the churches, the apostles often exercised a shared leadership among themselves and with the elders, a group that appears to have been added quickly to the leadership rolls. For example, the Twelve called upon the church of Jerusalem to select the Seven (Acts 6). When the Jerusalem Council resolved the schismatic debate over whether the Gentiles should keep the Jewish law, the issue was decided by "the apostles and elders" (Acts 15:4,6,22). On this or some similar issue, even the two apostles Paul and Peter initially came to conflicting opinions (Galatians 2:11–14). James Dunn aptly observes, "Apostolic authority is exercised not over the Christian community, but within it; and the authority is exercised . . . 'to equip the saints for the work of their ministry, for the building up of Christ's body'" (Ephesians 4:12).[14]

Since apostles were frequently mobile, local rule in the maturing churches seems to have been exercised largely by elders. In the Jerusalem church, the apostles were the sole authority figures early on (Acts 2:42; 4:37); but perhaps because of persecution and travel, they appear to have been less prominent over time. Peter reported the conversion of Cornelius and his household to the "apostles and the brothers" (11:1). The "apostles and elders" made up the Jerusalem council (15:6). When Paul returned to Jerusalem after his third journey, he called on "James, and all the elders" (21:18). Elders were certainly key authority figures in Jerusalem, as seen in Acts, and elsewhere as seen in New Testament letters. The absence of apostles on Paul's last visit to Jerusalem (Acts 21:18) is further evidence that as the Twelve dispersed, the Jerusalem church did not provide for further apostolic replacement as they had at the defection of Judas (Acts 1:12–26).

None of the New Testament letters are addressed to an apostle, as would be expected if each city had its own ruling apostle. One of the few letters that includes church officers in the title, Philippians, is addressed to "overseers [*episkopos*] and deacons [*diakonos*]" (1:1)—not to a local or city apostle. There seems to be no concern to place recognized apostles in residence in the various churches or regions.

The Marks of an Apostle

Striving to protect the Corinthians from the seduction of "false apostles," Paul pointed out characteristics (*semeion*, "sign," 2 Corinthians 12:12) that identified a genuine apostle. From that context and the larger New Testament background, the following are apparent:

1. The first and most important mark of true apostles of Christ was that they had seen the risen Lord and been personally commissioned by Him as witnesses to His resurrection (Acts 1:21,22; 1 Corinthians 9:1; 15:7,8). They were thus appropriately called "apostles of Christ."

2. The personal call and commission of the risen Christ had to be consummated in the baptism in the Holy Spirit (Acts 2:1–4 [for Paul, see Acts 9:1–17]), at which time the spiritual gift, or *charisma*, of apostleship was granted. This understanding is reflected, for example, in Paul's statements: "It was he who gave some to be apostles . . . " (Ephesians 4:11) and "I became a servant of this gospel by the gift of God's grace given me through the working of his power" (Ephesians 3:7). The Spirit with His power and anointing set apostles first among the leaders of the church (1 Corinthians 12:28).

3. Apostles were supernaturally equipped for prophetic preaching and teaching. To illustrate, when the Spirit fell at Pentecost, the disciples spoke "in other tongues as the Spirit enabled *[apophthengomai]* them" (Acts 2:4). Confronted with the confused and contradictory opinions of the watching crowd, Peter "stood up with the Eleven, raised his voice and addressed" *(apophthengomai)* them (2:14) in a masterful explanation resulting in 3,000 conversions. The Greek verb *apoph-*

thengomai is used to denote prophetic inspiration, which in this context is the immediate result of the Spirit's enablement.[15] Paul reflected much of the same awareness: "My message and my preaching were not with wise and persuasive words, but with a demonstration of the Spirit's power" (1 Corinthians 2:4).

4. With the apostolic gift came miraculous spiritual gifts (1 Corinthians 12:8–10). "The things that mark [*semeia*, "signs"] an apostle[16]—signs, wonders and miracles—were done among you with great perseverance" (2 Corinthians 12:12). The Book of Acts attributes numerous miracles to Peter, Paul, and the other apostles (Acts 5:12; 9:32–43; 13:6–12; 14:3; 16:16–18; 19:11; 28:7–9). Paul evidently regarded such miraculous ministry as an essential mark of a true apostle. He also taught and preached among them "with a demonstration of the Spirit's power" so their "faith might not rest on men's wisdom, but on God's power" (1 Corinthians 2:4,5).

5. The apostles were the authoritative teachers of the Early Church in both belief and practice. They were charged above all with the accuracy and purity of the gospel of Jesus Christ. As Paul wrote, "For what I received I passed on to you as of first importance: that Christ died for our sins according to the Scriptures, that he was buried, that he was raised on the third day according to the Scriptures" (1 Corinthians 15:3,4; cf. Acts 2:42; Romans 16:17; Galatians 1:8; Titus 1:9). The intent of their preaching and teaching is expressed in Ephesians 4:12,13: "so that the body of Christ may be built up . . . and become mature." The apostolic doctrine became the content of the New Testament canon. The apostles were understood either to have written the canonical books or to have been the primary sources and guarantors of their inspired character.

6. Apostles were commissioned as missionaries and church builders. Those the New Testament speaks about did this suc-

cessfully. The Great Commission (Matthew 28:16–20) was given specifically to the Eleven, perhaps in the company of the "more than five hundred" (1 Corinthians 15:6). The missionary impulse breathes through the accounts of apostolic commissioning (cf. Luke 24:47; John 20:21; Acts 1:8; 9:15; 22:15; 26:17,18; Galatians 1:15–17; et al.).

7. Suffering for Christ's sake seems to have been a major mark of the apostolic office. Paul validated his ministry and armed the Corinthian church against the seduction of false apostles with a lengthy personal history of sufferings on behalf of the gospel. "That is why, for Christ's sake, I delight in weaknesses, in insults, in hardships, in persecutions, in difficulties. For when I am weak, then I am strong" (2 Corinthians 12:10). "Now I rejoice in what was suffered for you, and I fill up in my flesh what is still lacking in regard to Christ's afflictions, for the sake of his body which is the church" (Colossians 1:24).

8. Apostles were pastoral and relational. Paul's love for his parishioners and his ministry associates flows through his letters. The warm and extended greetings at the conclusion of Romans are striking (16:1–16). He repeatedly uses parenting language (cf. 1 Corinthians 4:15; 2 Corinthians 12:14,15). On behalf of the Corinthians, he is "jealous . . . with a godly jealousy" (2 Corinthians 11:2). To the Thessalonians, Paul wrote that he loved and cared for them gently as "a mother caring for her little children" (1 Thessalonians 2:7). The language in the letters of Peter (1 Peter 4:12; 2 Peter 3:1, NRSV) and John (1 John 2:7, NRSV, et al.) emphasizes the same pastoral instincts.

The New Testament Prophets

"Prophets" are found immediately after "apostles" in one list of ministry gifts (Ephesians 4:11). and their activity is closely linked to that of apostles throughout the New Testament. Paul had a high view of their role: "And in the church God has appointed first of all apostles, second prophets . . . " (1 Corinthians 12:28). Further, the church is "built on the foundation of the apostles and prophets, with Christ Jesus himself as the chief cornerstone" (Ephesians 2:20). Along with the apostles, prophets were complementary gifts to the foundational era of the church.

The historical accounts in the New Testament affirm these complementary roles. New Testament prophets first appeared by name in Acts when a group, apparently residing in Jerusalem, went to Antioch and one of their number, Agabus, accurately predicted the coming great famine (Acts 11:27–30). Antioch soon had its own group of resident prophets— Barnabas, Simeon, Lucius, Manaen, and Saul (Paul) (Acts 13:1). Two other Jerusalem leaders and prophets were chosen to bear the council letter to Antioch, Syria, and Cilicia, and along the way "said much to encourage and strengthen the brothers" (Acts 15:22,32). On Paul's return to Jerusalem after the third missionary journey, he stayed at the house of Philip the evangelist, who "had four unmarried daughters who prophesied," and we learn women were active and recognized as prophets. At that time Agabus made his way down from Jerusalem to Caesarea and prophesied that the Jews of Jerusalem would bind Paul and hand him over to the Gentiles (Acts 21:10,11).

Paul's letters, written earlier than the Book of Acts, indicate the presence of prophets in the churches he had established as well as those he did not (e.g., the church at Rome). For example, he provided instruction on their activities in Corinth (1 Corinthians 14:29–32), saying their prophecies were to be tested by apostolic doctrine (1 Corinthians 14:37). Women prophets were active in the church at Corinth (1 Corinthians 11:5,6). The Romans were to exercise the gift of prophecy "in proportion" to their faith (Romans 12:6). The Thessalonians were cautioned not to "treat prophecies with contempt" (1 Thessalonians 5:20). The Ephesians letter stated Paul's understanding that, with the apostles, the prophets were foundational to the church (Ephesians 2:20). In that capacity they were, with the apostles, recipients of divinely given revelation (Ephesians 3:5) and a ministry gift to the church (Ephesians 4:11). To Timothy, Paul noted a prophetic message had accompanied the laying on of hands by the elders (1 Timothy 4:14).

The Book of Revelation is apparently to be understood as a prophecy, thus according John prophetic status (Revelation 1:3). Revelation also says the church was to be on guard against false prophets, in this case "Jezebel," who by their teaching and conduct perverted the apostolic gospel (Revelation 2:20).

These accounts make clear that (1) there were recognized groups of prophets in the early churches often closely associated with the apostles; (2) the apostles themselves (as Barnabas, Silas [both of whom on occasion appear to be recognized as apostles], Saul [Paul], and John) also functioned as prophets (Acts 13:1; 15:32; Revelation 1:3); (3) these prophets did travel on occasion from church to church; (4) both men and women were recognized as prophets; (5) prophets, while never appointed to ruling functions in their capacity as prophets like overseers/elders, did exercise spiritual influence with the apostles and elders in the belief and practice of the Early Church; (6) the integrity of the prophet was maintained by authentic inspired utterance that was true to the Scriptures and apostolic doctrine; and (7) there is no provision for qualifying or appointing prophets as a part of a church leadership hierarchy for succeeding generations.

The Gift of Prophecy

While there were recognized prophets in the New Testament era, even more pervasive was the gift of prophecy that energized the apostolic church. The Old Testament prophet Joel, moved by God, prophesied, "I will pour out my Spirit on all people. Your sons and daughters will prophesy, your old men will dream dreams, your young men will see visions. Even on my servants, both men and women, I will pour out my Spirit in those days" (Joel 2:28,29). Significantly, Peter, when explaining the Pentecost event and its evidential tongues, identified them with Joel's prediction of the outpouring of the Spirit and twice repeated that both sons and daughters, men and women, would prophesy (Acts 2:17,18). Peter's sermon was clearly a prophecy immediately inspired by the Spirit, as the verb "addressed *[apophthengomai]*" (Acts 2:14), which means "to speak as a prophet,"[17] denotes. When one examines closely the witness to Christ given by the early Christian leaders in Acts, the prophetic impulse is apparent—and doubtlessly intended by Luke. Peter's words to the crippled beggar (Acts 3:6), the temple crowds (Acts 3:12ff.), the Sanhedrin (Acts 4:8), and Ananias and Sapphira (Acts 5:1–11), to list a few, are filled with prophetic import. Stephen's eloquence and power are prophetic (Acts 7). The impact of the preaching of Philip (Acts 8:4–8) and other unnamed believers (Acts 11:19–21) was likewise Spirit-enabled. And so it is throughout the Acts account.

While it is too much to say every utterance of a believer is a prophecy, nonetheless, the theme of Acts is that every believer receives the power of the Holy Spirit to be a prophetic witness to the risen Lord Jesus Christ (Acts 1:8). Interestingly, John noted "the testimony of Jesus is the spirit of prophecy" (Revelation 19:10). All believers are inducted into a universal "prophethood"[18] and are endowed with one or more spiritual gifts, many of which have directly to do with wise, instructive, and edifying utterances (Romans 12:6–8; 1 Corinthians 12:8–10; Ephesians 4:7–13; 1 Peter 4:10).

Paul makes it clear not every believer will be a prophet in terms of filling a recognized "office," or, perhaps, even being regularly used by the Spirit in that way (1 Corinthians 12:28,29). The very identification of a separate gift of prophecy implies that. However, at the same time, he encourages all believers to "desire . . . especially the gift of prophecy" (1 Corinthians 14:1), for the person who prophesies does so for the "strengthening, encouragement and comfort" (1 Corinthians 14:3) of others. There is no statute of limitations on the Spirit of prophecy. In the words of Peter's prophetic sermon, "The promise is for you and your children and for all who are far off—for all whom the Lord our God will call" (Acts 2:39).

Conclusions

The purpose of this paper has been to study the roles of apostles and prophets within the Ephesians 4:11,12 ministry context and present findings both consistent with Scripture and relevant for this strategic time in the growth of the Pentecostal movement. The intent is not to be argumentative or polemical but to "make every effort to keep the unity of the Spirit through the bond of peace" (Ephesians 4:3). With these considerations in mind, the following conclusions are offered:

1. The apostolic nature of the church is to be found in adherence to the Word of God, which has been faithfully transmitted by the apostles of Jesus Christ in their foundational role, and in vital participation in the life and ministry of the Holy Spirit, who baptized, gifted, and led the first apostles.

2. Since the New Testament does not provide guidance for

the appointment of future apostles, such contemporary offices are not essential to the health and growth of the church nor its apostolic nature.

3. While we do not understand it to be necessary, some church bodies may in good faith and careful biblical definition choose to name certain leaders apostles. The word "apostle" *(apostolos)* is used in different ways in the New Testament: (1) for the Twelve disciples originally appointed by Jesus (and later Matthias); (2) for the Twelve plus Paul and a larger group (1 Corinthians 15:3–8) whose exact numbers are somewhat uncertain; and (3) for others such as Epaphroditus (Philippians 2:25) and the unnamed "brothers" Paul wrote about (2 Corinthians 8:23). Groups one and two, personally called and commissioned by the risen Lord, are often referred to in Scripture as "apostles of Jesus Christ" and are foundational apostles (Ephesians 2:20) with unique revelatory and authoritative roles in establishing the church and producing the New Testament. The third group, the "apostles of the churches," were assigned specific roles and responsibilities as needed by the early churches.

Contemporary apostles, of course, will not have seen or been commissioned by the risen Lord in the manner of the "apostles of Jesus Christ," nor will they be adding their teachings to the canon of Scripture. Presumably they will demonstrate the other marks of an apostle taught in the New Testament.

4. The title of apostle should not be lightly granted or assumed. Historically, apostles have been persons of recognized spiritual stature, stalwart character, and great effectiveness in the work of the church. Paul's warnings about "those who want an opportunity to be considered equal with us in the things they boast about," his assertion that "such men are false apostles, deceitful workmen, masquerading as apostles of

Christ," and his further association of them with "Satan [who] himself masquerades as an angel of light" (2 Corinthians 11:12–14) are sobering—reminders that unfettered human pride in seeking church leadership can blind one to the machinations of the devil. Persons lacking character may attach the title of apostle to themselves in order to assert dominance and control over other believers, while leaving themselves unaccountable to the members in their care or the spiritual eldership of their own fellowship.

5. The function of apostle occurs whenever the church of Jesus Christ is being established among the unevangelized. As Pentecostals, we fervently desire a generation of men and women who will function apostolically: to take the gospel with signs following to people at home and abroad who have not yet heard or understood that "God so loved the world that he gave his one and only Son, that whoever believes in him shall not perish but have eternal life" (John 3:16).

6. Prophecy is an ongoing gift of the Holy Spirit that will always be broadly distributed throughout a holy and responsive church until Jesus comes. The Spirit sovereignly chooses and directs persons who are open and sensitive to His gifts and promptings and endows them variously with an array of verbal gifts. Paul admonished, "Follow the way of love and eagerly desire spiritual gifts, especially the gift of prophecy" (1 Corinthians 14:1). Many persons of both sexes may be expected to exercise the gift of prophecy in various ways, as seen in the New Testament.

The New Testament does not make provisions for establishing the prophet in a hierarchical governing structure of the church; in fact, the content of prophecy itself should always be tested by and responsible to the superior authority of Scripture. However, the church should long for authentic prophecy with a message which is relevant to contemporary needs and subject to the authority of Scripture.

Finally, the Ephesians 4:11,12 gifts are both the historical and contemporary heritage of the Church. Some apostolic and prophetic functions flowing from persons directly commissioned by the risen Lord and acting in revelatory capacities seem clearly to belong to the foundational era of the Church. At the same time, some of those functions having to do with the revitalization, expansion, and nurture of the church ought to be present in every generation. We encourage all believers, led and filled by the Spirit, to allow themselves to be fully utilized as servants of the Lord, since all gifts are needed to edify and complete the body as well as to mobilize the body to reach the world. Then the purpose of all ministry gifts will be realized: "To prepare God's people for works of service, so that the body of Christ may be built up until we all reach unity in the faith and in the knowledge of the Son of God and become mature, attaining to the whole measure of the fullness of Christ" (Ephesians 4:12,13).

Practical Questions Regarding Apostles And Prophets

1. Does the Assemblies of God recognize present-day apostles and prophets?

The Assemblies of God recognizes ministers as certified, licensed, or ordained. The work of district councils and the General Council is overseen by presbyters and superintendents. Local churches appoint deacons. The Assemblies of God believes this practice is consistent with apostolic practice provided in the pastoral letters of 1 and 2 Timothy and Titus. The pastoral letters do not make provision for the appointment of apostles or prophets, nor does the Book of Acts indicate that provision for such was given in the churches established on the missionary journeys. The apostles appointed not apostles or prophets but elders (Acts 14:23). At the conclusion of the missionary journeys, Paul met with the elders of the Ephesian church (Acts 20:17–38). Clearly, elders are also given the functions of bishop ("overseer") and shepherd ("pastor") (Acts 20:28; 1 Peter 5:2).

Thus, within the Assemblies of God, persons are not recognized by the title of apostle or prophet. However, many within the church exercise the ministry function of apostles and prophets. Apostolic functions usually occur within the context of breaking new ground in unevangelized areas or among unreached people. The planting of over 225,000 churches worldwide since 1914 in the Assemblies of God could not have been accomplished unless apostolic functions had been present. In the Early Church, false apostles did not pioneer ministries; they preyed on ministries established by others. Prophetic functions occur when believers speak under the anointing of the Spirit to strengthen, encourage, or comfort (1 Corinthians 14:3). All prophecies are to be weighed carefully (1 Corinthians 14:29). A predictive prophecy may be true, but the prophet whose doctrine departs from biblical truth is false. A predictive prophecy that proves false leads to the conclusion that the person is a false prophet (Deuteronomy 18:19–22).

Finally, it must be noted that titles are not as important as ministry itself. Too often a title is worn in an attitude of carnal pride. The title does not make the person or the ministry. The person with ministry makes the title meaningful. Jesus explicitly warned His disciples against engaging in the quest for titles (Matthew 23:8–12). He tells us, "You know that the rulers of the Gentiles lord it over them, and their high officials exercise authority over them. Not so with you. Instead, whoever wants to become great among you must be your servant, and whoever wants to be first must be your slave—just as the Son of Man did not come to be served, but to serve, and to give his life as a ransom for many" (Matthew 20:25–28).

2. *What is the implication for the local church in the current emphasis on apostles and prophets?*

The Pentecostal and charismatic movements have witnessed various excessive or misplaced theological emphases over the years. We look with grave concern on those who do not believe in congregational church government, who do not trust the maturity of local church bodies to govern themselves under Scripture and the Spirit. Such leaders prefer more authoritarian structures where their own word or decrees are unchallenged.

In the current emphasis on Ephesians 4:11, verse 12 is being neglected: " . . . to prepare God's people for works of service [i.e. ministry], so that the body of Christ may be built up." The stress of the New Testament lies with every-believer ministry. The Protestant Reformation recaptured the biblical truth of the priesthood of all believers. The Pentecostal movement has spread like a fast-moving fire through the world because of the Spirit-gifted ministry of the entire body. The church must always remember that leadership gifts are not given for the exaltation of a few but for the equipping of all God's people for ministry.

3. *Should Assemblies of God churches welcome the ministries of apostles and prophets?*

We encourage our churches to give close heed to the following provision of the General Council Bylaws: Pastors and leaders of assemblies should make proper investigation of persons who seek to gain entrance to teach, minister, or pastor. Use of the platform should be denied until spiritual integrity and reliability have been determined. Since the use of non-Assemblies of God ministers may bring confusion and problems detrimental to the Fellowship, it is recommended that Assemblies of God churches use Assemblies of God ministers (Article VI, Section 3).

This bylaw provision is consistent with the oversight responsibility given to pastors (Acts 20:28–31) and leaders in the body of Christ (1 Timothy 5:22, 2 Timothy 4:3–5).

---

[1]Biblical citations are from the New International Version unless otherwise indicated.

[2]For simplicity, when Greek nouns and verbs are included they will usually be in the nominative singular and first person singular indicative.

[3]*A Greek-English Lexicon of the New Testament and Other Early Christian Literature,* 3rd edition, rev. and ed., Frederick William Danker (Chicago: University of Chicago Press, 2000), 122.

[4]Tractate Berakoth 5.5 and several other places in the Mishnah, the oldest portion of the Talmud. While the earliest rabbinical references date from the second century, it seems likely that the institution was much earlier. However, some scholars trace the concept to the "to send" language both of the Old Testament itself and secular Greek. See Colin Brown, gen. ed., *The New International Dictionary of New Testament Theology* (Grand Rapids: Zondervan, 1975), "Apostle," 1:126–136.

[5]See the insightful study of C.G. Kruse in Ralph P. Martin and Peter H. Davids, eds., *Dictionary of the Later New Testament & Its Developments* (Downers Grove, IL: InterVarsity Press, 1997), 76–82.

[6]It is frequently suggested that the Eleven erred in their selection of Matthias because Judas' place was reserved for Paul. Matthias, it is noted, immediately passes into oblivion. However, there is no hint of criticism in the text and few of the Twelve are mentioned after chapter 1. Paul's apostolic credentials are established independently of the Twelve

by both Luke and Paul himself (cf. Acts 9:1–30, especially vv. 26–28; Gal. 1:15–24).

[7]*A Greek-English Lexicon of the New Testament and Other Early Christian Literature*, 311.

[8]Some commentators identify the "super-apostles" with the Twelve; however, others suggest that the context more readily supports an identification with Jewish-Hellenistic teachers who came to Corinth with letters of introduction, perhaps from Jerusalem.

[9]See the discussion in E. Earle Ellis, *Pauline Theology: Ministry and Society* (Grand Rapids: Eerdmans, 1989), 38.

[10]"[M]essengers without extraordinary status." *A Greek-English Lexicon of the New Testament and Other Early Christian Literature*, 122.

[11]Gordon D. Fee, *The First Epistle to the Corinthians* (Grand Rapids: Eerdmans, 1987), 732.

[12]Colin Brown, gen. ed., *The New International Dictionary of New Testament Theology* (Grand Rapids: Zondervan, 1975) , 1:135.

[13]See, for example, James D.G. Dunn, *The Theology of Paul the Apostle* (Grand Rapids: Eerdmans, 1998), 578–579.

[14]*The Theology of Paul the Apostle*, 574.

[15] *A Greek-English Lexicon of the New Testament and Other Early Christian Literature,* 3rd edition rev. and ed. Frederick William Danker (Chicago: University of Chicago Press, 2000), 1:44. See also Gerhard Kittel, ed., *Theological Dictionary of the New Testament,* trans. and ed. by Geoffrey W. Bromiley (Grand Rapids: Wm. B. Eerdmans Publishing Company, 1964), 1:447.

[16]New American Standard Version and New Revised Standard Version, "signs of a true apostle."

[17]*A Greek-English Lexicon of the New Testament and Other Early Christian Literature*, 125.

[18]Roger Stronstad, *The Prophethood of All Believers* (Sheffield, UK: Sheffield Academic Press, 1999), 71–84.

24
Assemblies of God Perspectives on the Sanctity of Human Life Including Abortion and Euthanasia

The Assemblies of God bases its understanding of the nature of human beings on the Bible, which reveals that God created the universe, the world, and all living things (Genesis 1:1; 1:11; 1:21; 1:25). Humans are the highest form of God's creative activity, and He is intentional in both their creation and destiny. "'Let us make man in our image. . . .' So God created man in his own image, . . . male and female he created them" (Genesis 1:26-27). "The LORD God formed the man from the dust of the ground and breathed into his nostrils the breath of life, and the man became a living being" (Genesis 2:7).[1]

By making human beings in his own image, God set them above all other forms of life on earth. The "image of God," requiring both sexes for full expression, signifies that men and women are personal and spiritual beings, both rational and relational, intended for eternal fellowship with their personal Creator. Though marred when the first human pair fell into sin (Genesis 3; Romans 5:12), the image of God is still intrinsic to human nature (Genesis 9:6), insuring that men and women are capable of response to their Maker. Creation in the divine image is not only an expression of the incalculable value God places upon human life, it also signifies that God has sovereign power over life. He is both giver and sustainer of life; He alone has the power to determine its beginning and ending.[2]

The nobility of human beings is seen in the divine mandate: "Be fruitful and increase in number; fill the earth and subdue it. Rule over the fish of the sea and the birds of the air and over every living creature that moves on the ground" (Genesis 1:28). Superior to all other life forms, humans are to assume the role of responsible custodians of the earth.

Every human life, from conception through death, is therefore to be valued, respected, nurtured, and protected. Every human life is to be lived in obedience to God and His Word. The Bible describes a moral order to which all persons are responsible. At the end of life, all persons will stand before God to give account for their actions. "For we must all appear before the judgment seat of Christ, that each one may receive what is due him for the things done while in the body, whether good or bad" (2 Corinthians 5:10).

Therefore, human beings are responsible to bring the light of God's Word to decisions that bear on the sanctity of life. To this end, the Assemblies of God offers the following biblical perspectives:

The Beginning of Life

Contraception. The Assemblies of God, finding no clear

scriptural mandate, does not take an official stand on the appropriateness of contraception within a heterosexual marriage for purposes of regulating the number of children, determining the time of their birth, or safeguarding the health of the mother. These are matters of personal conscience as godly spouses prayerfully covenant with God about the growth of their families. While there are important ethical issues in determining to have a family, the prevention of pregnancy is understood to be qualitatively different from the termination of pregnancy since the sperm has not fertilized the ovum and human life has not yet begun. The biological processes themselves teach us that in God's creative design not every sperm or ovum is intended to survive and unite. It should be remembered, however, that some methods commonly regarded as contraception, such as the IUD and the morning-after pill, are actually abortifacients that terminate rather than prevent pregnancy.

The Bible teaches that in the institution of marriage, children are divinely ordered both to fulfill God's divine purposes for the race and for the repopulation of the earth. The mandate to the first pair was, "Be fruitful and increase in number; fill the earth and subdue it" (Genesis 1:28). Throughout Scripture, children are regarded as God's gift: "Sons are a heritage from the LORD, children a reward from him" (Psalm 127:3). There are certain circumstances where couples may choose not to have children for very good reasons. However, the use of contraception merely to avoid the demands of child rearing ought to be prayerfully examined in terms of the purity of one's motives and the personal implications of the divine mandate.

In Vitro Fertilization. From a study of the Scriptures, God's plan for human conception is sexual union between a man and woman in a legal marriage covenant. Children of such a covenant ought to be the result of a joyous and loving sexual relationship in which the husband and wife are responsible for birthing and rearing godly offspring. However, infertile heterosexual couples who have pursued without success all viable treatments may be confronted with a decision to utilize in vitro fertilization. There are numerous ethical issues to be evaluated in such a process, including the financial costs, the harvesting of sperms and ova, and the nurturing of multiple living human embryos, not all of which likely will be implanted in the uterus. The disposal of unused embryos is an acute ethical issue since they represent the beginning of human life. There may also be serious danger to the life of the mother in the event that multiple babies survive to full term and the abortion of one or more of them may be required. Before considering in vitro fertilization, careful and prayerful attention, with knowledgeable and godly counsel, must be given to all such issues, and believers must responsibly make decisions in good conscience with the guidance of the Spirit of God.

Reproductive Cloning. The Assemblies of God believes that reproductive cloning is immoral and a matter of grave concern. In the cloning process, the person is not conceived from the union of the father's sperm and the mother's ovum. The genetic material is drawn from only one person and manipulated in the laboratory before implantation in the "rented" womb of a cooperating female. Therefore, a cloned person cannot have both father and mother in the genetic sense. Moreover, there are serious questions about family identification, bonding, and nurture as well as personal identity for a person who is a genetic copy of another. There are also grave physical risks for persons who may be cloned. The cloning of animals has demonstrated the potential for birth defects and premature aging. Scientists have no way of knowing what type of horrors may be visited upon cloned individuals or upon humankind at large through such a process.

Abortion. The Assemblies of God views the practice of abortion as an evil inflicted upon millions of innocent babies and threatens millions more in the years to come. Abortion is a morally unacceptable alternative for birth control, population control, sex selection, and elimination of the physically and mentally handicapped. Certain parts of the world are already experiencing serious population imbalances as a result of the systematic abortion of female babies. The advocacy and practice of so-called partial birth abortion of babies is particularly heinous.

Sexual responsibility. Contemporary demands for abortion often flow from the practice of sexual freedom without corresponding responsibility. The Scriptures speak definitively against pre-marital and extra-marital sexual intercourse and declare such activity to be sinful (Exodus 22:16; Acts 15:20; 1 Corinthians 6:9,13,18; Galatians 5:19). To add abortion as an after-the-fact birth control device is to deepen and compound the sin with resultant guilt and emotional distress. The Assemblies of God affirms the biblical mandate for sexual purity and responsibility that, when obeyed, will eliminate many, if not most, situations where abortion is considered necessary or desirable.

The personhood of the unborn. The Scriptures regularly treat the unborn child as a person under the care of God.

1. The Bible recognizes that a woman is with child even in the first stages of pregnancy. When the Virgin Mary was chosen to be the mother of Jesus, an angel made this announcement to her: "You will conceive in your womb and bear a son *(huios)*" (Luke 1:31, NASB). The angel then informed Mary that her cousin Elizabeth was pregnant: "Even Elizabeth your relative is going to have a child (*huios*, "son") in her old age" (Luke

1:36). Scripture makes it clear that in the prenatal phase both Jesus and John the Baptist were recognized as males well before the time of delivery. Moreover, John before birth is recognized as a "baby" *(brephos)* (Luke 1:41, 44). This translates a Greek word used for children both before and after birth (cf. Acts 7:19). The Bible always recognizes the prenatal phase of life as that of a child and not a mere appendage to the mother's body to be aborted at will.

Even when pregnancy in Bible times was due to an illicit relationship, the sanctity and value of that life was not questioned. The daughters of Lot willfully became pregnant by incestuous relationships (Genesis 19:36), and Bathsheba gave birth to Solomon as a result of an adulterous relationship initiated by King David (2 Samuel 11:5). In none of these cases are the lives of the unborn considered to be unworthy and requiring an abortion.

2. The Bible recognizes that God is active in the creative process of forming new life. Concerning Leah, the wife of Jacob, Scripture says, "When the LORD saw that Leah was not loved, he opened her womb. . . . Leah became pregnant and gave birth to a son" (Genesis 29:31,32). When Job compared himself to his servants, he asked, "'Did not he who made me in the womb make them? Did not the same one form us both within our mothers?'" (Job 31:15). In pointing out God's impartiality, Job said He "'shows no partiality to princes and does not favor the rich over the poor, for they are all the work of his hands'" (Job 34:19).

God spoke through Isaiah: "'This is what the Lord says— he who made you, who formed you in the womb, and who will help you: Do not be afraid, O Jacob, my servant'" (Isaiah 44:2). And again, "'This is what the Lord says—your Redeemer, who formed you in the womb: I am the Lord, who has made all things'" (v. 24).

David summed it up, "For you created my inmost being; you knit me together in my mother's womb. I praise you because I am fearfully and wonderfully made; your works are wonderful, I know that full well. My frame was not hidden from you when I was made in the secret place. When I was woven together in the depths of the earth, your eyes saw my unformed body. All the days ordained for me were written in your book before one of them came to be" (Psalm 139:13–16).

3. The Bible recognizes that God has plans for the unborn child. Only He knows the potential of this new life. When God called Jeremiah to his prophetic ministry, He indicated the ordination was prenatal when He said: "Before I formed you in the womb I knew you, before you were born I set you apart; I appointed you as a prophet to the nations" (Jeremiah 1:5). When Zechariah the priest was ministering at the altar of incense, an angel announced that his wife, Elisabeth, would give birth to a son who should be called John. Then it was revealed that God had definite plans for this child. He was to be a forerunner of Jesus (Luke 1:11-17).

4. The Bible recognizes that God is sovereign in all things, including the quality of life of the unborn child. When people reject God, eventually they cheapen human life and make it relative. Some are considered worthy to live; others are considered expendable. Who but God knows whether someone destroyed in the holocaust might not have discovered a cure for cancer. Who but God knows what blessing millions of children killed before birth might have brought to improve the quality of life. When people set themselves up as God to determine if a life is worth living—whether before or after birth—they are usurping the sovereignty of the Creator.

There are also things finite humans cannot understand.

God's ways are above human ways. While today's medical technology frequently makes it possible to know when impairment exists in unborn children, it is important to remember they are still in God's love and care (Matthew 19:14-15).

The killing of innocent persons. God's Word is very explicit concerning the taking of innocent human life. "You shall not murder" (Exodus 20:13) is not only one of the Ten Commandments, but also a moral imperative that reoccurs throughout Scripture (cf. Matthew 18:19; Romans 13:9).

God inspired Moses to include in the Scriptures a law that brings the sanctity of the lives of unborn children into focus. "If men who are fighting hit a pregnant woman and she gives birth prematurely but there is no serious injury, the offender must be fined whatever the woman's husband demands and the court allows. But if there is serious injury, you are to take life for life, eye for eye, tooth for tooth, hand for hand, foot for foot" (Exodus 21:22-24).

It should be noted that the value of the life of both the mother and the child is such that even if there is no critical and lasting harm to either, the responsible party must be fined. However, if either the mother or the premature child is seriously injured or dies, then the severe penalties of the law are to be applied, possibly in this case those having to do with manslaughter (Exodus 21:13; Numbers 35:22-25). It is clear that the life of the unborn child is precious, and even a non-premeditated injury inflicted on the unborn is a serious crime.

God's attitude toward the killing of innocents is clear. No one is guiltless who takes the life of another, with the possible scriptural exceptions of capital punishment administered by a system of justice (Genesis 9:6; Numbers 35:12), unintended killing in self-defense (Exodus 22:2), or deaths occasioned by duly constituted police and war powers (Romans 13:4-5).

John Calvin expressed the horror of abortion in commenting on Exodus 21:22,23: "The fetus, though enclosed in the womb of his mother, is already a human being, and it is a monstrous crime to rob it of life which it has not yet begun to enjoy. If it seems more horrible to kill a man in his own house than in a field, because a man's house is his place of most secure refuge, it ought surely to be deemed more atrocious to destroy a fetus in the womb before it has come to light."[3]

Danger to the life of the mother. Those situations in which pregnancy seriously threatens the life of the mother raise a particular ethical dilemma for Christians who value the lives of both mother and child. If responsible diagnoses confirm that childbirth is likely to result in the death of the mother, historic Christian faith usually has favored the life of the mother above that of the unborn child since the mother is a mature person with established family and societal relationships and responsibilities. However, vague threats to the mother's physical or emotional health must not become an excuse to place the child at risk. Any intervention required must have the intent of saving the mother's life, not the prior intent of causing death to the child. As in any emergency, in such times God's children ought to fervently and earnestly pray for divine intervention. In doing so, the persons involved must prayerfully evaluate the medical diagnoses with the assistance of humane physicians and godly leaders and make, responsibly and with a clear conscience, what may well be a very painful decision.

The emotional and spiritual toll. The abortion industry rarely advises pregnant women of the potential impact of abortion on their spiritual and mental health. Desperate women who find themselves in an acutely embarrassing or inconvenient position because of an illicit affair or an unplanned pregnancy, and who are often coerced by selfish lovers and/or embarrassed families, are led to see abortion as a "quick fix." Nothing could be further from the truth. Women are usually unaware of the depression, guilt, and shame that may plague them for a lifetime. While God can and does forgive and heal the broken hearts of repentant sinners who come to Him for forgiveness, the actual deed can never be undone and probably will always be remembered with pain and regret.

The End of Life

Natural Death. The Scriptures recognize that death is the result of human sin (Genesis 3:2, 19; Romans 5:12) and comes eventually to all—except those believers alive at the coming of Christ (1 Thessalonians 4:17). Hebrews 9:27 clearly states death is an appointment. It is beyond the purview of human beings to schedule that appointment. Christians regard death as the "last enemy" (1 Corinthians 15:26), to be finally destroyed in the eschatological reign of the resurrected Lord Jesus. It is therefore not a "friend" to be sought and embraced, but it is nonetheless to be regarded as the final passage to glorious life with God. "Now we know that if the earthly tent we live in is destroyed, we have a building from God, an eternal house in heaven, not built by human hands" (2 Corinthians 5:1).

Families facing the impending death of a loved one and the frequent question of mechanical life support are encouraged to carry out the wishes of their loved one. However, in the absence of such knowledge, believers are encouraged to consider the guidance of Christian medical professionals and godly leaders, and prayerfully seek the wisdom of the Holy Spirit for a decision that will leave them with a clear conscience. The Assemblies of God respects the conscience of individual believers in these circumstances but does not find a biblical mandate for indefinite and artificial perpetuation of life in cases of persistent vegetative state or the prolonged cessation of biological function. In the providence of God, there is a time to release persons to go to Him.

Euthanasia and Assisted Suicide. The Assemblies of God condemns as immoral the killing of the weak, the physically challenged, the mentally ill, or the aged, whether by a deliberate act or by coercing or assisting a person to commit suicide.[4] God is both the giver of life and the arbiter of life. Fully informed and freely chosen suicide is the final usurpation of the divine prerogative. Humans are not empowered to take their own lives or the lives of others.[5] The sick and the weak must not be made to feel that they are a burden and have a moral obligation to relieve society of that burden. Their depression and illnesses often bring severe emotional and physical pain and raise serious questions about their ability to freely choose suicide. It should be remembered that many suicides occur in times of deep depression and great physical pain, when personal judgment and responsibility are seriously impaired. The Assemblies of God does not assume that all such persons are eternally lost.

Biomedical Research

The Assemblies of God affirms and encourages reverent and responsible scientific research intended to enhance the health and well-being of persons created in the image of God. Christian faith is not to be interpreted in ways that needlessly hinder greater understanding of the human body and the discovery of cures for and prevention of dreaded diseases and defects. However, there are many temptations to pursue the life sciences for ignoble reasons. Therefore, all biomedical research should be monitored and regulated so as to insure respect for the sanctity of human life and the essential dignity of human beings who are created in the image of God. All researchers are finally answerable to God

Stem Cell Research. Stem cell research shows great promise for the cure of numerous diseases and should proceed under appropriate ethical guidelines regularly reviewed and revised. There are stem cells available for research from legitimate sources that do not compromise the sanctity of human life. The practice of cultivating stem cells from the tissue of aborted fetuses perpetuates the evil of abortion and should be prohibited. Likewise, the cultivation of stem cells from the "left-over" embryos from fertility clinics raises serious ethical concerns for human life. Great care must always be exercised in the cultivation of stem cells to insure that the sanctity and dignity of human life are not compromised.

Genetic Intervention. The Assemblies of God is supportive of morally responsible genetic research and therapies. Genetic research conducted with reverence for life appears to have great potential for the health of human beings through the identification of and intervention in the genetic roots of hundreds of diseases. By the same token, used for proud and selfish ends, genetic screening and intervention also have the potential to bring great harm to the entire human race. In addition, the Assemblies of God believes legislation is necessary to prevent intrusive genetic screening and resultant discrimination as well as misguided experimentation and termination of life.

Christian Action

When abortion and other immoral life-threatening practices present themselves, Christians have an obligation to address these evils in public forums and to seek legislative and judicial redress. Among the steps Christians should take are the following:

Christians should pray earnestly for God's intervention and the wisdom and resolve to resist the degradation of human life, whether by abortion, assisted suicide, euthanasia, or questionable bio-medical research and experimentation.

Christians should provide biblical moral instruction in their homes and all possible public forums. The church, rooted in the eternal truths of God's Word, should seek to lift the standards of society by overcoming evil with good.

Christians should actively support candidates who embrace the sanctity of life and lobby on behalf of legislation to protect the unborn, the handicapped, and the aged, all of whom are endangered by a societal cheapening of life.

Christians should work through legislative and governmental agencies to insure appropriate ethical review of all bio-medical research and to impose constraints on that which is evil or misguided.

Christians should counsel those with unwanted pregnancies about alternatives to abortion, such as adoption. They should generously support responsible Christian adoption agencies with their prayers, finances, and time as well as facilitate placement of unwanted babies in loving Christian homes.

Christians should compassionately minister to those who suffer remorse and guilt from having had abortions or having participated in abortions or other life-destroying activity or research, reminding them of the words of Jesus, "whoever comes to me I will never drive away" (John 6:37).

Renunciation of Violence

Current laws virtually permit abortion-on-demand, at least in the early trimesters of pregnancy and, in some places, provide for other practices, such as assisted suicide, that destroy or endanger lives created in God's image. The Assemblies of God strongly believes such laws are immoral and contravene the law of God. Every legal means should be employed to reverse the effects of these laws and dismantle the immoral industries they spawn. At the same time, it should be remembered that the law only permits these evils. No one is required to participate in the destruction of life. Certain people freely choose to do so for reasons of their own convenience, and they possess certain legal rights that Christians may not abridge. While abhorring immoral laws that permit and protect the destruction of life, the Assemblies of God also denounces violent, lawless, and cruel actions against both the purveyors and the participants in these life-destroying acts, sometimes carried out by people claiming to be Christians. Christians in their quest to save life must not compound evil by harming or taking life.

Conclusion

The Bible teaches that every human being is loved by the Creator, who longs to bring each one into fellowship with himself. All persons must finally give account to Him for any actions that rob others of life, health, or dignity. With these eternal issues in view, the Assemblies of God intends to be both a witness to the truth of Christ and a healing and redemptive agency to assist, through its numerous Christian ministries, those who may be caught in these dilemmas.

---

[1]All biblical citations, unless otherwise indicated, are from the New International Version (NIV).

[2]The Bible does provide precedents for justly administered death sentences for capital crimes as well as for the exercise of self-defense and

duly constituted police and war powers (Genesis 9:6; Exodus 22:2; Numbers 35:12; Romans 13:4-5).

[3]John Calvin, *Commentaries on the Four Last Books of Moses,* trans. Charles William Bingham, 4 vols. (Grand Rapids: Eerdmans, 1950), 3:41-42.

[4]For a more extensive statement, see the Assemblies of God position paper "A Biblical Perspective on Assisted Suicide."

[5]See note 2.

Scripture Index

OLD TESTAMENT

NEW TESTAMENT

Subject Index